"NEVER HEEL UP"

“NEVER HEEL UP”

Michael
Busha

Disclaimer: Please note that the publisher and author of this book are NOT RESPONSIBLE in any manner whatsoever for any injuries that may result from practicing the techniques and/or drills described within. Martial arts training can be dangerous-both to you and to others-if not practiced safely. If you are in doubt as to how to proceed or as to whether your practice is safe, consult with a trained martial arts instructor before attempting to perform or copy any of the techniques and/or drills within. Since the physical activities described herein may be too strenuous in nature for some readers, it is also essential that a physician be consulted prior to practicing and/or copying the techniques and/or drills described in this book.

This memoir is a truthful recollection of actual events in the author's life and is portrayed to the best of the author's memory. Some names and characteristics have been changed, some events have been compressed and some dialogue has been recreated.

Printed in the United States of America

First Printing, 2020

ISBN: 978-0-578-49364-0

Library of Congress Control Number: 2020901840

For my wife Tomoko

Our journey through life is
analogous to the practice of karate
. . . we have to keep getting back up.

Proloque

This story has two-parts. Part-One is an attempt to show how very little I knew about aggression, fighting, and the necessary evils of how to protect oneself from the sad, pitiful behavior of a small minority of the human race. Part-One is also meant to describe my state of mind after a rather rough start to my adult life. I am convinced that had I not eventually started training in Shotokan karate, my life could have just as easily taken a very different and mundane, misguided and perhaps, tragic, direction. But ultimately, who knows whether the effect of negative events pushed me into the Shotokan world as a desperate last hope, or if the Shotokan world pulled me out of that sad existence by the sheer power of its overwhelming spirit. I'm guessing both scenarios worked together-Karma is like that. I do know that in some way-a person's past can skew their future-positively, if they pay attention. And I tried very hard to pay attention.

Part-Two starts with me on the plane heading for Japan in early Spring 1985. By that time, I was a strong Nidan, still relatively young and very excited to be on my way in what was simply a month's vacation from A.C. Spark Plugs where I had been an electrician for almost fifteen years in Flint, Michigan. This trip to Japan had a profound, pivotal effect on me. For my karate, of course, but also for helping me out of the malaise that was my life at the time. In addition, it introduced me to the rich cultural and spiritual experiences the Japanese people and the lovely country of Japan provided. And to the many non-Japanese, non-karate friends I made as well, all on their own personal journeys, and also brave enough to liberate themselves from their own brand of despondency.

I decided to include certain conversations in Japanese (with their translations) to better convey my disorientation and frustration with the language during my first visit to Japan.

"Never Heel Up"

Part One

Chapter One

(1969)

Baby Jennifer died a few days after birth. My wife and I had married at the start of the year and were happy, if not financially ready, certainly emotionally ready. But we were beaten down by the suddenness of her decline after a full-term pregnancy and the helplessness we felt when we had to push our way into the nursery just to touch her and watch her struggle to breathe. We spent hours at the hospital beaming over our little girl and months preparing for the big day. Now she was gone. There was nothing to do but say goodbye. The funeral director suggested we not spend the money and just take her directly to the cemetery. Of course, we refused his advice and had a regular funeral. It was a huge service with all of our family and friends in attendance to support us though they had not even seen her yet. For months afterwards, we lived mostly in a vacuum accompanied by only tears, sadness and silence. We recovered somewhat, forced to proceed with jobs, school, and in order to keep our friends from giving up on us. They were wonderful and supportive but we knew that they also had limits and that they had to concentrate on their own lives. We put on happy faces. The sadness did not go away but instead disappeared deep inside us. The expression on her face has never left me after all these years.

In December of 1971 we learned that we were again pregnant. We were delighted and the news helped us escape the depression of the last couple of years. We started planning again and setting up the baby's room. I had more money now and could buy a nice crib and dressers and paint for the walls of our new home and new carpet and bottles and blankets and all the things required by a new baby and its parents. Combined with Christmas events we were happier than we had been since first married.

Christopher Michael was born on June 23, 1972 and at six months, had worked his charm on everyone. I remember taking him to the Genesee Valley Mall. It was more to show him off than anything else. It worked, strangers walked up to me, peaked under his blanket and melted into his little eyes and nose. I felt good. We would visit our family and friends, displaying little Christopher and talking about his future. What will he be when he grows up? Who does he look like? I still have pictures of me holding him, my long hair drooping over his little face and my wife looking on smiling and proud. We hired our first babysitter, don't know why, maybe because it was what other couples did. I had no fun at all on our night out, just thinking about our little boy at home. All was well and my wife and I started enjoying our life together.

We took Christopher to the hospital on our Doctor's advice to find out why he seemed to be making a noise while breathing. We made several trips to the hospital and everything seemed to be going well but they did not want to release him yet. One evening as we sat watching him, I noticed that his little face was blue. I informed the staff and several of them went to check on him. They told us to wait in the lounge area. We sat there forever until we heard an announcement on the speaker for us to return to his bed. His little body was there but showed no life. My wife and I looked at each other but said nothing. Yet another part of both of us was lost that day. As we returned to the lounge an older woman who had also been visiting and who we had chatted previously with, asked what happened. I simply said "we lost him". My wife broke down crying and I went into automatic pilot, picking up our belongings and grabbing her by the hand and leading her out to our car, stopping briefly by the head nurse who asked about funeral arrangements.

It was another huge funeral service. We held it at Brown Funeral Home on Davison Rd. The director had arranged for a room for a small group of visitors. Within one day that room could not hold the traffic. Then, the day of the funeral, they had to transfer Christopher to the largest room. I chewed Tums, drank coffee, chewed Tums, and drank more coffee and was sick from stress. Pam sat between us and held our hands, keeping us as calm as she could. I have never thanked her. My wife was weak and white faced and broken. In January of 1973 we buried Christopher near his older sister.

Our marriage, although we stayed together a couple more years, also died that day. From the stress of the children's deaths, and from their mother and me slowly withdrawing to a protective mode so devoid of emotion that no one could help us through it. We never recovered.

The next few years were mostly spent in a daze, two children and then my wife, all gone. I cursed myself over and over for not being able to do better, to protect my children from dying and to save our marriage. "Why…why…why?" It was the only thing on my mind every day and every night. Over time my actions and attitude become less full of life and more just a façade that I carried off well enough at work but less skillfully with family and friends. More or less avoiding them rather than having to connect in any meaningful way.

With new women in my life I was demanding and unforgiving. New girlfriends did not last long. I was not able to relax and be honest with them and was quick to say goodbye. Even with buddies I could not completely let go and become their friend. Emotionally I was spent and retreated from the world in all but necessary activities that in my muddled existence could not be ignored. Eventually there were some drugs, never the stronger type, but too much beer and pot made me lazy and prevented me from climbing out of my hole and taking charge of my life.

(1976)

I moved to an apartment in a grand old house on Detroit Street in downtown Flint. The couple upstairs considered me as their elder and stopped by every once in a while. There was an inside door at the bottom of the stairs that connected my first floor to the stairs leading to their second floor. They would knock and walk in. It was never locked. My front room had a huge window. There were six wide concrete steps from my front door with a panoramic view of passersby and traffic, for what that was worth. The bedroom was just behind the front room with a four-foot by five-foot opening that, though it created a good space, also limited privacy. But in those days, at that time, privacy was not a big concern. There was a small kitchen carved out of the back porch. It worked. I remember cooking just one meal.

It was not in the best part of town. Over the one year I lived there, I became acquainted with three prostitutes. I would sit on the front porch and in the evening the girls would walk down the street trying to attract customers. They were young and their faces and eyes had yet to show the result of their life style.

One day the oldest, Cheryl, a very petite blonde, arranged for all four of us to have a party. The girls brought wine and I provided take-out Chinese. One of the girls, I forgot her name, brought a cake she said she made. I don't remember eating any of it. Mostly we stayed on the front porch, except for using the bathroom. They were happy, honest and loud, each telling stories from the road. None of them making excuses for, or hiding their life style, all of them giving me advice on my girlfriends. Never was I propositioned by them. But we had an interesting and fun relationship.

***

The call awakened me from needed sleep. It felt like it was pulling me from a deep fog. I tried to ignore it but the ring continued. It was Tuesday night. Sheila had panic and stress in her voice. "Michael, can I come over now? I need to talk to you." She was at my Detroit Street house in ten minutes.

"I was raped in the parking lot of MCC. He had a knife and forced me into his car."

We raced to the college and I drove all through the parking ramp over and over but we could not find the bastard. I have no idea what I would have done but I wanted to find him.

We drove to the hospital where we met a social worker who was called by the police. Sheila was taken care of by the nurses and the social worker talked her through what was to happen next. There were drugs given and samples taken, all professional but I felt they all blamed her.

I took her home and stayed with her that night. She had to explain why she was so late from college to her five children. She'd had four and her husband had told her "One more and I'm gone." She got pregnant again and he left before the youngest was born.

She recovered from the parking lot incident, kept the scars, of course. Three months later I was called to testify at the trial. My part was just to verify the timing and Sheila's state of mind and her story. It was over before lunch. He paid $85,000 for the attack and was sent to jail for three to five years. Before the trial started that day, she and I and a police court officer were sitting outside the court room. Suddenly the man who raped her walked in with his attorney, a woman. Sheila poked my leg and motioned towards him. I was up and at him in a flash. I was there, but the police officer had me, grabbed my arms and yanked me back to the bench. He pushed me down into the bench and stood there, between me and the pervert. I remember thinking later that day how it all was a blur. And that, what if I had reached him? Would I have been able to actually hurt him? I had never been in a fight before, had never really experienced aggression or physical threat. I shuddered "Good thing the cop stopped me." But that's not true. I had experienced aggression, kid style.

***

It was in ninth grade. In band class, ninth grade students had to take the bus from junior high school to senior high school to join the high school band. The class started at eight o'clock. We ninth graders would huddle together in the corner by the band room door waiting for Mr. Kolbe to arrive and unlock the door.

It was the habit of the 'bigger kids' to walk down to the end of the hall where we were, just to torment us. The bully who chose me as his victim liked to walk by and shove me, usually with an elbow in the ribs. He had two friends that would egg him on and push him to greater and more physical aggressiveness. I hated it. More than the pain from his attacks, I was embarrassed by the other kids seeing this happen. They did nothing to help. In one of the few serious conversations that I remember having with my father, he told me to "Just hit him back." "Don't put up with it. Nail him." Easy for him to say since he was an amateur boxer in the Marines.

He did not teach me how to hit nor did I make a plan. It all happened spontaneously. Jeff and his friends were walking down the hall again. It was a Thursday at a quarter to eight. I was standing, kind of leaning against the band room door. I had put my books down on top of my saxophone case.

"Here they come again." My buddy said in a kind of whisper. Jeff got to within about five feet of where I was standing. I did not wait for him to reach me. With aggression born of frustration I threw a wild right hand punch with a running start that caught him, without any warning, just below the rib cage. It was unfair of me and unprovoked.

I remember him doubling over in pain. He couldn't breathe and was gasping. I knew I was dead. I knew he and his friends would kill me. I stood there. But they didn't kill me. The two friends were gone. Jeff was straightening up a little. All eyes were on us. I stood there. Just minutes later Mr. Kolbe walked past and unlocked the band door and we had band class. We walked out of class one hour later to get on the bus back to junior high school. I expected Jeff to be outside the door waiting for me. He wasn't. They never again came down the hall to harass us. I saw him a few times on the way to the bus. He ignored me. Two years later, I was a junior and he a senior. We never became friends but did talk to each other once in a while and stayed in touch until work and life got in the way.

While still living on Detroit Street, I decided to try learning martial arts. Three friends and I had met at each other's house to watch the one-hour Kung Fu show a few years earlier. We would meet an hour before the start, drink wine and smoke a joint. Then the show started. For me it was another world. Not just the Kung Fu, but the whole Asian culture. I didn't know anything about it, did not remember learning about it in school. But I was entranced, with all of it, the Kung Fu, the Confucian culture, and the search for peace. Watching with close friends just enhanced the experience. Kwai Chang Caine wanted peace but always found aggression and animosity. It was a perfect display of the differences between Americans and the Asian cultures. After the show we would talk about the episode and then about other things that would come up, stimulated by the show.

Before that it was the Billy Jack movies. Billy used Hapkido which at the time seemed quite similar to any other martial art. I know now it is quite different. Billy also wanted peace for the Indian school and for the general community in which he and his girlfriend lived. Of course, like Kwai Chang Caine, peace was an illusion that was not easy to come by. I loved the attempts by the Indian school to temper his anger and aggression, wanting peace but able to resort to violence. The concept was new to me. The first Billy Jack movie was a year or so before Kung Fu and I learned a lot about peace and its opposite, violence. Already convinced that peace was the higher road, I learned that to have peace, it was necessary to have strength. If there is strength then the options are many. If no strength, others dictate the options.

So, here I was. The receptionist at the Taekwondo dojo on N. Saginaw Street in Flint took my name and my entrance fee. He sent me over to one of the black belts. The black belt showed me how to make a stance, keep my hands up, and move across the floor. After thirty minutes, he paired me with another student, told him to "show him some moves" and walked away. The student knocked me around the floor for the last 30 minutes of class. I learned nothing. I spent another three months trying to acquire Billy Jack or Kwai Chang Caine-like skills. Looking back after a few years I guess I did learn a few things, but their dojo atmosphere was not what I wanted so I did not renew the contract.

Chapter Two

We were standing in line to see a movie. There were six of us, three couples. The two guys in front of us were drunk and loud and making rude comments about every woman who walked by. Nobody in line wanted to hear their nonsense. But nobody said anything to them.

I had heard enough and asked them to be a little careful about their language. I gave no threats and was quite polite. The bigger of the two looked at me, then at the woman I was with, staring her up and down with his tongue hanging out while making suggestive gestures. Then he started cooing and describing her body parts in some of the worst language I'd heard.

"Knock it off. She's not comfortable with that." I said. "No one here likes your behavior." He was in my face in an instant, using his height to impose more fear and threat. Taller and bigger men do that. I was to learn later on that height is a major factor for men, mostly for men who do not have anything else and have little education. They tend to impose themselves onto others in order to claim one piece of territory for themselves in their life. It seems almost a handicap if you look at it the right way, never having to develop in other parts of life, never worried about social skills like restraint and tact. Others just did their bidding out of fear.

"I want you to stop harassing us." I said this in an overly aggressive voice. In a voice straight out of fourth grade he said "make me." He was still standing there, his breath still polluting my space.

The threat was real. I was duly intimidated. "I don't want to make you do anything. Just stop, ok?"

"If you don't like it, do something about it, right here. Come on!"

Of course, by that time, all eyes were on us. In his best grade-school manner, he shoved me in the chest and threw me off balance. I stood there, not knowing how I got into this situation and with no idea how to stop it.

"I just want you to stop." I said. I don't want to fight.

"Well I do want to fight. Come on chicken shit."

I really did not want to fight him. And I had no idea how to handle this aggression. Looking back, maybe there were moments in which how I behaved or what I said might have helped defuse the situation. But I was not prepared for his violent behavior and was totally defeated by the overpowering threat. I stood there, silent.

"Come on!" he said. "Show me what you can do."

"I don't want to fight you." I said quietly. "We'll just leave."

"That's right chicken shit. Just leave. Leave with your chicken shit friends."

He shoved me and again I lost my balance. "Get the fuck out of here."

I turned to my friends, "Let's go", my voice soft and beaten. They said nothing. We left and went to another movie. They all comforted me and said there was nothing else I could have done. But I was totally shattered. I felt completely helpless and of course, embarrassed. I had no options, no way to deal with this threat. The fear I felt was something new in my life. I remember thinking shortly afterwards, sitting at home, about why a person would act like that? Why is he so different than the average person? Did I cause the situation? What could I have done differently to stop it from escalating? I had no answers. I was a Psychology major and did not know what to do. There was nothing I could think of that would have changed the outcome. I did not fight him. That's what I should have done. But I didn't have a clue how to fight. And the guy was so big and so strong I would have been crushed. What's worse, to fight and lose, or to back down? Both were bad options.

Chapter Three

(1977)

Walking from the far parking lot to class at the Flint campus of the University of Michigan, I could hear the noise. It sounded like nothing I had ever heard. It got louder as I walked past the red brick building. The door was open. Even today I don't know why I walked into the building. Always I kept to myself, not entering the space of others. It was out of character for me to enter. But enter I did.

Inside was a long hall with dark wood panel on both sides. There were two openings, not really doors, leading into the right side of the building. There was a wood floor with some square painted shapes, same in black and some in red. On the far wall, opposite the openings, there were two flags, one American and one, Japanese. Between them but a little lower was a portrait of a small, white haired man who looked somewhat like a scholar or professor. On other walls were various pictures and illustrations. The wood floor was very clean. In one corner were stacked some wooden sticks, gloves, a heavy bag and pads.

The noise continued. But now it echoed off the walls and bounced off the floor. The source of the strong, piercing noise was a very small man. He was older than me and a little shorter. But the movements he performed were fluid and showed more power than one could expect from his size. He was further down the floor, towards the back. I stepped up onto the floor through the front opening. He ignored me and I stood there watching. Suddenly he stopped, stood at attentions and bowed. Turning to me, he smiled.

"Can you please take off your shoes?"

I backed up, removed my shoes and stepped again onto the floor.

"Sorry to bother you. Are you doing a martial art?"

"Shotokan. It's Japanese. I'm Tony." Shaking his sweating hand, he seemed strong, confident and a little different. We talked about his

Shotokan style and about this karate club. He showed me a few more katas. He had a kind of hunch back when standing and talking but it disappeared during the katas. We talked about karate for ten minutes and he told me more about the club. It was not actually on the University of Michigan, Flint campus, but it was called the University Karate Club. Tony said there was a class starting in two weeks. If I was interested, I should give it a try.

"I might do that."

We shook hands and I walked out to where my shoes were, stepped into them and walked outside. It was an autumn day, great for walking on campus. Sitting down on the lawn, I pulled out *Critique of Pure Reason*, I remember, and started to read. After a few more minutes, Emmanuel Kant's writing was being overpowered by thoughts of Tony's powerful, guttural shouts. It was a perfect day, nice breeze, sunny skies, a day that would finally show me a way forward, out of the fog that was my life and set me on a journey to perfection that I know I will never achieve. But the path has been so sweet.

With Tony – Practicing Kicks and Balance

***

I pulled my car into the small, gravel parking lot on the east side of the University Karate Club. Mine was the only car and I sat there waiting. It was five-fifteen on a Tuesday evening. Tony had said the beginner's class started at five-thirty. The flyer he handed me said the same. So, I waited. At about five-thirty another car pulled into the lot. A woman, who looked younger than me, parked the car one spot over from where I was parked. I nodded at her. She acknowledged me with a smile. We both waited a while longer. It was past five-thirty. I got out of my car and walked around to the front entrance. She also got out and followed me to the front.

"Are you the karate teacher", she asked.

"No!" I laughed. "I came to try the beginner's class. But I don't see anyone here and the door is still locked".

"Me too." She had the same flyer in her hand.

"It's supposed to start at five-thirty".

We talked for a while. She was a student at the campus, was married, and was interested in studying a martial art, any martial art. She had no idea of styles or cultures involved. They were in town for a couple years while he attended GMI (General Motors Institute). While we were still talking another car suddenly turned into the lot and parked next to my car. The driver swung the door open and hurried over to whcrc wc were standing.

"I'm sorry to be late. Here, I'll open the door. Come in." Dan Smith was a little older than me. He seemed hurried and a little disorganized. But he also seemed friendly and full of energy.

"It looks like you two are the only ones here tonight", not looking at all disappointed. He handed us both a disclaimer form which we signed, then we all removed our shoes and socks and walked onto the floor.

"Let's sit down", he said.

The three of us sat in the middle of the floor. Dan explained a little about Shotokan karate and about the club, some of which I had already heard from Tony. He explained that the club was part of the Mid-America karate region which was part of the International Shotokan Karate Federation, which, in turn, was a part of the Japan Karate Association (JKA), with headquarters in Tokyo, Japan. Fifteen minutes later, Sensei (he explained that Sensei was whoever was teaching at the time, "don't call me Sensei outside of class"), started the class.

"OK, ready? Let's line up here. We stood in line at where Sensei pointed. The first lesson started.

"Here's how to make a fist. Hold both hands out in front of your body, about chest height, palms up. Roll your fingers up into your palms, one at a time starting with your little finger, and lock them down with your thumb, like this. Now, turn your hands over, palms down".

He showed us how to form a straight line at our wrist, not bent up or down. He showed us how to do basic punches. Then he showed basic stances, first with hands on our hips, just concentrating on good form, then adding basic lunge punches as we moved forward, then backwards, which was much harder. Towards the end of the one-hour class, I saw other students start to arrive. They shouted a greeting, "OSU", strongly and with confidence. I would go on to shout this same greeting thousands of times over the years that followed. Sensei acknowledged them one by one with the same strong "OSU".

The students would change into karate uniforms somewhere in the back, walk up the rear entrance to the floor, bow, and then step onto the floor and start stretching. Any talking was in a whisper, no loud chatter. Lastly, Sensei taught us the front kick. First, in place with the feet shoulder width apart, then from a stationary front stance, then, while moving forward. Class was over. We lined up and Sensei taught us how to bow out. Tony walked over to greet me.

"I knew you would be here. What do you think?"

We talked for a few minutes, almost in a whisper. Someone said "line up" and Tony excused himself and went to join the rest of the fifteen or so students, including four black belts. I could not keep my eyes off the black belts.

The black belt at the head of the class said something, in Japanese, I assumed. Everyone kneeled down on the floor. Another command was given. The entire class was silent. After about a minute, another command was shouted. The Sensei and students bowed towards the photo on the wall of the old white-haired man and then to each other. I was to find out a short time later that the "old, white haired man" was the founder of Shotokan karate, Funakoshi Gichin.

Then it was everyone up and spread out across the floor in even lines, black belts directing the patterns, ordering students to do this or that. One of the black belts was chosen to lead the class in warm-ups and stretches. All of this was done in rhythm, counting in sets of ten. Then the black belt stopped the warm-ups, had the class come to attention and bowed to the Sensei, who walked to the front of the class and bowed.

What happened next is what sold me on this style of martial art. The Sensei commanded something, again most likely in Japanese. The entire class moved in unison into a stance. I recognized it from my beginner's class. Then I witnessed a series of punching and kicking techniques, all with a set of slow-speed and then high-speed moves across the floor. No talking. No joking around. Everyone doing exactly what they were told, and doing it as good as they could. The level of effort was amazing, as was the level of respect.

Sonya was the woman who stood with me at the locked door before the first class. We watched the advanced class until the end and left as they were bowing out. Some of the other students left with us. Others stayed and talked to each other, wiping the sweat off their foreheads and practicing moves. Some were sparring.

Sonya and I came back on Thursday and then on the following Tuesday and Thursday. Each time we stayed a while to watch the advanced class. I was always awed by that class, especially the higher ranks. Their moves were clean and powerful and their sparring was fearsome, with occasional injuries and bloodied noses. Which is why, on Thursday, I was startled when Sensei said Sonya and I could enter the next class now, after just two weeks in the beginner class.

She and I looked at each other, fear in our eyes. I asked Sensei, "really? I don't feel ready".

"Me neither", said Sonya.

"I know the beginner's class is supposed to be eight weeks but you two have had private instruction for two weeks. Don't worry, you will be fine".

With that, we joined the next class.

Sonya and I walked out of that class and went directly to Churchill's, a bar in downtown Flint. We had become good friends and had already formed a pattern of going to karate class and then going out for drinks, either to Churchill's or Doobies. We eventually became friends with some of the advanced class students and they often went to the bar with us.

Chapter Four

We trained hard, eager to improve, and had a good time with the other karate students. But we had the best time when we were alone together. We would pick a bar for Friday and Saturday. We would eat and drink and sit and talk for hours. Sonya was anti-Reagan and liked to blame him for all the ills of the world. I agreed with her on many topics. After a lot to drink, she would become more and more argumentative. Her gestures, which were at times, even without drinking, erratic, would turn staccato after a couple of hours of drinking.

After one karate incident, I needed to talk it over with her as soon as we arrived at the bar. Joe Ferguson had punched me square in the nose. My eyes watered. My nose was bleeding. I couldn't see anything. He seemed fierce to me at that time. He always stepped in fast and his punches and kicks were so close I could feel the power. As a white belt, most of the advanced students were easy on me. He was not, except for making contact. He normally stopped his punches and kicks just short of contact.

Tonight-he had made contact. We were doing three-step sparring. One person steps in three times with a basic punch while the other steps back and blocks. On the third step-in, the defender blocks and then counter punches. Joe stepped forward once, twice, and then a third time, and I felt his fist slam into my face. I had never before felt a direct hit to the head. Now I know it was actually a controlled hit and not full power, but at that time I could see, not stars, but darkness.

"Get up", he said. "Get up and continue. Get up and finish, it's not that bad."

I got up and finished the drill. Joe ran to the corner and brought back some paper towels.

"Here, clean up a little."

There was no "I'm sorry", no "are you OK?" After class he told me I had good spirit. Sonya and I talked for many hours.

"He doesn't like me", I said.

"Why?"

"I have no idea."

In fact, there wasn't a reason he would dislike me. The abuse continued for another couple of weeks. Joe punched and kicked me in the three-step sparring drills. I was unable to block effectively and more bloody noses followed. During a kicking drill I didn't hear the command to start. Joe did. The pain exploded inside me. I could feel it start as a low kind of ache and rapidly expand into my legs and arms as if some kind of pain pump was turned on. Finally, my stomach was cramping and I felt I would black out. I felt sick and thought I would throw up. The problem is that I have never been able to throw up. The final trigger never comes. Instead I usually just gasp, choke and bear the pain until it goes away, which is what I did. Holding my stomach and bending over, the Sensei came over to me and put his hand on my stomach as if to remove the pain. Then Joe walked over and held me upwards.

"I'll take care of him", he said.

He took me over to the corner, sat me down and put one hand on my stomach and one on my upper back. He gently massaged both areas and ordered me to control my breathing. Sensei was explaining and demonstrating the next drill. Outside my cloud of pain, I could see the drill. Sensei had the students go over the next moves slowly and then told them to try it at fast speed.

I jumped up to join the class. Pain was still inside me but somehow, I just wanted to fight my way out of this situation. Joe attempted to stop me but I shook him off and got back in line. He followed me.

"You sure you're alright?"

"No. I'm not".

I still felt like vomiting and had a headache that was making my eyes squint.

"Let's just do it", I said.

"OSU" He replied.

We went through the drill. The line rotated and a new partner stood across from me. The class finished the drill. Sensei then started to work on kata. We started with Heian Shodan, the first kata, and worked through it by the count, then did it again with no count at slow speed and then at fast speed. The brown and black belts were told to walk around and help the beginners. Of course, the black belt that was to help me turned out to be Joe. He was slapping me here and there, forcing me to "straighten your back leg", "push off and transfer your weight the front leg", then "push off with your new back leg".

"Bend the front knee-deeper"

"Stance is too narrow"

"Stance is too wide"

"Shoulders facing front"

"Elbow a fist away from your body"

Heian Shodan was over. Now we started Heian Nidan. I had only just recently learned the moves. We started out by the count. Turning left into a double block combination in *kokutsu-dachi* (back leg bent stance), I formed a left arm block to the side and a right arm block to the front. Joe was there in a second. "Here we go again", I thought.

But something changed. He gently guided my blocks into the correct positions, pushed my right hip down while adjusting my stance. Then he stood in front of me. Moving slowly, he stepped in with a lounging punch to show me the *bunkai* (application). Then he quickly moved to my left, coming in again to show me the application from the side. Then he showed me the entire application of catching a punch, pulling it in and finishing off with a short punch and hammer fist to the head or stomach level.

He was quite expertly manipulating my body, forcing me to be in the exact location and explaining the whys and the hows. Now the individual moves made more sense to me and I could apply more speed, putting the moves together with more power. Joe was there with me, bouncing effortlessly around me, both playing the part of the attacker and victim to my blocking and counterattacks.

"Last time, with speed and power!", Sensei commanded.

I could feel the blocks working correctly. I could imagine breaking the arm of an attacker. My turns seemed dead on.

Sensei shouted "*yame* (stop)". I felt good inside.

"Heian Sandan". Sensei shouted.

I had not yet learned the moves. Joe again walked up to me.

"Go over in the corner and work on Heian Shodan and Nidan"

He stayed in the center of the class and started helping the other students. The class went through the Heian katas. Joe worked with the other students as he had with me, positioning their blocks and stances, forcing them to relax when necessary and tense as required by the kata.

Anyone under brown belt was told to line up against the back wall. Brown and black belts stood, facing us, in *yoi* position. First kata was Bassai Dai. It was and still is considered to be the gateway from the Heian and Tekki katas into the more advanced katas. It has a powerful first move and requires strong, fast hip rotation. A few years later, in Japan, I witnessed a Japanese Sensei tasked with building a kata team to compete at a Tokyo karate tournament. There were over twenty students from which he had to choose to be on the team. A total of five would be chosen, three for the team and two alternates. The sign on the dojo door said "Kata to be performed for elimination-Bassai Dai." But in fact, no one was allowed to perform the entire kata. Sensei stopped every participant after the first move.

"If the first move of this kata is powerful, the rest will be good and so will thc othcr katas".

I watched as a little over twenty students walked up to the center of the dojo, bowed, and performed the first move. From *yoi*, right fist cupped into the left palm and positioned in front of the body, one has to surge forward after a slow, kind of lean forward initial move. Nakayama Sensei said a few years later to let gravity help with the initial movement and don't hurry it. The right hand would be forced out in an inside-outside block and stop just as the right leg and left leg met after driving forward, the left leg supporting the right and the left hand supporting the right hand. The idea was to think of drawing a sword from the left side. From the initial push off to a complete stop, standing mostly on the right foot, took immense focus, power, timing and balance. Sensei judged each of us on just that move. Sensei said he would choose the final three-man team after a few months of practice. The team practiced weekly for three months. The tournament was held. Our team won first place. Such is the dynamic nature of Bassai Dai.

Back at the University Karate Club, I watched along with other lower ranks. The upper ranks had to perform the kata to the best of their ability in front of Sensei and in front of us. It was important to have this kind of pressure. Also, though, we had the opportunity to see what good karate looks like. Sensei gave the command, "*hajime* (begin)". There were a few seconds of silence. Then one black belt lept forward into the opening move, the others followed. It was clear even to me that the skills were of a much higher level. A few were far superior to the others. One of them stood out as an example that I decided to copy. It was Joe. He was the one that the others waited for at the opening move. His kata was a blend of power, speed, balance, hip rotation, timing and dynamics. This was the first training for me that offered the chance to see the higher ranks at their best and I was awed. Looking at Sonya, we both rolled our eyes in a silent communication of "oh my God-what are we doing here?"

Other advanced katas were performed by the group. Bassai Dai was followed by Jion, Empi, Kankudai, and Hangetsu. Each student was good at some of the katas and better at others, except Joe. Every kata was performed with the same amount of speed, power and grace.

The class ended. We sat in seiza, recited the dojo kun, and bowed out. We lower ranks grabbed damp towels and wiped the floor clean. Back in the changing room, the higher ranks were already stuffing their bags with wet karate *gis* and getting ready to leave. Joe was still there and was on his way out the door when I walked in.

"You OK?"

"Yeah, thanks for helping me"

"No problem. What are you guys doing tonight?"

"Who, Sonya and me?" Everyone assumed we were a couple. It was basically true but just friends and drinking buddies.

"We were going to Churchill's and have a few beers".

"Do you mind if I come along with you?"

Chapter Five

Joe met us at Churchill's. Generally, we parked on Saginaw Street and walked the two blocks to the corner where it was located. We saw Joe park a few spaces behind us and waited for him so we could all walk together to the bar.

"I've never been here." He said as we walked up to the door. "I never come downtown".

"We come here at least once a week, almost always after class on Thursdays."

"Beer is better than aspirin?" he asked.

"Sometimes that's the way I feel. Usually it's more out of frustration than from bruises and head shots."

We walked through the double doors. Both Sonya and I turned our heads to the right, on the hopes that our regular table was empty. It was. We had started to call it our crisis table because of the many discussions we had following karate class. The table was in a small section behind the door as it opened. It was a minor inconvenience now because it had been getting colder. Sitting at this table meant a short, cold draft each time someone walked in. Maybe that's why it was often not occupied. It was also more private then the rest of the tables in the bar. It offered the potential of occasionally standing up to demonstrate a karate move when the conversation ultimately turned to that, without the other patrons getting too freaked out. In the future this would become useful as Joe often became one of the regulars, along with some of the other more serious students.

We sat down. Immediately our favorite waitress came over to serve us.

"Who's this?" motioning with an empty beer pitcher towards Joe.

Sonya and I introduced Joe and told her a little about him.

"He's the guy that smashed you in the face?" We cringed.

"Yep. That's him. See Sensei, you're famous". We all laughed.

Sonya and I had no idea who Joe was and knew nothing about his past, his likes or dislikes. We were nervous. Maybe Sonya was more than I, since she had a hard time getting to know new people and a real distrust of people's intentions.

We ordered a pitcher of beer. Joe didn't have a favorite so he told us to order whatever was good. Since Sonya and I had started coming to this bar, and since we often sat at the same table, we noticed other regulars. Often, they also had their own favorite tables. Humans tend to follow patterns of behavior even in the most mundane, basic activities. We introduced Joe to several other people, with occasional replies on the order of "the guy who smacked you?"

The beer came. I grabbed the pitcher and poured the beer.

"Cheers". Joe was holding his glass up.

"Cheers". Sonya and I reciprocated.

"And thanks for your help tonight." I added. "The kata isn't as difficult as I thought. I learned a lot".

"It's a tough kata to learn. Heian Shodan is our most basic, simple blocks and punches, a couple of basic stances. Heian Nidan has more interesting blocks, some kicks and different timing. You did good, you too, Sonya."

As the night progressed, we came to know Joe better. He was now my Sensei. I had decided that night, after alternately calling him Joe, then Sensei and then clumsily addressing him as Sensei Joe. Years later, even after he and I traveled to clinics and tournaments together, I would still call him Sensei. That's Japanese karate.

Sensei worked at a GM plant in downtown Flint. He worked on the line as an assembler. He said there was always a little time to sneak behind the line somewhere and work on kata. He had a long-time girlfriend who had a young son. In the future we would also become friends with her as she came to many karate events. Joe would eventually marry her. "I want to give her a better life" he would say at the time. Many of us karate students went to the wedding. It was held at a railroad theme park in the north east side of Flint. It was a perfect day. Sensei and his new wife were very happy and content. As we learned more about Sensei that evening, he became less of a threat to me and more of a tough-love buddy.

Sensei did not like to discuss politics much. This bothered Sonya a little, as she was always interested in talking about "puppet politics", as she called it, and certainly liked to trash anything related to Reagan and republicans. Sensei had simple logic, a deep thinker but with no use for rationales or excuses. What I liked best about him was that there was no judgement. He accepted people as they were. "They could be wrong, but they are who they are", he said. Sensei drank his beer slowly. Sonya and I easily drank two to three times what he drank. He was reserved and relaxed.

A guy from a table against the wall on the opposite side of the bar wandered over. I had talked to him briefly before, a few weeks before, and did not like him much. He was quite drunk, as he usually was, and loud. He liked to be the center of attention at his table and usually took over the surrounding tables as well. Straight to our table he headed with his beer in his hand.

"Someone said you were a karate Sensei". He was talking directly to Joe.

"Yes. He is one of our Senseis", I replied. I introduced them. Sensei smiled and said hello. The jerk did not.

I do Tae Kwon Do. What do you think of that?" He looked at Joe.

"It's a good system, lots of tough fighters."

"You think yours is better?" He was still staring.

"Nah-just different. But Tae Kwon Do has lots of great circular techniques and beautiful kicks. Sensei was trying to praise the guy's system and his ego, which was clearly needed.

"I could tap you on the head before you get up out of your chair"

"I'm sure you could. But why would you want to?"

"Just to show you. You guys think I couldn't do it?" He looked at us. He was more threatening now. I remember thinking how can I get rid of this guy? He roughly sat his glass of beer on our table.

"I know you can do it. We just want to have a few beers and enjoy ourselves. Your style is great and I know you train hard. But can you please leave us alone?" I answered.

"You don't think I can do it, do you?"

With that, he started bouncing up and down in a loose stance. It was a clear pattern of faking, which is usually a sign that a kick is coming. I found this out later from Sensei.

The kick was fast. I hardly saw it. I'm sure it was intended for Sensei's head - the level was perfect as was the arc. The problem was that Sensei was no longer there. He raised his arms to block the kick, spun out of his chair while grabbing the guy's leg. With a right hand over the left twist, Sensei forced the leg down in a locked position. The guy had no choice but to go down with it. As he fell to the floor, his leg was still controlled by Sensei, who held him there, on the floor, for everyone to see. The manager was at our table instantly.

"What's happening here?"

Sensei, not missing a beat, simply said "just demonstrating some moves", letting go of the leg. Head still stunned from the forceful 'fall' to the floor, the jerk staggered up. Staring at Sensei, he slowly reached out, took his beer from the table, and started walking back to his table where his friends were trying not to stare.

"Sorry for spilling the beer", Sensei said. "We got a little carried away". Sonya was already wiping up the spill with the napkins on the table.

"Everything's OK?" The manager was looking at both of us. He knew us both since we were there often.

"It's OK" I said. "Sorry about the commotion." He left, walked over to the guy's table, had a few words with the group, and then went back to the bar.

I noticed that the guy was sitting quietly, not talking to his friends, just deep in thought. The other people at his table were also quieter than usual, not looking directly at him.

"Sensei, how did you do that? I didn't see it coming at all."

"I saw something was coming when he first came up to the table. It was only a matter of when. I could see his eyes and read his ego. Also, the people he is sitting with were all looking over here. The script was already written. You didn't see that?"

"No. I thought we might have to diffuse the situation but never thought he would pull that."

"He had limited choices, especially tonight with everyone looking. To me, there was no doubt he would do something stupid."

"I can't believe he was not able to kick you. There was no warning at all."

Sonya had known the guy for several months. I'm not sure about their relationship but she was always very friendly with him. I didn't like him much but he was never that much of an asshole since I met him a month before. Every time I saw him, always at Churchill's, he was friendly and talkative. Mostly he was trying to talk up Sonya. They must have had something, or he was trying to make it happen. I didn't know at that time and didn't care. Sensei was very relaxed, as if nothing had happened.

"Sensei, talk to us. How did you do that?"

"You guys." He started. "I knew he would do something. I didn't know what, but something. The most important thing is to always be ready for someone like that. In a way, he had no chance. I knew something was coming and was ready. I didn't even know what he was saying when he first walked up to the table. It was just a bunch of noise."

"How do I learn that?" I asked.

"You're doing the right thing. Training in karate will give you far more than physical benefits. If you're looking for just exercise, go to a gym, maybe lift weights and run a few miles a day. That should make you tougher. But with the study of karate, you will also read many books and so learn a different way to look at the world and the roughness that exists in it. I have books you can read."

"Can I borrow some of your karate books?"

"Sure, but some of them are not karate books."

"What do you mean? What kind of books? Some are about boxing?"

"Naw. You should read a lot of martial arts books, of course, but other stuff is good to learn also."

"Like what?"

"Try reading some stories about Zen, they have a ton of information that can add balance to your karate training. If you want, I'll write down a couple of titles for you."

But I was looking away from Sensei. The guy that Sensei had just dropped to the floor was walking over again.

"Sensei", I said.

"I see him. You stay in your seat."

But Sonya was up and, reaching over me, trying to warn the guy.

"Matt. Stop. Don't be stupid"

"Don't worry Sonya. I'm OK"

"Come on. Let's go outside for a few minutes. You need to calm down."

"No. I don't need to calm down. I am calm."

Indeed, he did look calm. In fact, he seemed like a different person now.

"It's OK Sonya. He slowly moved her hand from his shoulder.

"Joe, right?" He was now looking directly at Sensei.

"That's right. Sensei was looking at Matt, seemed to be staring deep into Matt's eyes.

"I owe you an apology."

"OK. Let's hear it."

Matt, shocked a bit to hear Sensei's response, stared back.

"Yeah, OK. Um, I apologize for being a jerk." Matt was still looking straight at Sensei.

"And I accept."

"Alright then", turning to Sonya, "and I'm sorry for my stupid actions." He was already turning around. He started walking back to his table.

"Hey, wait a minute." It was Sensei.

"Can you sit down for a few minutes?"

What followed was amazing. Sensei asked the waitress for another glass.

"Go ahead. Sit down for a couple of minutes."

"Sure, I guess so." Matt sat down on the chair closest to the door, the chair that had been knocked over during their scuffle. The glass was delivered. Sensei slid the glass over to Matt. Reaching for the pitcher of beer, Sensei reached it and moved it over to just above Matt's glass.

"Share some beer with us?"

"Maybe not a good idea!" Sonya said. She was looking at Matt with a face that said "don't you dare screw this up."

But Sensei motioned to Matt to raise his glass. Matt did. Sensei poured and they clicked glasses. Each had a sip of beer.

"Your arm OK?"

"Yeah, it's OK". The side of my face is swelling up though."

"Let's see"

Sensei reached over, gently felt the left side, just below the eye. It was badly bruised where it made contact with the floor.

"You guys get me some ice!" Sensei commanded.

"I'll get it", I said. There was ice in the table that held the last of the salad bar veggies. It was mostly melted but was the quickest and easiest to get. I grabbed one of the containers, dumped the remaining mostly-dried-out cucumbers into another container, scooped up some of the melted ice and headed back to the table.

"Get some clean ice" Sensei ordered. I went to the bar, quickly asked for and received a metal bowl full of new ice. Almost running, I handed the ice to Sensei.

"Sonya, give me your napkins."

Sonya handed over the napkins. Sensei laid one on top of the other until there were four of them stacked. He poured some of the ice onto the flat space, folded the corners upward, stood up and then applied the ice pack to Matt's face.

"Hold this against the area, about here."

Matt did as instructed. Sensei had him move the ice pack downward about an inch.

"That's better. I've had a little experience with bruises too."

I saw a weak smile develop on Matt's face.

"You were pretty fast." Matt said, switching hands on the ice pack.

"Saw it coming, maybe even before you knew."

"How?"

"Don't really know for sure. Just knew that something was coming. It had to be a high technique because of the table."

"But how did you know what kind of block to use?"

"It would have been the same block no matter what attack. The difference was just the counter. I had my own limitations. The attack would come. It would be high. And from the way you were standing, it would be from the left side. The door is too close here, right?"

"Yeeeh, right."

"The counter was just whatever worked. We do hundreds of blocks and counters every training. I do more in between trainings. It becomes automatic."

"I can see that." Matt again switched hands on the ice pack.

"How does it feel now?"

"It's better, thanks."

"When you get home tonight, take three aspirin. You'll feel even better in the morning."

"I'll do that, thanks."

With that, Matt walked back across the room and sat down at his table. There was talk but this time the talk was at a lower volume, with many glances over to our table.

I was totally stunned by the incident. Both Sonya and I just sat there all through their conversation. I expected another, much more aggressive encounter. It didn't happen. Sonya told me later that Matt was known as a tough person who never listened to anyone. Usually he tried to show off, especially bragging about his skills in Tae Kwon Do. Part of her interest in martial arts came from knowing him.

The night was coming to a close. The manager was putting chairs on top of tables in preparation for the morning cleaning crew.

"Ready to go?" Sensei asked.

I wanted to pay the entire bill but Sensei reached into his back pocket, pulled out his wallet, found ten dollars and handed it to me. I argued as best I could but Sensei would have none of it. I took his money and paid the bill. We got up from the table and started out of the bar. As I opened the door, Sensei stopped me.

"I'll go first."

Sensei walked out and looked up and down the street. Sonya and I followed him. We walked down the street to our cars.

"Thanks for coming with us." I said.

"I enjoyed it a lot. I'll give you some book titles next week."

He had remembered that small conversation.

"Great. Thanks. See you next Tuesday."

We all shook hands. Months later it become hugs all around.

Sonya and I went back to my house.

"Let's try to do that."

We sat down at my kitchen table. We took turns trying to recreate the incident at the bar, first me standing and kicking at her head, then her trying to kick me. Both of us working on the block and counter that Sensei performed.

“If that’s what I’ll be able to do, I’m going to get more serious.”

“Me too.” Sonya said. She was picking her keys and purse up from the table. We were together four to five times a week but she always went home.

Chapter Six

Tuesday came. We were all stretching before class. A few, including me, were doing light free sparring. It was still a few minutes before class would start. I had just finished sparring with a blue belt. I did very well, I thought, and was feeling good. Then Sensei Ferguson walked up and asked me to spar. After the incident at the bar, I felt at ease with Sensei and was all for it, thinking that since we were friends now, he would take it easy on me.

The jab caught me by surprise. My head was thrown back. Then came the foot sweep. I don't remember seeing it, just remember my legs going out from under me and floating to the floor. Sensei reached down and helped me up.

"Let's go!" He ordered.

The next two attacks were similar, with me ending up on the floor. I was frustrated, but there was no damage or pain, just exhaustion and embarrassment. Then Sensei stopped the foot sweeping and started using another set of attacks. He would fake a foot sweep and then attack with a reverse punch, short roundhouse kick, both to my stomach. Again, not much pain or damage. But the snap of the kick did sting and added to my frustration. Then, suddenly, he stopped.

"Take front stance." He commanded.

I did what he said, left leg forward in a down block position, front knee bent deep.

"No, this is free sparring. Not so deep, hands up like this." He demonstrated.

He manipulated my left hand upwards and my right hand lower, both hands in front of my body, elbows a little inward. He turned around beside me in a free sparring stance.

"Like this." He repeated.

He turned my body more sideways, bent my legs a little, while raising me up in stance.

"I want you to use this stance for a while. Later you can adjust to suit yourself."

He turned around to face me as my opponent.

"Now, jab with your left hand." I did as he ordered.

"Pull back with your opposite hand. You can generate more power and speed."

I tried it again.

"That's better. Now jab again and follow with a reverse punch. I did this ten times with Sensei correcting me and adjusting my body for good, efficient technique.

"Now I want you to push off with your back leg while doing the jab, let your front leg slide forward and the back leg catch up, then push off again with the back leg, use your hips, for the reverse punch. Push off hard and don't come up in your stance, like this." He again stood next to me to demonstrate.

We practiced a few times. Back in front of me now, he told me to attack him with the same speed and power we had just practiced.

"I'm your target. The jab should be at my face level. The reverse punch should be at my stomach."

Backing up to make distance from me, he instructed, "you have to reach me with the jab. It has to be real. It can be a feint or it can connect. Either way it has to look real."

We practiced for a few minutes. Then Sensei had me change to right leg forward sparring stance. We practiced the same drill again. It was not as easy as before.

"Start out slowly. Whenever you are learning something new, start slowly, get it down right, then speed up." We practiced until I could do the drill fairly well.

"OK. Now we'll try some free sparring again. This time, I can do whatever I want. You can only use the jab/reverse punch combination we just learned. Whenever you see an opening, take it. Don't forget to block!"

We started sparring. Sensei attacked. I tried to block. When I thought there was an opportunity, I pushed forward hard with the jab/reverse punch combination.

"Get your hands up!" He said, as he tapped me on the chin with his own jab. It stung. I raised my hands. He gave me openings. I attacked. Mostly he would let the attack in. Sometimes he would block and counter it. A few times he would again foot sweep me.

"Just keeping you honest," he joked.

I knew he was teaching me and not just beating me up. My frustration was gone, replaced by focus and effort.

"Hai, yame!" He ordered. Class will start soon. Take a break."

I was sweating hard, but still had an hour-long class to get through.

"OSU" I said, and bowed.

"Stretch some more before class starts", he said, after returning the bow.

Sensei left and went over to the entrance area. A new student was standing there. It was Matt. He was standing there in a black karate gi that was covered in patches. On some of the patches were names of companies, presumably past sponsors to events. He also wore a black belt. Sensei was there in a flash.

"OSU" he said while simultaneously bowing and holding out his hand. Matt bowed, shook Sensei's hand vigorously and walked out onto the floor.

"You cannot wear that belt yet, not here." Matt did not hesitate. Off came the belt.

"And as you can see, we wear a plain white gi." Matt backed off the floor.

"But today it is OK, Sensei motioned. "Wait here."

Sensei walked over to the corner cabinet, opened the glass door and pulled out a white belt.

"Here you go."

Matt pulled the new belt out of its plastic wrapper, removed the rubber band holding it together, and started to put it on.

"Please turn around" Sensei interrupted. "You can't dress in front of the seniors."

Matt obliged. Finished, he stood there.

Sensei Ferguson walked Matt over to Sensei Church, who was the teacher for the next class.

"This is Matt. He wants to start training here today. I think it is OK, even though it is between programs. He has some prior experience."

Introductions made, Sensei Ferguson told Matt to warmup and get ready for the next class. I walked over and said hello. Sonya was already there. She was clearly surprised.

"Matt called me over the weekend. He wanted to know Sensei's number. I gave him the dojo number. He said he wanted to stop by and observe a class. "

"Looks like he's doing more than observing." I replied.

The class was called to start. We all lined up. Matt took his place at the end of the line. I thought it would piss him off, but if so, he didn't show it.

As this was the intermediate class, after warm-ups the first training was Heian Shodan. Matt did not know the kata at all. Sensei Ferguson told him to take a place in the middle of the group and copy the moves from the other students.

We did the kata three times, first, by the count, second, by the count but fast speed, third, no count with speed. I was watching Matt. He was intense. He copied the moves and seemed to learn the moves quickly. By thc third run through, hc did wcll, making crrors in direction and in technique, but better than the other beginning students who had already learned the kata. Matt kept coming to our dojo and did very well until he left the state for a better job. We held a going away party for him and let him know how much we enjoyed him in our classes. He stayed in Shotokan karate and for many years later I was still meeting him at the annual Master Camp.

The class went by quickly, as always. It was time for the forty-five-minute advanced class. I bowed out. But Sensei Ferguson yelled across the room, "Busha. You stay."

I was shocked-and scared. I looked at Sonya who was already outside in the hall. She grinned and mouthed "good luck!" I gave her a look that showed my fear. The advanced class started immediately. Again, we lined up, me at the far left. Everything seemed different. The mood was more serious and intense. This time the class was led by a visiting teacher from Ann Arbor. He was traveling to Flint in order to train and spar with Sensei Ferguson and the other higher-ranking students. He was going to take the Nidan test in a few weeks.

What followed was the hardest forty-five minutes of my life to date. At the start, we were told to find a partner. A strong brown belt ran over to me, as if to quickly claim his victim. I knew I was going to get killed, and I was even more scared. Sensei barked out orders. Starting with one-step sparring, we went through a dozen different attacks.

Then we were told to raise our stances a little, push off from our back leg (I'd heard that before), and relax. The rounds were three minutes each. We fought three minutes, took a thirty-second break, and started again. This we did ten times. Then we changed partners. Next was a black belt, for another ten rounds. I had four different partners. It was a hard and brutal training and I was getting killed each time.

But I tried hard. When I was foot swept, I got up fast. Attacking as fast and as hard as I could, I had a few successes but a lot more times where I was knocked around, thrown around and hit mercilessly. Always the intent was to control the punches and kicks. In reality, because of the intensity, contact was often made. I had more than my share of that contact. And then it was over.

Or so I thought. Sensei Ferguson stopped me from leaving the dojo floor. He also stopped a couple others, three in total, and told us to stand at the opposite side of the floor. All the others bowed out and left. I had no idea what was happening, not did anyone else.

"You three need to take the kyu test. We watched you during the last class. Any objections? Can you stay a little longer?"

Nobody objected.

The test for all three of us took no longer than thirty minutes. Later I found out that all of us had passed before we took the test, which was just a formality. I was now a yellow belt and one of just two that were invited to the advanced class.

"Your technique needs a lot of work. You have to pay attention to details. In a lot of ways, you are sloppy-but then you are still a beginner." Sensei Ferguson said.

"So why am I going to the advanced class?" I asked him.

"You've got a lot of guts for a beginner. We'll make sure you clean up your technique. This is best for you. But you need to practice more. That means almost every day. Can you do that?"

"Yes."

From that night on I attended the intermediate class and then the advanced class. And although I was very busy with school and work, I did manage to train more outside of class, a habit I continue to this day. This of course, prevented Sonya and me from driving together to the bar after karate. There was nowhere to really sit and watch the class, and anyway Sonya was not a watcher. She became bored quickly. She started leaving after intermediate class. I would meet her after the advanced class finished. Of course, by that time she was already a little drunk.

With Sonya, it was best to start drinking together. The conversation could be controlled or guided better. By the time I arrived, after idle chatting that kept me at the dojo for a few minutes beyond the end of class, Sonya had been sitting at our table and was often in a foul mood. Without me to bounce her numerous daily political complaints off, she stewed over a pitcher of beer by herself. I tried my best, when I finally did arrive, to calm her down. Sometimes I could. Most times I just let her rant on.

Joe Ferguson – Denver and Swartz Creek Dojo

With all the extra training, both inside and outside the dojo, I progressed much more quickly. Sensei pushed me hard. Why he took so much interest in me, I don't really know. He never asked me if I wanted to learn more, maybe a new kata or a new technique. He just called me over to a corner and taught it to me. Besides the intermediate class and the advanced class, I was sometimes told to stay after class and work out, less formally, after the doors were closed. At these trainings I learned techniques that were not taught in any of the regular classes.

We learned, and practiced, how to attack vital points of the body, what pressure points were best, and how to maneuver a person into position to be able to strike them. From these sessions I received many bruises. But I started feeling stronger, and my body changed. Three months later I was a blue belt, then green.

Chapter Seven

"This dojo will be closing soon." Sensei announced at the end of the intermediate class. Sonya and I looked at each other. With the difference in belt level we were no longer standing next to each other.

"I will be moving out of state to start a business. But don't worry. Sensei Church is opening up a new dojo. Sensei Church…."

Sensei Church stepped out of line. He was there for every class and was a fierce fighter. An inch or so shorter than me, he attacked as fast as Sensei Ferguson. I didn't like sparring with him much. He was a great person and later we would become friends. But at that time, he lived and breathed karate. He never held back and, though he agreed in principle with the idea of *sun-dome*, his energy and spirit usually got the best of him. This resulted in many split lips, black eyes, jarred teeth and huge bruises. It seemed at the time that he treated me the same as the black belts, though I was a green belt.

Sensei Church told us where the new dojo was, on South Saginaw Street, all the way across town. This dojo would be open another month. The new dojo would open at about the same time. Sensei Church would keep the "University Karate Club" name.

Sensei Church, finished, stepped back in line. We bowed out. Usually there was a silent break for a few minutes while the intermediate class filed out. The rest of us would do some stretching or light free sparring. This time, everyone was talking. There were many disappointed and angry students.

Sensei Ferguson was at my side.

"You're coming to South Saginaw Street, right?"

But life at the current University Karate Club was not yet over. The following Tuesday, Sensei Church introduced us to a new black belt. Don Elford had been training in Fort Lauderdale with Takashina Sensei for nearly two years. Now a nidan, he was soon to compete in a regional tournament in the South Atlantic Karate Association. The entire evening was dedicated to helping Don by providing him with numerous victims on whom he could practice his techniques.

It was fun and scary to watch. Sensei had us make a large circle. Don stood in the middle. We were instructed to kiai loudly and attack strongly. Don's job was to listen for the kiai, turn towards it, and defend himself. This he did very well, rarely missing a block and counter. Only our Sensei and Sensei Ferguson were able to score on him.

I had my turn also. With a loud kiai, I pushed forward as hard and fast as possible. The next second - I was on the floor. Don helped me up and asked if I was OK. I remember starting to answer but then another loud kiai rang out from the other side of the circle. Don turned around to successfully block and counter the attack.

Jim Nelson was there. He was a purple belt and he attacked strongly. The next thing I saw was a powerful round house kick that landed on the side of Jim's head. The force of the kick knocked him across the floor and down onto his knees. Jim remembers Dan whispering to him, "That's why we don't do that drill very often." Jim took over the Swartz Creek dojo in 1983 and ran it continuously until 2018 when he turned it over to Carol Glenn, but he still kept training. He has been a main player in the Mid-America region of the ISKF since that time.

Jim Nelson – Swartz Creek Dojo

Sensei Carol Glenn – Teaching Women's Class at Corunna Rd Dojo Mid 1980's.

It was a special night. Sensei Ferguson and Don sparred. Although he certainly gave Don the best fight of the evening, Don's technique was more advanced and showed the benefits of training with Takashina Sensei, a graduate of the JKA instructor school, and one of the most prestigious and tough Senseis in the world.

Don was in town visiting his family. He stayed two weeks and attended every class, teaching two of them. Don eventually became a police officer and then a detective. From 2003 until the end of 2018 he worked at the CIA and said he had many challenging and assignments which allowed him to see much of the world, including places he never wanted to see again. But all in all, for a retired police detective, he told me he never imagined himself in many of the places he went. Don's classes were hard, but for a different reason. He would introduce a technique, say something like step back with rising block and reverse punch, then step forward with front snap kick and another reverse punch. We would do the technique slowly by the count, perfecting each move. Then we would speed up, still by the count, gradually improving the power and speed. Lastly, we would be instructed to go full speed and power, performing the entire set at each count. When finished, we would simply change legs, this time right leg forward, and go over the entire drill again, training the other side. A couple years later I learned that this was classic Takashina Sensei training. Don told me that Takashina Sensei could go weeks and barely acknowledge your presence, classes were very hard but rewarding.

Sensei would teach the same class for two to three months at a time. The good part of that is you could see your technique improve. The bad part is that once you realized what the class was, you knew what was to come. No matter what the technique, when you started with one side you knew you were going to do the same with the opposite side. He was a professional and knew how to teach.

Don Elford & Author – Corunna Rd. Dojo

Don Teaching Class in Swartz Creek Dojo With Jim Nelson & Glen Glenn

Denver Tournament

Don also told me another wonderful story about a New Year's training party in 1977/78.

"We trained from 11pm to after midnight. Then we showered, dressed and a party ensued at the dojo. During the party Takashina Sensei said it was time for all to sing individually. Now, I can't carry a tune with a backpack and I'm aware of that. So, Ron (Don's friend and dojo mate), his girlfriend, and I, did our best imitation of Diana

Ross and the Supremes 'Stop in the name of Love'. Laughs were had by all. Sensei sang some god-awful song and it was then that I realized that as bad as I was, there was one thing I could do better than Sensei - sing! After the party, the die-hards, think it was Steve, Ron, Paul Leong and maybe one or two others and I, were invited to Sensei's apartment. There his wife provided some food and then retired to let the boys have fun. We drank with the realization that every time Sensei opened a bottle of liquor we couldn't leave until either it was finished or he was asleep. During this time, Sensei reached for his samurai sword but would not unsheathe it because if he did, he explained that blood would have to be drawn. Good decision. After he opened a bottle of Courvoisier. I thought all was lost. During that bottle Sensei thankfully fell asleep and we all quietly slithered out and headed to an IHOP. After eating we headed to Ft. Lauderdale beach and as the sun came up, we fell asleep there. I woke up later with half my face in the sand, saw the water and started to crawl towards it only to realize that while we slept, the beach had become crowded and many were staring at the sight of us and how we welcomed in the new year."

***

Takashina Sensei would be the guest instructor at many of the annual Michigan summer camps a few years later. He would also become what I considered to be my personal Sensei, even though I only studied with him at camps, regional trainings, at Jim Nelson's dojo in Swartz Creek, and at the dojo that Don and I briefly opened in Flint. He would write a letter of introduction for me to his friend Kondo Sensei in Ueno a few years later when I was living in Japan. I remember visiting the States and attending the Michigan Camp after having lived in Japan for a couple of years. We talked for a few hours, in a mixture of Japanese and English.

Takashina Sensei – Master Camp

Author with Takashina Sensei – Michigan Summer Camp

Michigan Summer Camp

"Busha" (he always called me by just my last name), "Japanese is good *da kedo* (but), *sonkeigo, kenjougo, to teineigo mo benkyo shite kudasai ne.* (please study the other forms - respectful, humble and polite forms also)." Of course, I began to study them upon returning to Japan.

We had another conversation, mostly one-sided, with Takashina Sensei lecturing me on budo. And it is from him that I learned the meaning of budo and the difference between budo and "just" karate. I could have listened to him all day long, always mixing serious discussion with laugh-out-loud jokes.

We moved to South Saginaw Street. The club got bigger as more visitors started to drop by. That was one advantage to relocating outside the campus area. Don returned to Florida. For now, the South Saginaw street dojo was led by Sensei Church. Sensei Ferguson also started teaching more of the classes. About this time, we started to meet and become friends with karate students from other parts of the region, roughly Michigan, Ohio, Indiana and parts of Kentucky and Pennsylvania. It was called the Mid-America region and led by Sensei Greer Golden.

We traveled to each other's dojos and went for special clinics and tournaments, even some open tournaments, meeting many excellent people who remain my friends thirty-years later. Friends I would trust in any situation. We would fight each other hard, but always respectfully. Afterwards we would joke and drink with each other. They are the most respectful, tolerant, understanding and least bigoted group that I know. And one can find them in all parts of the world.

Author – Open Tournament Tennessee

Shodan (Black Belt) Test Ann Arbor With Doug Goldstein

Shodan Test Ann Arbor

Shodan Test With Sensei Golden & Don Elford

Great Instructor & Friend

The South Saginaw street dojo was home for a few years, from green belt to Shodan. My shodan test did not seem very remarkable at the time, since we were all participating in clinics and tournaments almost every weekend. It was held in Ann Arbor. Sensei Golden was a main force at the time. He was still very active in the region and would travel to give clinics and help run tournaments. He taught great classes, very hard basics with good sparring drills. He had one of the best front kicks I've seen, even in Japan. At a clinic in Ann Arbor, we were fooling around between classes. Sensei Golden called the black belts over to the side of the gym. He lined them up, had them take fighting stance, and then, one by one, went down the line and attempted to attack each of them with a front kick. They were told it would be a front kick and they were free to defend any way they wanted. Not one of the fifteen black belts were able to stop or otherwise block his kick, which found its way to the mid-section every time, making even seasoned nidans and sandans bend over with pain. It was the topic of conversation at the after-training party that evening at the Cottage Inn in downtown Ann Arbor.

After picking Sensei Golden up from the airport one summer so he could teach at one of the Michigan Karate Camps, he stayed over at my house in Flint. In my living room he taught me what he called 'the alphabet of techniques', knocking over furniture and slipping on rugs that covered my wood flooring in the process. And of course, we talked about training in Japan.

My wife remembers a great story about Sensei Golden. It was at a regional clinic in Delaware, Ohio. She was sitting high up in the bleachers reading a book when Sensei Golden walked in (this was before she started training in karate). He placed his karate bag on the lower bench and my wife walked down to say hello. Finding herself standing above him looking down, she immediately recognized the impropriety of the situation and stepped down below him to continue the conversation. He was moved, and his entire demeaner changed, "transporting me back to my years of training in Japan", he later told us.

Chapter Eight

(1984)

Master Camp was and still is held every year in June. All the masters from the ISKF came and stayed at camp Green Lane outside of Philadelphia. Nakayama Sensei and sometimes other Senseis from Japan also came. There were three trainings a day. We were awakened every morning by Bob, the loud camp coordinator, with his whistle. Bob and I had many great conversations once we got to know each other. And he played a very important part of making the camp run smoothly. We also heard his tweeting before each meal and at lights out in the evening, usually at ten o'clock.

The morning run started right after the six-am greeting by Okazaki Sensei, a short meditation and a warm-up. The *mokuso* session was always wonderful. The birds were singing loudly and there was usually a cool breeze. Then, already glowing from the run, we would fan out to our respective training areas determined by belt level. There we would find out which master would be the instructor. The masters would rotate through each training site so that all ranks would have each Sensei at least once. It was a good system. The camp was excellent. Karateka from all over the world would travel to Philadelphia, make their way to the main dojo, and get shuttled to the camp.

Master Camp in Philadelphia

There was also a friendship tournament that included sparring and kata. And of course, there was a *dan* test (black belt grading). The dan test was always well attended as there were only two or three venues from which to choose for the higher-ranking students. The judges were an impressive panel that included all the attending masters. It was a great opportunity to see that level of skill from all over the world.

The camp was looked forward to each year by many students. I was able to attend many times and enjoyed every one of them. Usually either me or another karate student would drive as we both had vans. There would be anywhere from four to eight of us crammed into the van. We would talk loudly and energetically, often singing along with songs on the radio. Driving from Michigan, it took about fifteen hours to arrive at camp, including bathroom breaks. We would drive the first nine hours and find a hotel. Always wanting to save money, we would send one person in to register, then all of us would sneak in and stay in the same room. There would be two beds and deciding who would take the beds and who would have the floor was always eagerly debated and subject to much joking. Usually it would come down to whoever was the oldest or whoever was the highest rank. Other times, when women were also along, we gave them the beds.

Arriving at camp the next day at around noon, we would usually have to wait until registration started at one o'clock. Getting there early meant you had your choice of bunk beds in the cabins. The cabins themselves were reserved in advance. I tried to get the lower bunk to the left, just inside the door. There was a little more space and more importantly, there were two windows, one in the front and one on the side, both forming a corner that allowed for a good breeze at night. In addition, further back in the cabin meant more traffic at shower time and dressing time. There were three toilet stalls, two urinals, and two shower stalls. Early morning and just after training proved to be the highest traffic patterns. The front was much less crowded.

The cabins were old, built in the 1950s. They were sturdy enough, as verified by summer storms that sounded as if they would tear the walls down but didn't. There was nothing extra though, just rectangular buildings with wood shuttered windows that would flip down by means of a rope and pulley system for when it rained hard, and became too windy or cold. None of us really wanted to close the shutters though. Any time there is a group of men sleeping together in one place, it is best to have air circulating.

Master Camp in Philadelphia

We signed in, hauled our bags to the cabin, unloaded our gear and parked the van in the small lot at the entrance to the camp. We were told not to leave cars inside the camp area as that would create a chaotic arrival scene and lead to safety concerns in the event of emergency. We picked out our bunks, unpacked our gear, putting most of it in either the small dresser provided or inside a drawer that slid out from the bottom of the bunk. Then parked the van in a gravel lot next to the entrance into the camp.

Finished with the unpacking, we were free to relax and watch the other campers arrive. This was fun for me because with the new arrivals came a host of different languages, cultures and races. It was and still is a diverse and international gathering of some of the most polite, hardworking and, again, tolerant people I have ever had the pleasure of meeting. This would become another trigger in my eventual relocation to Japan. I enjoyed the cultural differences very much and with each passing camp I grew more curious of other cultures. I also became more dissatisfied with my life in America and, especially, in Flint, Michigan.

Meeting the different karateka was always fun. As a black belt, one never knew who was opposite you in partner training. Black is black. They didn't know you and you didn't know them. Everyone wants to be their strongest and to show their skills, which led to overly energetic training at times.

Yaguchi Sensei taught the first training for my group at four o'clock. We did some basic techniques and then some sparring drills. After an hour Sensei told us to get a partner. I started looking around but was immediately grabbed by a tall, very serious looking guy who I had previously noticed during the basic exercises. I noticed him because of his fierce and fast moves and because of his no-nonsense approach. Others would train hard and do the basic techniques as well as they could. Between drills they would relax and talk. He did none of that. He stood in kamae stance and waited for the next drill, from dead calm to full force.

And then he was in front of me. He had grabbed me by the sleeve of my gi and pointed with his index finger, "you, me, OK?"

"OSU", I said, trying to be neutral and show no emotion. But I felt fear.

Sensei Ferguson had told us to pair up with someone new, someone from a different dojo or a different country. "You are too comfortable with people you train with every day. This is your chance to see how you compare with others. We all practice Shotokan but dojos are different and the Senseis are also different."

OK-so here I was, paired up with someone new. Not someone I chose, but definitely someone new, and someone scary.

After working on the sparring techniques separately, we were expected to know what to do. My preference was to always go through the technique, once with a partner, slow a few times and then fast, kind of work into it. Yaguchi Sensei did not do it that way, however. From the first attack, everything was at fast speed.

It was simple. Side A would step forward with a front kick and lunge punch face level. Side B was to step back with *gedan barai*, then raise the blocking hand straight up to also meet the oncoming punch.

Finally, side B was to reverse punch and side A was to block *soto uke* and reverse punch. Not an extremely difficult set of techniques. And not something I had never done a few hundred times at our dojo.

But my partner was not fooling around. His attacks were meant to make contact. His first front kick struck me in the stomach. The follow up punch caught me squarely on the chin. It was controlled somewhat but hurt like hell. I tried to reverse punch as the final part of the drill but his block stung my forearm and his follow up reverse punch again caught me in the stomach. This was just the first set. And just the first half of the first set since the next half would be me taking the role of attacker.

We did ten repetitions. I was getting beat up, hurt all over and was sweating heavily but kept trying harder to block his punch and counter attack. Every time I was out-matched. He came in hard and fast. Every technique made contact and hurt. I tried to go even faster and did make better technique after a while but that just made him concentrate more and the contact got worse.

We did ten, then twenty, then thirty sets. I was exhausted and beaten. "Change legs" Yaguchi Sensei commanded. This was torture. I was already spent. I knew there would be thirty from this side also. It started again. Now the other side of me would get bruised up. He stepped in, this time with his left leg and left lunge punch. I tried to block the first punch but was too slow. It slammed into my face. I went down.

Quickly getting up, we started again. Time after time his fist caught me in the face, his kick penetrated my mid-section, and my counters were rendered weak and ineffective. I was not only exhausted but frustrated and on the verge of passing out.

"Change attack person." Sensei shouted. This time I had to step forward with a lunge punch and front kick. He had to step back and block both the punch and the kick. I was tired but tried hard. I wanted to make contact with the punch. It was the first time I ever actually tried to make contact. But every time, he just effortlessly stepped back and blocked hard. The first time he dropped down with the block to jam my kick, his block caught my leg on the shin bone. Falling down from the force and the pain, I got back up and attacked again, with the same result. This happened twenty-nine more times.

"Change legs."

From right leg forward sparring stance, I kicked the floor as hard as I could off the left leg, changed to my right leg, and extended my kick as much as I could. He just batted it down as before. But when setting down, I thrusted my left hip forward and my left hand out, stretching into an extreme hanmi position, pulling my right hand back to my hip as hard and fast as I could. The punch caught him on the jaw. He staggered backwards and fell to the concrete floor. He did not get up.

I was completely surprised. The attack seemed effortless and felt almost like slow motion. It might have been the most perfect technique I had ever performed. His rising block was worthless. I don't know if it even made contact. I do know that I had to do something to stop the bruising he was giving me. All the lessons from previous trainings came back in an instant.

Yaguchi Sensei ran over to us. Another black belt was also there. Sensei asked my partner if he was OK but there was no answer. I bent down to try to help but the black belt with Sensei told me to stay away. I found out after class that he was a doctor and was assigned to our class. There always seemed to be a few doctors in residence at the camp, for insurance purposes, I suppose. The other students continued to train while the doctor worked on my partner. He moved over to his side and tried to stand. The doctor did not allow this though. I watched as two more black belts were ordered to take him to the infirmary.

The requested thirty sets were completed. All eyes were on us. Yaguchi Sensei walked up to me with a scowl. "You, find another partner." Then he returned to the front of the class. We trained another thirty minutes.

That was the first class. The rest of the week was much the same. Some partner training was hard but controlled and respectful. Some was not controlled and if there was respect, it came only from being as strong, or stronger than the partner.

Basically, I liked it all and grew much from the training. I did meet the guy from the first training again. We talked a while and I apologized a hundred times for my lack of control. Though I meant it when I apologized, at the time of the incident I felt both relief and pride in having dealt with him successfully. As I look back it was juvenile at best. He was an OK guy. We had one more partner training opportunity and we were both different. He was more controlled and, though he still made contact, did not attempt to do damage. I was much faster and was able to block many of his techniques.

I also did not fear him as I did before, partly because he was different with me now, and partly because I found myself moving faster and with more power than ever before. It was a great feeling and a big step for me in my karate life.

Chapter Nine

I was single. There were many female karateka at camp. In my world in Flint, Michigan, women were not exactly a snapshot of the country, that is, a small percentage of them were slim and healthy. A larger percent was overweight and would have trouble walking the length of a football field. But to be fair, I was not exactly a happy guy in Flint for the last few years, still living in a deep fog of dismal memories which surely tainted my perspective. Here at camp, the majority were thin, strong and energetic. And the cultural differences, even if they were from the USA, were striking.

The next morning, I woke at five AM, walked down to the small creek that ended at the base of the camp with the Shotokan rock watching over all of us. The rock was painted over every year by a handful of campers with the new date and a fresh version of the Shotokan tiger.

My purpose for waking early was to meditate alongside the creek. Meditation was still pretty new to me but I liked it and wanted to enjoy the peaceful early morning calm. I found a spot just below the rock on the bank of the creek, sat down on the cool grass, and narrowed my eyes, swinging forward and back, then side to side, gradually slowing until I was still, settling into a pleasant state of awareness.

At some point I became aware of motion and the sound of breathing, not my own. Opening my eyes enough to spot the source, just to the right, about twenty feet away was a most beautiful sight. Niki, as I found out later was her name, had come down to the creek. She was wearing her karate gi pants but had on a tank top instead of the gi top. It was a thin top, made more for a yoga class. It was short and ended just a few inches above her navel.

I knew she was the women's national karate champion, both kumite and kata, from seeing videos of her. She was practicing slow kata, I think it was Gojushiho Dai, but it was long before I knew the more advanced katas. I do remember her doing an advanced kata in a tournament the previous year. She was in the finals and during one quick, powerful turn, a barrette flew from her hair and made a loud clang on the floor, which was more pronounced since everyone was watching her performance in complete silence. She completely ignored it and carried on with her kata, eventually taking first place. Funny, the things one remembers after nearly forty years!

She was breathing in deeply with one move and then exhaling with the next. It was a magnificent sight. I was no longer trying to meditate, instead just watching her. The sun was rising, which created a sort of silhouette effect that made her look like a goddess. She went through a number of katas. Then she turned around, reached for a rolled-up pad behind her, spread it out and sat down, and started to stretch, at first on the pad with long yoga-like postures. Then she stood and did the "looking at the sky" pose that I recognized. It was lovely. While stretching, she looked over my way. I still had my eyes narrowed. I don't know if she was fooled or not. She continued to stretch and then, finished, rolled up the pad. She walked over and sat down across from me, not bothering to use the pad, adjusted into cross-legged position, just two feet away, and joined me in meditation.

Something strange was happening. I again tried to return to single-point consciousness where all noises, senses and, in this case for sure, thoughts, were to be ignored. We sat in silence for quite some time. I was aware of the birds waking with their excited chirping, a little of the breeze that was rustling the leaves above us, and of her.

She was breathing shallowly. I could feel her breath, not just hear it, and was acutely aware of her presence, yet it did not dominate. I was very deeply meditating. After a time, she said softly, "let's not be late for training". I opened my eyes fully. She was smiling and reached out both hands. I stretched out my hands to meet hers.

"Very nice meditation, thank you."

"My pleasure"

"Are you here every morning?"

"This is my first year here but yes, I will be here every morning."

"Can I join you then?"

"Absolutely. That would be great." I don't know if I was drooling or not.

Thus, we started to meet every morning. She would go through her slow training first and then walk over and join me. At the end of the week we were sitting closer and holding hands during meditation. It was a powerful experience. We became friends and although I would like to say we became more than that, it would be a lie. Close friends we were, but she was not interested in anything more. It was one of the few times in my life, up to that point, that I had so much respect for a woman. After that week, and with more involvement in karate, I was to meet many more women that would instill the same feelings of respect and real friendship.

In fact, from about that time and maybe a little before, with Sonya, I began to be interested in mostly karate women or at least women who had some kind of passion in their life. Karate women are strong, energetic, confidant and have a higher level of self-esteem than the average woman I have ever met, even today. They can be funny and also serious. In short, they can be anything they want because of their inner strength and beauty.

I have seen women fighting with men. They push themselves just as hard. I've seen them get foot swept, jump back up and get swept again. I've seen them get so banged up and frustrated that they had tears in their eyes. But they still got back up and fought. And they didn't quit until the teacher said "yame."

Niki was like that. She was at camp with a small contingent of students from Trinidad. I always wondered what their dojo training was like because all of them were good at both kumite and kata. They could often be seen together working on technique between classes. And every night they would hang out in one of the cabins until Bob blew the whistle.

But there were many women at camp. I was fortunate to meet and become friends with some of them. Sara was at camp without her husband. They both operated a dojo in North Carolina. He stayed home to keep the dojo open while she trained for the week. She was tall and thin and had long brown hair that fell simply over her shoulders. She was a vegetarian and already a Nidan. I met her the second day of camp. Part of the training, as Okazaki Sensei said was "to help with serving at mealtime."

My first waiter experience was lunch on that day. She was there along with ten others. After cleaning the tables, around forty of them, and setting out plates, silverware, cups, water pitchers, juices and bread, the waiters could sit down together and eat before the crush of the other campers arrived, then the waiters became busy serving food and picking up empty dishes.

We were both sitting at a table near the kitchen. I had noticed her before, when she was carrying plates and supplies to the tables. She was smiling and greeting everyone and looked like she was having fun instead of dreading this camp requirement. She wore a long cotton dress and a thin top. We exchanged glances, then smiles and then hellos. When it was time to eat the hurried lunch, we sat next to each other.

"Here's to more salad, yum-delicious."

"Not much here if you want to eat healthy foods." I replied. I was not, as yet, concerned much about the type of food I would eat. She was.

"What are you doing after lunch?"

"Just relaxing" I said.

"Would you take me to a grocery store? I need to buy some healthier foods, and need a little more variety.

"Sure. Do you know where a good grocery store is?"

"No. But I will find out. This is my third meal of lettuce and tomatoes. Thought I'd buy some carrots, beans, onions and other stuff, whatever I can find."

"OK, let's go. Let's meet at the bottom of the stairs at 12:30."

Bob's whistle announced the beginning of lunch for about two-hundred campers, usually a few less than breakfast or dinner. Many went out for lunch or slept.

The campers rushed in, trying to get a table with their friends and also getting a spot in the salad line and steam tables. Our job was to deliver two or three large serving bowls of hot soup to our assigned table, then hurry back to pick up dishes of meat, potatoes, sandwiches, or whatever else was on the menu for that day. In between trips to deliver first servings, we had to pick up empty bowls or plates and grab seconds for those that had already been emptied. It was a busy hour or so.

I never minded being a waiter and always announced to my table, in a pleasant voice, "Let me know if you need anything."

The Senseis also came to lunch, unless they were golfing. Okazaki Sensei was always there. I don't know if he didn't golf or just thought he needed to stay at camp and participate. The campers would file in, take their place at the tables, try to pick up something from the salad bar discreetly and then wait for the Senseis to arrive before starting to eat, which followed a rowdy "OSU" greeting. At the end of the meal, campers had to wait until Sensei stood and said "*gochisosama deshita*". Most thought it was "OSU" because everyone ran it together, rendering it indecipherable, but it was a traditional after-the-meal Japanese saying, not "OSU". This was emphatically pointed out by Sensei Golden one night after dinner. He made us repeat it a few times.

When the meal was over and the campers started filing out, the waiters had to take all the dishes back to the kitchen, empty them into the garbage can and set them down where the kitchen staff could reach them to follow up with washing. The tables had to be thoroughly cleaned with wet towels and the towels had to be rinsed and placed in a pile where they would presumably be washed and disinfected by the staff.

I liked lunch duty as it went very fast with most people wanting to get back to their cabins to take a nap or just walk down by the creek with their friends. Some would go to one of the dojo areas and work on kata or do some light free sparring. Since there was a dan test at the end of camp, some wanted to get in as much training as possible.

Sara was there at 12:30. We walked to the dirt parking lot, climbed into my Chevy van and maneuvered ourselves out of the lot and onto the main camp road. It was a narrow, gravel road and ran between a few old houses and barns that had been there at least a hundred years. Driving out onto the county road, we started talking and she pulled a joint out of her purse.

We talked about many things, her husband and their dojo, life in South Carolina, philosophy and my favorite at the time, psychology. We had a long discussion about behavior modification. She thought if there were strong enough leaders, or, if all households had morally and ethically sound heads, society would naturally develop and improve. The heads of State or of the family would know how to mold behavior, allowing the people to keep their personalities and all that makes them special, but changing them just enough to cut out the violent fringe.

My argument was that, yes, that might work, but where would we get those kinds of leaders? And where and how would each family be able to create a "moral and ethical head"? As far as I could see, morality and ethics are like a 'if I win the lottery' kind of dream. It's kind of like shooting a gun to celebrate New Year's. You feel safe shooting into the air because it seems like nothing is there, no one to hit. Of course, it comes back down to earth and risks hitting someone or something. "It is a false safety. The risk is just afterwards. One could argue that when it falls back to earth and causes harm, it had nothing to do with you shooting it into the sky.

"You have to have more faith in humanity." She said. "If we were to insist on moral and ethical behavior, and study ways to develop and promote it, there would be gradual change."

"Sure. But who says what is good behavior or acceptable behavior and what isn't? How could we, a mixture of personalities and cultures with very different values, goals and beliefs, agree on one "good" behavior scheme?"

From behind we heard the long blast of a car horn. We laughed. No telling how long we had been stopped at the intersection. I looked both ways, thinking that a car could come sailing through at any time. Another horn blast, I was moving but probably too slowly. Driving through the intersection, I pulled over to the right shoulder, and waited for the car to pass. He passed, with another long horn blast and a wave of his middle finger. I waved back but with my entire hand, mentally erasing the appropriate fingers.

Sara and I took this drive almost every day for the rest of the camp. We became very close. In the evening, when all camp activities were over, I walked her back to her cabin or she would walk me back. Often, we continued to talk and would often hide to keep Bob from seeing us after 10 PM.

***

It was a remarkable week. I was one of the nervous karateka that had a date with the examiner on Sunday. It was time to test for nidan. I had passed shodan just under two years prior to camp.

The time for the test arrived. Lined up at the head table were all the masters, Okazaki Sensei, Yaguchi Sensei, Koyama Sensei, Mikami Sensei, Takashina Sensei, Golden Sensei, Fields Sensei. There were fifteen shodans lined up to take their nidan test. We all sat in seiza position, that's the way it was then, until our name was called.

I waited as one group of three, then another and another stood up and took the test. I remember some sloppy tests and some excellent tests and thought at the time that I should be OK. My chosen kata was Hangetsu. Not much danger there, I had performed it more than a thousand times.

Nidan Test - Master Camp in Philadelphia

It went well enough. Okazaki Sensei then called out Jion kata. My heart skipped a few beats. I knew the kata but had practiced it less than a hundred times. "Make strong beginning!" Takashina Sensei had said at our Michigan summer camp. "Show dynamic changes, and *kime*."

I slammed my left leg backwards and blocked strongly and hard with upper right hand ude uchi and left hand gedan barai. Slowly I turned to the left with both arms extended into a spreading block, trying to show tension, then, exploded into the kick and triple punch combination, trying to show power and a solid stance.

It was over. I was told to get back in line with the others in seiza position. I tried to look back at my performance of Jion. Lots of doubts crept into my mind. Was my kibadachi good going down the embusen? Were my high and low blocks lined up with my body on the turns and not misaligned in front stance and in back of my body plane?

My name was called for basics. We were told to stagger ourselves to make room, stand on the marks facing to the right so as to do the techniques across and in front of the assembled masters. We went through numerous basics, all of us trying to be as low in our stance as possible, while still moving with power, speed and focus. The group before us did the same techniques. But I noticed that when they came to the end of one set of moves, I think it was the one where they started in kibadachi and stepped across with side thrust, then a turn and continue to step across with a side snap kick, the three of them ran into the audience of other karateka who were there to watch. Some of them would do the technique and then end up juggling in between the legs of the onlookers. Some would awkwardly try to dodge them by turning forty-five degrees towards the back of the dining hall, away from the judge's table. It all looked amateurish to me. A few even stopped and asked the judges "what should I do now? Is this enough?"

When it came my turn to perform the same techniques, and had reached a point where I would soon end up inside the audience, I shuffled back enough to make room, and then continued, hearing a couple of the judges say "OSU."

Then came sparring. We were called up two at a time to do first one-step sparring and then, the last part of the test, free sparring.

One-step sparring went well. I was paired with a guy from another Mid-America dojo who I knew fairly well. We had trained together a few times and got along well. We pushed each other as usual with both of us attacking strongly and counterattacking fast and hard.

My next sparring partner was someone I didn't know. He was about my size but more powerfully built. He attacked strongly also but took a side step before each attack. He would move his back leg over to the right and push off at more of an angle. I guess he thought it would confuse me. It didn't. Actually - it just made his attack slower.

The second time he did it, I also slid to the opposite side-that made us a good distance apart. When he surged forward the angle was so acute that he could not possibly make up that distance. I shot a rear leg round house kick to his mid-section that brought him to his knees. In truth it was probably too hard. It even surprised me. He was back up quickly though and we finished our one step sparring test with no major mistakes. He did not use the side step move again.

Then it was time for free sparring. I was thinking the same as everyone else, "who will I be sparring?" Watching as others go through their matches only makes it worse. Every time there is contact or someone is foot swept and hits the floor, it makes you feel less and less confident.

A good friend from a dojo in Ohio was up next. He was sparring a taller opponent from the East Coast Karate Club, Master Okazaki's dojo. And he was getting creamed. He hit the floor three times in the first minute. The third time he was hit in the head with a left round house kick and then swept with the right leg. It looked brilliant. He was getting up slowly and I could see blood trickling from just above his right eye.

The referee stopped the fight. He was helped off the floor by one of the medical staff. They carried him off to the infirmary about a hundred yards down the concrete path.

My name was called again. My opponent would be another guy from Okazaki's dojo. This guy I knew would be hard to fight. He had been one of my training partners in the regular classes and was tough and did not have much control. We took fighting stances. He attacked quickly, first throwing a jab that would have nailed me in the face had I not forced myself backwards and just barely managed to block it. Immediately his left foot shot out but from an upper block it is easy to drop down and block a low kick. My reverse punch counter caught him square in the chest.

Again, we faced each other. This time he did not attack, instead throwing a series of fakes and then moving back and forth and sideways. It looked impressive, I guess. I was waiting for a chance to match one of his side moves with one of my own, much as I had done in the previous one-step sparring match. That chance came, but my timing was way off. I shuffled to the right and pushed forward with a round house kick but found myself on the floor. He caught my kick and pushed through it while sweeping my support leg. I did not see it coming and had no defense for it. The referee called time and asked me if I was alright. I jumped up with an "OSU".

We faced off yet again. I had to do something that showed I was up to the challenge. So far, he was dominating me, except for the first half point. I stepped in with a fast round house to the head, more of a feint, unless it happened to connect. It hit him on the upper arm though. We kept fighting. He jabbed and it landed just above my left eye. The referee called a halt. We bowed to each other and to the referee and then to the table where the Masters sat. We both ran to the edge of the test area, turned and bowed again to the referee and to the table. My opponent and I then shook hands. He grimaced in pain. "Got to get to the infirmary. I think my arm is broken." "I'll go with you", I said, and started to help him through the crowd.

"It's OK. We'll take him down." His dojo mates were already clearing a path and putting a jacket around his shoulders. I stayed for the rest of the test.

The results would not be known until breakfast the next day. I would have to wait and go over in my mind all the missed chances and mistakes. But Sara was there and was cleaning the blood from over my eye. She took me down to her cabin and found antibacterial cream and applied it along with a bandage, then whispered, "You looked good."

Chapter Ten

It was a long night and I did not sleep at all. The more I thought about it, the more I knew I had failed the test. Hour by hour, just lying in bed, my mind went over every mistake and every move that showed lack of power, speed and spirit. Finally, I got up, put on a pair of shorts and a T-shirt, and walked outside. Going down the hill to the pool, I climbed over the fence and sat down on one of the lounge chairs. "Everything is OK", I thought. "If I don't pass, I'll start training again for the next test in December."

I started going over the test again in my mind. "They have to judge me in relation to the other testers. If they do, I should be OK. What did I do badly enough to fail? But where did I do good enough to pass?"

There was a slight breeze that felt good after the heat of the previous couple of days. I worried and fretted more, and then, fell asleep.

"Hey you, did you spend the night here?" It was Niki. She was talking through the chain link fence that surrounded the pool. "Your test was good. I'm sure you passed."

"I'm not sure at all. But I've been worrying about it too much."

"Come on. It's time to sit. This will be my last day. I fly out after lunch."

I climbed back over the still-padlocked fence, scrapping my hand on the top link. Blood was dripping slowly. Niki grabbed my hand and led me down to the creek and sat me down at our usual spot. We faced each other and she grabbed both my hands. She noticed the blood and calmly wiped it off with her towel, took my bloody hand, wiped it clean and then said softly, "be sure to put something on it". We meditated together for thirty-minutes. It was time to go to training. I still don't remember what the training was that morning. It was just a blur.

Back in the cabin we were showering and getting ready for breakfast. Four other people in our cabin had tested and it was quieter than usual. We were mingling with the other campers outside the canteen, waiting for Bob to blow the whistle. Soon we were inside, sitting at the tables and the waiters were serving the food. We talked and I tried to appear normal. Sensei Ferguson and Sensei Elford, Sonya and a couple others from our dojo were sitting next to me. “Everyone quiet down”. It was Bob, yelling as usual. “Sit down and listen up”.

Okazaki Sensei started to speak. “Yesterday we had a special training. Everyone did the best they could. Some people passed and some people must train a little more. For those that did not pass-ask your Sensei to help you with weak points. Always just keep training. You will surely pass next time. Do not give up.”

I knew he was talking to me.

“For those that did pass, my advice is the same. You still need to train more. Do not relax and think you are better than those who did not pass. Only-you did better on one day. Maybe today, if another test, you would not pass. Karate is like that. Just keep training.”

He reached down to the table and picked up some papers. “OK. So now we will read the results. We will read the names of those who passed. If you do not hear your name, please train harder and try again. When you hear your name, please stand up.”

He first went through the new black belts. There were fifteen or so that passed. They stood, listened to the results, bowed and sat back down. There was applause after each. My hands were sweaty and my stomach hurt.

Then came the nidans. Slowly, Okazaki Sensei read names aloud. Three, then four…then, my name. I stood up on rubbery legs. “Nidan” Sensei said. There was applause like the others. My table was especially boisterous. I bowed toward Sensei and sat down.

I hadn’t eaten any food. But after Joe and Sonya and the rest of my table mates congratulated me, I started feeling hungry. While the rest of the names were called, I started to sneak a few bites of the food in front of me. Reaching for the salt and pepper, I started to shake the pepper, stopped, felt the top of the shaker, tightened it and continued.

“Excellent” said Sensei Ferguson. “Guess you really are a nidan!” He had unscrewed the cap.

The rest of the test results were announced and Bob was yelling out the day’s schedule. Looking up, I felt a set of hands on my shoulders, “told you, no problem!” It was Niki.

Sara was standing over my other shoulder. “Congrats” she said. “Are we still going for coffee today?”

It was awkward but wonderful. Sara then spoke, “Niki-come with us”.

We had an excellent time together. Niki and Sara talked more to each other than to me but that was OK. I knew Sara and I knew Niki. They hadn’t known each other until now.

“Sara and her husband have a dojo in South Carolina”, I said to Niki. And Niki’s dojo is in Trinidad”.

“Trinidad?” Sara was very interested in this news. “I’ve always wanted to go there. Do you think I can visit sometime?”

“You are welcome anytime. Both of you are welcome.” She motioned to me.

“So, Niki-I hear you and Michael get together every morning for meditation.”

“Yes. We meditate and talk a little before morning training.” We sat there and chatted for another few minutes, the three of us touching hands on the table. Niki finally had to go. “Have to get to Philly by 6 PM” she said. It was already 2 PM.

Sara looked at me. “Let’s take her to the airport”.

“No-that’s OK. There’s a shuttle from camp.”

“No way. We’ll all go together. Are you all packed?”

“All packed and ready.” We drove back to the cabins, picked up Niki’s gear, and started for the airport. There was another training at 4:30, we would make it if the traffic wasn’t too bad. I drove my van. Sara sat in the passenger seat. Niki was in back. “Niki-come on up here.” Niki dragged the cooler up between the seats and sat between Sara and me. We talked about the week’s activities. They continually harassed me about my injury and about me knocking down my opponent, “very tough guy!” Sara said. “Think he could take us both on?” My mind was racing.

We barely made it to the airport on time. I wanted to sit awhile with both of them, but there was no time. We stood outside the gate. The rest of the passengers had already boarded. “Well OK. Guess we’ll see each other next year?” Niki said. “If not before!” said Sara.

"I enjoyed out morning sessions. I'll try to keep up the discipline from now on."

We all joined hands. I couldn't help myself and hugged Niki. Then she was gone. Sara and I left the airport and headed back to camp. We arrived at camp but sat in the van talking for way too long in the parking lot. In the side mirror I could see people walking across the road to the training halls.

We never made it to the 4:30 class. We took a long walk down the road leading away from camp, the same road we used for the morning run. We talked about everything. It was our last full day and we wanted to make it last and not leave anything missing.

It was getting cool and was already late. Bob had long ago blown the lights out whistle. It was totally dark on the road. We had no flashlight. Holding hands, we walked slowly. Gradually we came out of the wooded trail and arrived at camp. We walked through camp to her cabin. We were still holding hands but were no longer talking. Very reluctantly, I separated my hand from hers and started to say goodnight. She stepped after me, grabbed my hand again, and started walking me away from her cabin.

***

It was the last day of camp. Many campers were packing up their cars. The cabins were crowded with karateka hugging and shaking hands goodbye. The shuttle vans were parked in front of some of the cabins. The last training was light. Okazaki Sensei went through a summary of the week's drills. Sara and I partnered throughout the entire class. And she was attacking hard. Some of her kicks landed and hurt. But each time she smiled. How kinky this karate stuff could be!

After class was over, Sara and I said our goodbyes. It was hard to do. "Can we meet again soon?" I knew it was the wrong thing to say.

"We'll see. Things should go naturally. If we get together again, it would be good. But we can't force anything, OK?" I understood immediately. As discreetly as possible, I squeezed her hand. She returned it with a close hug. All this was acceptable in a group of karate people. We were all close, with men hugging men, women hugging women and group hugs everywhere. It is the same today among karate friends, even more pronounced as we have grown older together and known each other through births, deaths, marriages and divorces. Something about training hard and sweating together that breaks down many of the boundaries that exist in normal social situations.

"See you next year!" she said loudly. With that, she smiled, turned and walked back towards her cabin, turning finally, to wave one last time. Then she actually skipped across the lawn to her cabin.

My cabin mates were mostly all packed to leave when I arrived so I hurried and stuffed my things into bags. We made it to the van, threw the bags in, and started out. The ride home was quiet after so much activity. Everyone was tired and more than ready for a clean and private shower and some downtime. We drove the twelve hours home with just a few stops for gas, food and restroom breaks.

***

I was not prepared for what happened at the first training after summer camp. It was normal, I was to learn, that after passing to the next grade the newly promoted karateka was to be rewarded with personal training from all the seniors. That meant sparring lessons, of course! And they were all in attendance the first Tuesday back. I thought at the time that it was a little strange that all of them were present that night. We had the first class as usual, attended by the lower ranks. It went quickly, with the higher ranks all demonstrating spirit and power to the lower ranks.

We had a five-minute break. Sensei called the next class to order. "I have an announcement to make before we start class." Everyone was quiet. "We have a new nidan, second degree black belt, just back from Master Camp. If you haven't had a chance to attend yet, you should make plans for next year." He went on to explain about the camp and how it was structured. He then continued… "So, tonight we have a newly promoted nidan. We have a custom for promotions among black belts. We do this with new black belts and at each promotion after that. So, if everyone would make a circle."

The class formed a small circle, some of them not knowing what was going on. The higher ranks pushed them backwards into a larger circle. Sensei ordered me into the middle. Then I knew what was going to happen.

"We'll have three-minute rounds. Nobody will stop until I say stop. Everyone must attack as strongly as possible. If you aren't strong enough, you will do ten pushups. We'll start with the lowest ranks and progress to the higher ranks. Do not take the time to bow after each session. When I stop the round, I will call out the name of the next person. The next person will move quickly into the circle and start the attack. Now, everyone bow to the center."

The next hour was exhausting. The first fifteen-minutes went easily enough because it was the lower ranks. Then the brown belts stared. Brown belts are dangerous. They have a good bit of power and speed but lack control. Therefore, I had to use precious energy to keep a good distance and to avoid getting hit. I was starting to get tired though, and lazy. "Fight!" Sensei Ferguson said. "OSU" I answered.

Through with the brown belts, the black belts stared attacking. I started taking punches and strong kicks to the stomach and face. I was sweating hard and my legs were getting rubbery. Sensei Ferguson was next. His first technique was a fake jab and then a foot sweep and I was on the floor. Back up, I did my best to attack, with admonishments from the other black belts. When I was put on the floor, they would yell at me to get up and fight harder.

But I was fighting as hard as I could. Eventually I was just getting beat up and could do nothing much to defend myself. They kept coming. All of them tried to foot sweep me. Most were successful. I would get up and start fighting just to be swept down once more, all the time hearing the other black belts yelling and prodding me to go harder.

Then the mood changed. The higher the rank my opponent was, the more the shouts became "good attack-come on, you can do it, you're doing great, now attack…."

Jeff was next. Students would skip class if they knew he was teaching that night. He was an excellent karate man, with speed, power and lots of spirit. He started out like the others, by sweeping me. Then he forced me outside the circle with a series of attacks that I was powerless to defend against.

And then, he slowed down, just a bit, and let me block and counter his attacks. Softly he told me to "attack with combinations" and to "use distancing". He was teaching me. In the middle of the storm he was making sure that I learned and took something home from this.

And so it went. A non-stop barrage of attacks that left me totally tapped out. But step by step they stopped belittling me and began to spar with me as an equal, more or less. They were instructing me in front of the class. My energy came back and I was attacking with more power. "Relax", one of them said. "Stay low", said another. "Keep your hands up." The fake should look real." and on and on.

And then it was over. I bowed to the circle of karateka, and at Sensei's order, the class sat down, still in the circle. "Very good," Sensei said. "This was a demonstration of spirit. Everyone should know that if you train well, you will also be capable of performing non-stop fighting like this. The Japanese have a saying, 'if a nail sticks up, we must hammer it down.' The saying does not just mean that if someone thinks they are special or acts like he is better, then we must hammer them down. It also suggests that people need to be on the same relative level as everyone else. You can think of it as a railroad. If the nails that hold down the wooden rails start to stick up, the train cannot run down the track. It takes all the rails being even to allow the train to travel down the tracks. The one rail is noticed and must be adjusted to conform to the others for the good of the train. This is what we did today. We didn't make him fight to show that he is not special, everyone is special, you, and you, and all of you". Sensei pointed to students in the circle. "We wanted to show him that he belongs to this group and that he must work with all of us so we can all progress. But in some cases, we use '*Deru kui wa utareru*', which means to be one with the group and society. If one member stands against the rest, he or she must be pounded down. That's where the hammer comes in!"

Chapter Eleven

Over the next couple of years there were many clinics and tournaments and camps. Then I became friends with Jim Oberschlake. I had known Jim from previous karate events. He had built a dojo near a county road, just in front of, and on the property of his parent's golf course. Jim participated in many tournaments and was close to Sensei Golden and another karateka that would become national champion a few years later. And he was an expert with the foot sweep that won him many tournaments. With excellent timing he was able to lure his opponent forward or force him backwards and then sweep the front leg, the back leg, or both. He would finish off simply with either a reverse punch or jab. Often the technique was so good that it was deemed "Ippon'.

Master Camp - Sensei Jim Oberschlake, Yaguchi Sensei. Chiho Bare, Author. Both Photos on This Page Courtesy of Daniel Bare

Jim Oberschlake – ISKF National Tournament San Francisco (Okazaki Sensei & Yaguchi Sensei, Marty Vaughan Sensei, Dave Tally Sensei and Jeff Weber Sensei in Background)

Jim was an English teacher and had a clear schedule with time off each summer. This allowed for karate training on a regular schedule and provided flexibility for trips to other dojos and, most importantly, to Japan.

He told us stories about his trip to Japan and his training at the Honbu dojo in Tokyo. He told of getting beat up by the Japanese karate men, and how difficult it was to train because he was a foreigner. His tales included details of assorted bruises but also the cultural differences such as the food (didn't like it much but got used to it), the people, the subways, the temples and the strange language. To me it all sounded exotic and mysterious and a little dangerous, especially the karate training. Though many of his stories were told in front of a group, I always tried to catch him alone so I could get more details. I was extremely interested in his Japan experience, and wanted to know more.

***

Sonya and I joined a Japanese language class at the International Institute in downtown Flint. Rachael was the teacher. She had lived in Japan for four years, attending Sophia University in Tokyo. She was a good teacher. I quickly learned hiragana and katakana (very easy to do-takes just a few dedicated weekends).

We learned basic sentences like 'this is a pen' and 'where is the bathroom'? Very simple sentences but it was Japanese and I loved it. At the beginning there had been eight students. It dropped to four and eventually just Sonya and I were left. We never missed class. Sonya and I actually did our homework assignments at my house and, of course, at Churchill's or Doobies over much beer.

Sonya and Rachael got along well. They were similar in many ways. Both of them were extremists in terms of their beliefs in religion, politics and their world views. Both were very liberal and both loved to drink. After the first eight-week session ended, we joined the second. We also started to go together to Doobies after class. Sonya would talk about karate to Rachael. Rachael would talk about Japan to us. We learned much of our Japanese from her at the bar and practiced it while we drank beer. It was a great time and we all became friends.

Rachael and I started dating. Sonya more or less gave us her blessing. Once in a while, when we were out, Sonya would ask me if I had seen Rachael lately and how she was doing. But then she would start drinking faster. It was obvious that she both condoned the situation and tolerated it at the same time. I avoided mentioning Rachael unless she asked.

After a while I met Rachael's family. Her mom was blind. Her dad worked at the local Fisher Body plant, now long gone, a blue-collar family. We all went out after class on Mondays and Wednesdays. With karate on Tuesdays, Thursdays and Saturdays, my schedule was full. It was a healthy schedule, except for the alcohol.

Before long it was summer again. I had four weeks' vacation time saved up. Rachael and I made plans to travel to Little Tokyo in Los Angeles by car. I built a wood-framed-bed in the back of my van for sleeping. It was close to the roof of the van and we had to kind of duck and scoot in to avoid hitting our heads. But it allowed for lots of storage beneath. The rest of the van would serve as our living room. I missed Master Camp because of the Little Tokyo trip that Rachael and I took, but at that time there were lots of clinics and lots of tournaments. I kept up my questioning to Jim Oberschlake. He told me more about Kimi Ryokan. It was a small inn just east of Ikebukuro station. From Ikebukuro it was only a twenty-minute ride on the Yamanote Line to Ebisu. It was crowded, he said, but the trip was short so it didn't matter much. "It is run by two brothers that speak excellent English. They enjoy having foreigners stay at their inn because they both have experience living in the States. They will help you with everything. If you need to book a train for travel throughout Japan, they will help. If you need help with a place to stay in a different city, they will help, also with good places to eat and drink and all kinds of sightseeing. They were kind to me."

That summer, after returning from Little Tokyo, I participated in a number of tournaments and started winning some of them. I did OK in the kata competition but really did well in the kumite. I was talking seriously to Jim about making a trip to Japan. He was giving me more practical information now, that I could use on my trip. It was a given that I was to go to Japan. Sensei Golden also pushed me to make the trip.

Hard drugs were never a big issue for me since I always had to have control. But it was the Seventies in terms of growing up for me, and they were readily available. I enjoyed the freedom and the liberal atmosphere that my friends and I had but eventually started to feel that something was missing. I still thought daily about my now ex-wife and my two children and about how I had not been able to prevent any of it. That, and the Flint, Michigan insular union environment and the closeted feeling it gave me to be part of the union and its "do what you have to do attitude". I felt myself giving way to more and more escapism and began to feel more and more isolated. Drugs were there, but they were just one ugly part of it. I needed something more to ensure they did not take hold of me any more than they had already.

I met and married a great woman and we had a good couple of years. She was smart and had a heart of gold. But I was not psychologically ready to give her what she wanted. We talked very frankly several times about our issues and we parted more or less as friends. But something had to change. I was tired of my life, tired of my job, and tired of my situation, and could sense the outcome if I did not make a change.

Finally - I bought my airplane ticket, went to Chicago to get my visa, called Kimi Ryokan and made a reservation. I had a letter of introduction to the Honbu dojo from Okazaki Sensei.

I was training harder than ever. Jim instructed me to get as tough as I could. He and I did not train together regularly but when we did, he would coach me in kumite. Then we would talk more about Japan. He tried to teach me what to do and what not to do. He told me to never back down or show any weakness. He gave me lots of this kind of advice which I modified as I learned more about the culture when I started to have my own experiences.

Passport - First Visit to Japan March 1985

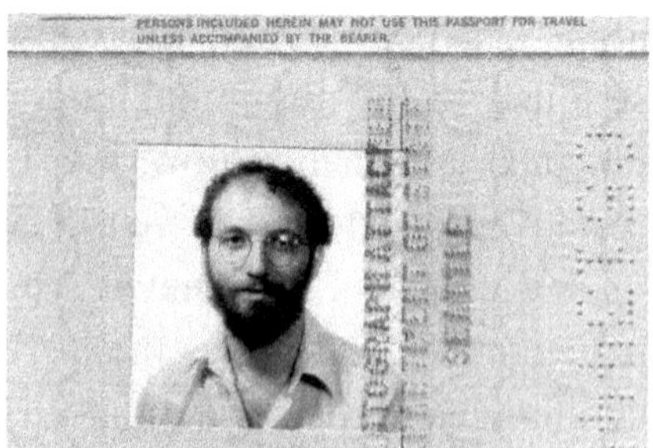

Passport Photo (Would You Allow This Person Into your Country?)

Part Two

Chapter One

(Japan – March, 1985)

My flight to Japan left from Detroit on Air Canada through New York and then non-stop to Narita. I had one large duffle style bag and a backpack. My karate gi took a lot of space, that and two pairs of jeans and some shirts and underwear. Everything was checked. All I had to do was relax on the plane. In New York there was a four-hour layover. The layover itself was longer than any flight I had ever experienced. I was already tired when the flight to Tokyo departed. It was impossible to sleep. The air was thick with smoke and dry and it was hard to breathe. There was a movie starting. The stewardess came down the aisle from first class section. She was carrying a small basket full of mini bottles of wine. I had wanted to make this trip all about being healthy and training, to stay strong and keep my body clean. "This is not working!" I thought to myself and motioned to the stewardess for some wine. She gave me a plastic glass, two bottles of wine and reached in and pulled down my tray table. "Let me know if you want more", she said, as she touched my shoulder, smiled, and continued down the aisle.

I opened the first bottle and filled the glass. It was red, unsure what variety, maybe Cabernet. It didn't matter. It tasted good. I was in the middle bank of seats in coach, on the aisle on the left. Next to me there was a Japanese family, in fact, most of the passengers were Japanese. The wife was sitting next to me, then two children and the husband at the far end. The husband had probably been drinking since the flight left New York. He was now sleeping. The wife was at first either shy or, I thought, didn't like foreigners. She sat sideways in her seat, facing away from me and towards her family. With her children now asleep, she started to relax a bit and sat facing the front and even turned towards me a little when she wanted to stretch.

She was facing me now, and watching me. I could tell because as I reached into the seat pocket to get the other mini bottle our eyes met. She didn't look away. I smiled at her. "Want some wine?" I asked.

"No thank you. You cannot sleep?"

"No"

"Where you go?"

"To Japan"

'In military?" I would hear this question many times.

"No, going for karate."

"Karate? Ah, I see. Why you study karate?" This was the first time I heard the word 'study' used for karate training. Her family was returning to Japan after three years in New York.

"Are you happy about returning to Japan?"

"Yes. But longer in your country would be good also. My husband, he want to stay three more years."

"So why don't you stay?"

"He must take another job at company. He has no choice."

"So, he was promoted?"

"Ah, yes, promoted. But he still want to stay more in your country."

"Maybe he will have a chance to work again in the States in the future."

"That is possible, yes. How long you stay in Japan?"

"I have about one month."

"Just you go to Tokyo?"

"I'm not sure. Maybe I can visit some other areas. I would like to see some famous sites."

"Sites?"

"Yes. Like Daibutsu."

"Ah yes, Daibutsu. It is a popular place, even for Japanese."

"And Nikko."

"Yes, but I think it is still very cold. It is very near to mountains."

"OK. Maybe not."

"She laughed. But you can still go."

"I don't have warm clothes so maybe not a good idea. Any suggestions?"

The stewardess returned with her cart. "Would you like some more wine?"

My new friend nodded yes. The stewardess poured wine directly from a regular bottle into my glass, then handed us another glass after pouring it half full. Then with another smile she handed me the bottle, still half full. "Enjoy."

We talked on and off for several hours, sharing the wine. She told me what to expect upon arrival and how to find the taxis. She also taught me the challenges of raising children in the USA all the time knowing they would return to Japan someday. Japanese language classes were only half days on Saturdays with a close-knit Japanese community. Weekdays were spent guiding the children through American primary school, made more difficult because of her incomplete grasp of English. But made a little easier because of the support group of longer-term Japanese that had been through the school experience many times and could offer advice on just about anything. She was thankful for the community but also complained a little about having to attend events in the lives of the community members.

"When America *jin* (person) come, very nice party. But if no America *jin*, *danna san* (husband) just drink and become, how you say, *yopparatte*."

"Drunk?"

"Hai hai. Drunk."

I decided I'd better stop and try to sleep. She must have read my mind.

"You should sleep now, only maybe three hours before land."

"Yes. It was very nice talking with you. I wish you and your family good luck with your new job back in Japan."

"Thank you very much. Nice talking you too. Have nice visit to our country." With that, she squeezed my arm and patted it twice. Then she turned towards her family and was quiet.

I did sleep and woke just as the stewardess nudged me to have me raise my tray table and seat back for landing. I had missed breakfast. No matter, I was finally arriving in Japan. Wiggling out of my seat, I walked down the aisle ten rows to the bathrooms, waiting in line for a few minutes. Everyone seemed tired but happy to have the flight over with. Most of them were now home. I turned sideways a bit to fit through the tiny door and looked in the mirror. "Pretty rugged", I thought, studying the red in my eyes. "Guess I should have slept more." I had no toothbrush so just rinsed my mouth well, splashed water on my face, and tried to make myself presentable by massaging my face muscles, cupping some water and holding it to my eyes which felt good.

Mindful of the line that was growing, I cleaned up the small sink counter and mirror, checked the toilet seat, and opened the door. Looking directly at me was my seat mate. She smiled but did not say anything. She hustled both kids into the bathroom with her. "Glad I cleaned up after myself", I thought.

Forty minutes later the plane touched down at the New Tokyo International Airport in Narita. The plane taxied to the gate. I couldn't see that well from my seat but noticed a lot of fenced off areas, very high fences with barbed wire at the top. It reminded me of prison yards in the movies. One line of fences, then another about twenty yards away, and then another. Rows of what looked to be soldiers stood in front of the fences with helmets and shields. I learned later that they were actually riot police in place since the airport had been built. They looked ready for battle. At that time only one runway was open after the left-wing political parties and local farmers and residents joined together to protest the rest of the project. This scene continued inside the terminal, no fences but security everywhere. The airport was huge. But there were signs in English showing me where to go through customs and immigration and to find my baggage.

With the duffle bag slung over my shoulder and the backpack strapped on, I followed the signs to the taxi area. "*Ikebukuro,*" I repeated to the older gentleman standing next to his taxi, cloth in his hand, wiping down his front fender. "*Eh?*" He said for the second time. A previous taxi driver had motioned me away, arms in X shape in front of his chest, down the line, refusing to even deal with me. Surely my pronunciation was not good but I also showed both of them a map. Finally, another older person with an arm band motioned me over. He took my map, studied it for a minute and then placed it down on the hood of one of the taxis.

"Ikebukuro. Tokyo?"

"Yes, Tokyo."

"*Hai Hai. Matte kudasai* (please wait)." He walked down another two taxis and talked to a driver who was also busy polishing his mirrors. The old man told me to come over to where they were standing. The trunk magically opened. Each of them took one bag and stuffed it in. Loaded, the passenger door opened. The driver motioned for me to get in. As I reached to close the door, it started to close on its own. He was soon also into his seat. He punched a button on his meter, looked around at the traffic, and drove off.

I was nervous but convinced that they knew where I wanted to go and would take care of me. Years later I would depend on taxi drivers and other service professionals in many situations. I would be seldom disappointed.

The rain came down just enough to force the use of wipers. It was steamy. I was tired and just wanted to get to my hotel. We drove. The traffic was heavy and moved slowly. Soon, an hour had passed. "*Ikebukuro*?" I asked, getting worried. "*Hai, hai. Mo sugu* (ok, ok, soon)."

Another half hour passed. Traffic got better, then again became heavy. I looked at my pocket phrase book. "*Mada desu ka* (not yet)?" The driver pointed to a sign that read "Ikebukuro *Eki* (station)". "Ikebukuro", he said with a big smile. Clearly, we had arrived. Now he stopped, pulled my map from his pocket and studied it. He crawled down one side street and then another. The streets became even narrower. Then he stopped.

"*Ikenai Okyakusama. Eeto*… cannot go." He pointed to the street in front of us that was crowded with people and outdoor market stands. "Stop here?"

"OK." I answered.

The passenger door opened and I got out. "*Ikura desuka* (how much)?" I asked. He had a clipboard with various charges written down. He tried to explain them. I knew he had taken a couple of toll roads so just accepted the total of 22,000 yen as my fare. It had taken almost two hours. I had been traveling for more than thirty hours and just wanted to sleep. He set my bags on the sidewalk, said "*sho sho matchi* (wait a minute)" and disappeared down the street, running. "*Hai hai.*" He was back. "Come here." He picked up my biggest bag and motioned for me to follow.

Kimi Ryokan was only a minute's walk from where the driver had parked. He walked up the three steps and turned, holding the door open for me. I walked in. "*Daijobu?* (are you ok)", he asked. "*Hai, arigato gozaimasu.* (yes, I'm ok, thanks)" He bowed and left.

Kimi Ryokan's lobby was beautiful. The hallway was narrow and the floor was highly polished wood. It looked like wood taken from a ship's galley. It was weathered with age and accented with inlaid stones about a foot in diameter. The stones were also smooth and I slipped on one after taking my shoes off, something I learned from Jim. On the walls were photos of temples and scrolls with calligraphy that looked like the washi paper I had studied. I could not read it yet, of course. In the corner, just past the front desk, a miniature garden grew out of the woodwork. There was gravel with a raked pattern, two small rocks seemingly protruding from the ground, and a cherry tree that was blossoming into bright pink flowers.

Without the taxi driver, I felt alone and out of place. No one seemed to be here. "Hello." I said over the counter. No answer. I waited a minute. "Hello?" This time I stretched out over the counter and raised my voice. No answer. "Great, now what?" I thought.

In through the door rushed a young-looking Japanese man carrying several plastic bags in each hand. "Sorry. I saw you arrive but was buying some groceries down the street." It was impeccable English, with an accent but still very clear. "You are Michael? I am Nemura"

"Yes. Hello." I reached out to shake his hand. He had to shuffle groceries but met my greeting and shook my hand strongly. "You must be tired. Let me put these down." He piled the grocery bags onto the counter, took my two bags and said, "follow me."

"I recommend that you take a nap for a few hours. When you're ready, I will give you a short tour of the hotel and tell you about some good places to eat."

"That sounds great." I could feel a huge blanket falling over me and just wanted to crash. He showed me to my room, pulled the futon from the closet, and placed my bags in the corner. I was asleep before he closed the door.

Waking the next morning to the sound of voices in many different languages, Japanese, French, maybe Spanish, and certainly British or Australian English, I looked at my watch. It was seven o'clock and I stretched out straight, feeling my joints pop and crack, and sat up in my futon.

I hadn't noticed my room at all. Now, as I looked around, I could see the same simple, clean lines and décor as in the lobby. The room was about eight tatami mats. There was a small dresser on one wall. In the corner was a one-foot square garden, complete with a blossoming cherry tree. All along the side was a closet with a sliding shoji screen, painted with scenes from the Meiji period.

It seemed that everyone was headed somewhere and the excitement was evident. I wanted to just listen for a while but I had to go to the bathroom. When I reached the communal toilet, there was a line of six people. Standing in line I was able to meet and talk with many of the other guests. We would chat, and then they would go into the bathroom, sometimes in pairs. The bathrooms were coed and there were three stalls. One of them opened the door after entering to tell me there was one extra stall. It was the first of many times I was to share bathroom space with total strangers of the opposite sex, not a big deal to me now, but remarkable then.

Finished with that, I went back to my room. I wanted to make the 10:30 training. The Honbu dojo at that time was located in Ebisu which was eight stops on the Yamanote line. I had time but didn't know how to get to the station. Mr. Nemura was ready to help. He led me out the door and onto the street, me carrying my backpack with my gi and a change of clothes. We arrived at Ikebukuro station and he showed me how to buy a ticket and how to calculate the fare based on the distance traveled on the map above the ticket machines, very easy. In Tokyo and all the surrounding stations, the signs were all printed in English. It was actually in *Romanji* (English letters), that was kindly translated from the kanji. It was 120 yen to Ebisu. He told me to keep my ticket after it was punched by the attendant. Then I was to hand it over to the attendant at the destination station. In the future this would become more and more automated, eventually ending up with no attendants at all, one would just buy the ticket, place it into the automated machine which would spit it back out for you to carry to the destination, then you would again place it into the machine. If the amount paid was correct, that would be the end of it. If not correct, a buzzer would sound and the gate would lock. You would have to see a real person to pay any additional fees. But that was after privatization of the JNR. In 1985, everything was done by an attendant. Most of them were kind to me. Others were rough and cold, kind of like life everywhere.

I was on my way. It was nine o'clock and the trains were overflowing with office workers. I skipped two trains in hopes of finding one with more space but it became apparent that there would be no such chance. So, I followed the lead of the other commuters, walked up to the train doors, stepped up onto the train car and turned my back to the inside, then gently pushed back away from the doors into the crowd of passengers already squeezed about as much as I thought possible. I was wrong. Over the next few stops more people got on. They dutifully waited almost until the others got off but just as the last of them were exiting, they forced themselves onto the car. It was fairly efficient and most people followed what I figured were unwritten rules of etiquette.

I was standing in the loading and unloading area just in front of the doors. At every stop I was twisted and turned and shoved and jabbed in various parts of my body with briefcases, purses and umbrellas. I found a place just inside the doors, about one step away, pressed up against the outside wall that worked. I could hang onto the luggage rack and kind of sway back and forth as needed, still squashed, but not as badly as being directly in front of the doors. I was to learn the next day that from 6:30 to about 9 am is the worst time to board the train. That's when the platform employees put on white gloves and helped the passengers by gently pushing them into the car to ensure they don't get their clothes, purses, briefcases or umbrellas caught in the doors as they close. This went on for twenty-five minutes. Finally, the conductor announced "Ebisu."

The rain was coming down hard now and the wind was forcing it horizontal. I stepped down off the train onto the concrete platform, then walked to the stairs and down through the station, following the crowd of people, with no idea at all where to go. Then, in unison, everyone popped open their umbrellas. It was an amazing site. Different colors and sizes and people holding the umbrellas at precise angles calculated to be able to walk, still shoulder to shoulder, but without poking each other in the eye. I, of course, had no umbrella, and couldn't remember ever owning one. Everyone exited the station and walked to the corner. At the corner, they all dispersed in many directions towards their offices. I stood in the rain at that corner, already soaked.

"May I help you?" It was a middle-aged man in a suit shielded by a huge umbrella. He held part of it over my head, protecting me from the rain. "It is raining very hard, isn't it?" He said this in good English.

"Yes. Thank you. I have a map. I'm looking for the JKA headquarters. I pointed to the location on the map. Somehow, I thought everyone would know where the world headquarters of the JKA was.

"Ah. Let me see." He took the map in the same hand that was holding the umbrella. Then he pivoted with the map in his hand, trying to orient himself. "*Eeto* (umm)…I think we go this way." His index finger pointed from his briefcase handle. "OK, let's go." He pivoted back around so he could still hold the umbrella over me. "Not too far." It was not the only time Japanese people went out of their way to help me. In many situations over the next few years they helped me often, sometimes with simple favors, but often it took considerable effort and time. We walked, and then walked some more. He asked a few people on the street. We could not find the dojo.

He was getting wet and I knew he would be late for work. I felt very bad for him.

"It's OK. I have lots of time to look for the dojo. Thank you very much for your help."

"I am very sorry." He was looking at his watch. Maybe map is not correct?"

"No problem. I will keep trying. Thank you very much."

"I'm sorry." He said. "Here is a place to avoid the rain." It was a KDD office. He guided me to the entrance which was covered.

"OK. Please go to work. Thank you for your help."

"OK. Good luck. Goodbye." He handed me the map.

The rain was still pounding downward onto the sidewalk. I asked a few people, all who listened patiently to my Japanese language. Some of them made the X mark with their hands but most at least tried, looking at my map for a few minutes and then giving me the 'I don't know' gesture.

I stood under cover of the KDD office entrance, shielded from the rain but already soaked. Then my savior, the postman, appeared on his bicycle. Double satchels hung over the left and right side of the fender and over the rear wheels, full of packages and envelopes, some just barely sticking out, but everything was covered with a vinyl sheet.

He was walking the bike, probably because of the heavy pedestrian traffic, or the rain. Pushing the bicycle, he turned into the office entry, parked, pulled the vinyl off to one side and began looking through one of the pockets, gathering the day's mail for the KDD building.

"*Sumimasen* (excuse me)." I walked up to him with my map held out in his direction. "*Kono jusho o sagashite imasu* (I'm looking for this address)."

"*Eeto. Chotto matte kudasai* (wait a minute please)." He transferred mail from one of the pockets to his satchel that was strung over his shoulder. Then he turned to me. "*Misette* (show me)." He reached for my map.

"*Eeto. Sochi desu yo* (that way)." He pointed in the direction I had already tried a few minutes before. But the rain was confusing everything and I was no longer sure where I had walked before.

"Sorry." I said in English. "Could you help me?"

"*Eh? Ah, Hai. Chotto matte, ne*. (huh? Oh, ok. Just a minute)" He pointed at his satchel and then into the KDD building, taking my map and putting it into his pocket, then disappearing into the building with his load of mail. For a moment I panicked with my map now gone. But then I realized his bicycle was still there so relaxed a little. He was back in ten minutes.

"OK. Come!" He motioned me to follow. He looked up and down the street, paused a couple of seconds, turned the map and started out. We walked around a huge block. He had no umbrella but was protected by a full body rain suit. I had nothing but it didn't matter now. We walked more. He looked at the map and then looked at the small address plates on each building. He looked confused. "*Chotto matte* (wait a minute)." He said.

Walking into a building which, according to the display in the window, was a bakery, he was out in less than a minute. Then he walked me next door and pointed upwards. There, in small letters, was a JKA sign with its rising sun logo. It was hard to see because of the rain which is probably why the others could not find it for me.

I smiled widely at the mail man, who looked very proud and happy also.

"Domo arigato." I said.

"You are welcome", he said in English, handing me the map.

Chapter Two

I remember smelling fresh baked goods, and being soaked and tired but still feeling good at having found the dojo. Walking up the two flights of stairs, the metal steps clanked loudly. At the top was another small sign, reinforcing the fact that this was the dojo. A single door led to an entrance area. There was a small window, much like an old theater ticket window. Behind the window sat a young man who was facing away from me towards the others in the office area. He was bowing from his sitting position and saying "*hai, hai*" over and over again.

I looked at the others in the office and immediately recognized Tanaka Sensei, Asai Sensei and Osaka Sensei. Tanaka Sensei, who had just been berating the young man, yelled again and the young man quickly turned towards me. "*Hai, nan desuka* (yes-can I help you)?"

"Konnichi wa" I said. I handed him my letter of introduction that Okazaki Sensei had written for me. I did not know what was in the letter. Nor did I know what was written on the outside of the envelope.

He sat straight up when he read the envelope, rose from his chair, ran over to Tanaka Sensei, handed him the letter and stood there. Tanaka Sensei looked up at me and then started to open the envelope. He pulled the letter out, unfolded it and began reading, looking at me several times. Rising from his chair, he walked towards the clerk area, the clerk following close behind. At the window, Tanaka Sensei held the letter up to me. "You, Michael?"

"Yes"

"How long train?" He said.

"One-month Sensei."

"One-month. No, how long?"

"Oh, sorry. About five years".

"Train hard?"

"Hai Sensei", I said, projecting my voice as far into the office area as possible.

You train all days?"

"Hai Sensei."

"Best kata-what?"

"Um…best kata?" I had never thought of which kata was my best, so I chose Jion.

"Ah, Jion. You show me sometime." He was smiling.

"Hai Sensei."

"You train today?"

"Hai. Is it OK?"

"OK. He show you." Sensei pointed to the clerk.

"You train hard." This time he was not smiling. "I watch."

"Hai Sensei. I will."

Tanaka Sensei turned, said a few words to the clerk and started back to his desk.

"Ah, Sensei!" I said this a little too loudly. "Please." I was struggling to find the right pocket of my backpack. Finally, I was able to pull out a fifth of Jack Daniels, still in the gift box.

"Please," I repeated, and held it out to him.

"Oh. Thank you very much." He smiled again as only Tanaka Sensei can smile, then headed for his desk. I was told by many karate friends to take a gift. I was glad for that advice.

The clerk opened the door next to the window, walked around to the entrance area, and motioned for me to follow. "Come here." I followed him into the dojo.

The dojo had been converted from an old bowling alley, probably about eight to ten lanes. It was long and had a clean and polished wood floor, mostly leftover from the bowling alley. At the far end of the floor, about where the pins would be, was a shrine with a photo of Funakoshi Sensei at the center, watching over the entire dojo. The shrine was set off by an offering shelf that held a *mikan* (orange) and a small cup of sake. Around it was a wooden fence-like barrier. To the left of the shrine was a large Japanese flag. On the other side were several flags of different countries. Along the entire right wall, running from the front all the way back, was a line of five *makiwaras* (striking posts).

Directly in front of me, to the left, was a sitting area, left over from the bowling alley I supposed. There were rows of plastic chairs staged just behind a three-foot partition between the dojo floor and the sitting area that also included shelving on the sitting area side. The shelves were for shoes, bags and anything else brought into the dojo. Just behind the sitting area, against the wall, was a line of three vending machines, one with snacks and two with drinks. I would patronize the Pocari Sweat machine almost daily for the month. In front of the sitting area, in the corner by the cracked mirrors just before the step-up to the dojo floor, was a heavy bag hanging from the ceiling. The toilet paper I was to use so often was also in that corner.

Cracked Mirror (Yahara Sensei In Background)

"Shoes off." It was more an order than a request.

"Hai." I slid to the left into a chair, removed my shoes and placed them into one of the shelves.

"OK. Come." I followed him, stepping up onto the dojo floor, remembering to bow, and half running to catch up with him. He opened the door at the back of the dojo. All across the back, just behind the shrine area and separated by another wall, was about a fifteen-foot long area with shower stalls to the left, a small maintenance room and then the locker room at the far-right hand side.

As we entered the locker room, I noticed a small area with the lockers and ten or fifteen gis hanging beneath a high shelf. By the smell, it was easy to tell the gis were not freshly washed. "You, clothes change. Go to dojo. Stretch." Then he left.

There were already three foreigners changing into their gis. They were not talking. I introduced myself to them and discovered they were from different countries and spoke different languages. Antonio was from Spain and could speak English. He would become a good friend during my stay in Japan. The other two couldn't or didn't want to speak. I was able to glean that the two had been there just a few weeks but that Antonio had been living in Japan for almost three years. I was hoping to get some advice from one of them but they were changed and ready to go before I could ask. Finding an empty locker, I sat down on a bench and started to pull off my still soaked clothes. Other students arrived. They greeted each other and nodded at me but not much was said.

Gi on, I stuck my backpack into the half-size locker and walked out the door into the dojo, bowing as I stepped out onto the floor. I remember thinking to myself that something new was happening in my life, that I must focus on karate goals and not let anything else get in the way. As before when something new, challenging or scary was in front of me, I took a long, deep breath and exhaled completely.

Walking over to where the others were gathered, I started to stretch and warm-up. It became a little noisier with every group of students that arrived. Two or three at a time walked in, took off their shoes, stuffed them into a shelf, bowed and walked up onto the floor. I did notice that they walked quietly across the floor.

There were now twenty of us on the floor, warming up. It was 10:15. Class started at 10:30 AM. Some started to spar lightly to help warm-up. I was still down on the floor, trying to stretch the cramps out of my legs from the long flight and the cold trip from Ikebukuro.

It was 10:20. From the entrance area, a group of men, already in gis, walked in, kicked off their slippers, slid them under the chairs, walked onto the floor and bowed. Without warming up or stretching, they started to free spar. I learned that they were instructor trainees and assistant instructors. One of them was the young clerk that had showed me around the dojo, and he was walking over to me. "OSU." He said. "OSU." I said, thinking he was just being friendly.

"*Asobimashoo*?" He said. "Um, sorry?" I said, not knowing what he meant.

"Kumite?" He pointed to another couple of students who were free sparring.

"Ah. Hai." I'm sure my smile disappeared.

"OK. Come." He led me away from the warm-up group. "*Hai. Jyu kumite* (free sparring), OK?" He bowed. "Hai. OK." I bowed back. We both took *kamae* (ready) stance.

I was slow and did not see it at all. He faked a left jab and came across with his left leg and swept me hard to the floor. I got back up, smiling, "very good!" I said. He was not smiling.

That was the pattern for the next few minutes. I remember hitting the wall at least twice. I also remember that during one exchange, we were too close to the shrine area. He pushed me back with a series of attacks. Suddenly he changed tactics, slid to my right side, grabbed me by the shoulder and right arm, and pulled me away from the shrine area. "Come." He said as he directed me towards the center of the dojo floor. At that point I noticed that many students were now watching us. We started to spar again and then I heard a loud "Hai, OK." It was Tanaka Sensei. He would teach this class. I heard a couple days later that he was not scheduled for that class, so he must have swapped with another instructor after reading Okazaki Sensei's letter of introduction.

I was glad there was only that ten minutes of sparring. I was already tired and sweating. But also, I felt kind of invigorated and ready for the class. I hurt all over but it was very much like some of the encounters I had with Joe Ferguson back at the University Karate Club. I felt good.

Sensei sat seiza in front of the line that had quickly formed at his command. Several assistants were off to the left, slightly ahead of the baseline we formed. We bowed to shomen, Sensei turned and we bowed to him. Then Sensei ordered one of the assistants to lead warm-ups. I noticed the group of students that had entered the dojo already dressed in their gis were lined up in the back, behind the regular class. The instructor trainee class started at noon and many of them participated in the 10:30 class as a warm-up. Officially they were also there to help teach us spirit and proper technique. I learned the most about spirit from them. Always they were high energy and never let us slack. They were no-nonsense, serious karateka and they did not waste time on those who did not train hard. I did what they told me to do, without question. They gave me all they had in terms of instruction and pushed me hard. Sensei was the technical instructor. They were the enforcers. Many of them became the high-ranking senior instructors that we all know. I owe them mightily for their patience and effort.

After warm-ups were finished, Tanaka Sensei shouted for us to take kamae stance. I was slow to move, not because of skill but because I expected some kind of announcement or lecture. Not to be. A nidan, I was maybe a little tired still from the trip, but basically in good shape. I was not, however, prepared for the cloud of intensity that hovered over the class.

We went through basic punches and kicks. The class was lined up so that we were doing drills lengthwise from the back of the dojo to the front, exactly the length of a bowling alley. That meant between twenty and twenty-five techniques forward and the same back.

There was nothing difficult about Sensei's class for the first thirty minutes. Basics, with a few twists like stepping forward with a lunge punch and then shifting off forty-five degrees. But I was quickly running out of gas. At home, between sets of techniques, which was usually five or six forward and back, we would have a break of at least thirty seconds. Not much, but plenty if you were training regularly.

Basics were over. Tanaka Sensei again told us to take kamae. He had us practice sparring techniques for ten minutes.

"*Jaa...paatanaa* (get a partner)" he shouted. We all moved quickly and found a partner. My partner was another foreigner who, I found out later, had been in Japan for almost one year. I was to know him better a year later. We bowed. Sensei called an assistant to help him demonstrate. They both took front stance. Sensei had his assistant step in with mae geri to the stomach and Sensei stepped back with a down block and reverse punch. The assistant, however, blocked the reverse punch by simply dropping his forward blocking hand downward. Then Sensei raised his right front leg and shot out a cutting kick, stepping back down with a back fist and reverse punch. Sensei demonstrated the drill three times. “Hai.” He said. The assistant ran back to his own partner. “*Jaa. Yatte mitte* (try it and see),” Sensei said.

My partner told me to me to practice the drill slowly for a few minutes. He explained and helped me understand the techniques. “*Hai. Supeedo* (ok-with speed).” Sensei shouted.

What followed was something I never before had experienced. My partner transformed himself into a Yakuza. He charged forward with the first kick, burying it in my stomach. I had no chance to step back and block. This happened a half-dozen times and then I was finally able to move backwards fast enough to block it along with a reverse punch. He dropped his block so hard it pulled me downward and way off balance. But I tried to do the cutting kick which had always been a good kick for me. It would have been successful had it been on target. But it wasn’t.

We started again. This time I was ready for the block to my reverse punch, gripped the floor and shot out my cutting kick which caught him in the kidney area. The back fist was sloppy. The follow up reverse punch was weak. But I did finish the set. In total we did the drill twenty times and I was exhausted. “*Hai, suwitchee* (switch)!” Sensei shouted. And I became the attacker. I tried to stretch out my initial *mae geri* (front kick) and nail him but he was way too quick. His reverse punch though, was right on target and I was again sucking for air. “OK?” He said. But I couldn’t answer.

Sensei was there in a second. “*Daijobu* (are you ok)?” He asked.

“Hai, Sensei. Daijobu.”

“Stop?” He said.

“No Sensei.”

“OK. Go.” With that, he grabbed my shoulders and pulled me straight up. “Too high.” He said in English. “Cannot move fast, stay low, like this.” He demonstrated, and proceeded to beat the crap out of my partner. I could see his face and spirit dwindle as Sensei made him do the drill over and over. He was never able to block one of Sensei’s techniques. That did not please me at all though. I wanted only to do the techniques well. I remember feeling bad for him, though not that bad. “*Wakkatta* (understand)?” Sensei asked. The nearby students were watching us now. "*Hai, Sensei. Arigato gozaimasu* (yes, Sensei. Thank you)."

"*Hai. Paatana switchee* (switch partners)." We rotated to get a new partner. Then it got worse. From the beginning it was fast speed. But I was energized and tried to move fast, twisting my hips while moving backwards, pushing off the back leg to make power and distance. I was working with my partners now, all of us pushing each other.

Then came what my friend Jim Oberschlake had warned me about. I was face to face with Shinna sempai. He was one of the instructor trainees and was in the class just to warm up.

At the command to start, Shinna attacked quickly and strongly. He did not, however, stretch his kick to penetration. I stepped back and blocked his kick and threw a reverse punch. What followed was another lesson in the difference between karate, and karate in Japan. Shinna stuffed my reverse punch with his right hand and then shot the same hand square into my face. I continued with my cutting kick which landed on his right side and which he completely ignored. With the same hand, he blocked my back fist and my reverse punch. But of course, he did not stop there. Immediately after that he pushed his right leg outwards in an arc and reverse swept my right leg, dumping me to the floor. He followed this with a stomp kick to my side which I felt for weeks. "OK," I thought. "Guess anything goes." So - I also abandoned the rules.

As I was to learn, depending on who you were partnered with, you either did the drill as instructed or you did part of it and then adlibbed. That was one of the most important lessons I learned during my stay in Japan. Karate was indeed a violent art, and unpredictable.

From this first training I learned flexibility, toughness, aloofness and reciprocity. Basically, if my partner did the techniques as instructed, I responded in kind. But if my partner liked to modify to enhance the drill and add techniques just to have the upper hand, I eventually learned to follow suit.

Shinna and I continued, he practicing karate, me providing a reluctant target. I had no energy left. Tanaka Sensei noticed. He shouted at me from only a foot away. "More speed!"

"Hai Sensei." I said. I tried hard but nothing more came. "More speed!" He shouted again. Still I had no more. There was nowhere to reach in a grab for an ounce of stamina.

Shinna spoke. "Relax, *koko kara.*" He was lightly pounding his stomach. "*Hara.*" He reached over and back handed me just below my belly button. "*Koko kara. Kore....ja nai...* (from here, not from here)." He posed as if flexing his muscles. "*Koko kara, soshite*....low. Stay low." It was a mix of English and Japanese that I have never forgotten. "Hai sempai. Hai Sensei." I bowed to them both.

"*Hai suwitchee.*" At Sensei's command the entire class rotated counter clockwise so that we each faced another partner. Now I was looking into the eyes of the young clerk again. There was no smile. I didn't really expect it. But there wasn't even an acknowledgment, other than the bow, which was "*giri* (obligation)" at best. "*Hai..sutaato.*"

I didn't even have the time to take a stance. I remember, not clearly, being more or less dragged to the area just off the floor. One of the assistants stayed with me. He tried to sit me up on the floor. I did not want to sit up and struggled against it. He gently placed his left hand on my stomach and his right hand on my back at the shoulder level and coaxed me up. Then he rubbed both areas, so expertly that I was able to relax a little. Gradually I got my wind back. He then pulled my gi back and looked at my chest area. He called another assistant over to help. I don't know what was said. The two of them helped me up and walked me off the floor into the office area. They laid me down on a short sofa at the back of the office. I remember strong cigarette smoke and all eyes towards me.

I had limped into the office supported by the two assistants. Probably I could not have made it without their help. Opening my eyes, there was a small group circled in front of the sofa. Again, I could not understand what was being said. There was a very kind young lady, a secretary I think, who sat down on the sofa next to me. She held out an opened bottle of Pocari Sweat. "Drink?"

"Thank you." I reached for the bottle but a bolt of pain shot through my ribs and I shouted out. "Sorry." I said. More talking in Japanese. "You stay here." The secretary said. "Doctor will come."

I wanted to say no, to say that I was OK. But I wasn't so sure. It felt like my ribs were broken. Every time I moved the slightest, the pain pierced my body. "Just wonderful-my whole month is shot". I tried to reduce the pain by not moving and thinking of something else.

"You… OK?" It was Tanaka Sensei. I started to get up from the sofa but he stopped me and pushed me back down. "You stay. Doctor come. Today-finished."

"Hai, Sensei."

It was only a short time before the Doctor showed up. He stood next to Tanaka Sensei and they talked about me. Sensei explained what happened. Then Sensei reached down, opened up my gi top and pointed. The Doctor opened it a little further, placed both hands on my chest and began walking his fingers over my ribs.

It was like a dream, me, in pain, looking up at five people all examining my chest and making grunting noises and oohs and aahs while the secretary still held the bottle of Pocari close by, in case I suddenly wanted it.

The Doctor found the right spot, my entire body contracted which forced my legs to straighten out, come off the sofa, and hit Tanaka Sensei in the thigh. "I'm sorry!" I knew it probably hurt. But Sensei said nothing.

The Doctor talked to the secretary and Tanaka Sensei. Then he spoke in slow, basic English. "I think bones not broken, maybe moved a lot, um trauma", pronouncing it "traooma". Very bad bruise, not broken." He repeated. He walked over to a chair opposite the sofa, sat down, opened his medical bag and took out a pen. Then he pulled out a pad of paper and started writing. When he was finished, he walked back to the sofa.

"You stay here. She will go to purchase items."

"How much? I have money." I tried to turn over to get my wallet but realized I was still in my gi. "In the locker room", I said.

"It is OK. No money necessary. Just rest and wait."

I didn't argue. I was still out of breath, tired, sore and beaten and fell asleep immediately.

The secretary was nudging me awake. She had returned with a package in one hand and the Pocari Sweat in the other. The Doctor was still there. He removed a small box from the package, tore it open and opened the bottle inside, placing four tablets in my hand. "This is for the pain." He said. I thought to myself that this was exactly what American Doctors would say. "Every day, take four tablets, three times, total twelve tablets. Do this for three days. The secretary handed me the Pocari and I swallowed the pills, my ribs crying out.

"You can wear this." He pulled out an elastic wrap, similar to what I had seen in the States. "Put on like this." He demonstrated by holding the elastic over his head and pretending to pull it down over his shoulders and tight over the rib area. "You will be very pain, um, sore."

"Can I train?"

"Maybe not good idea."

Tanaka Sensei came over to the sofa. He was now changed into jeans and a T-shirt, covered by a light jacket with the JKA logo. "You no problem go home, OK?" He asked.

"Yes Sensei, no problem."

"Need help?"

"No Sensei. I'm OK.

"Go home. Rest."

"Hai Sensei. Thank you for your help." Sensei turned to the Doctor. They talked some more. Then Sensei talked to one of the assistants seated at a desk near the sofa. It was arranged for the assistant to escort me to Ebisu station.

The assistant walked me back into the dojo, across the floor and into the locker room. He waited while I changed into my street clothes, which took such a long time that the secretary was called in to help me into my jeans and shirt. No one seemed to notice the whole time she was in the locker room. Then the three of us walked back across the floor, through the lobby and down the stairs into the street. The kind lady said goodbye to me there, handing me a new bottle of Pocari Sweat. The assistant was very good to me, I'm sure under strict orders from Tanaka Sensei. He guided me to the train map. "Where you stay?"

"Ikebukuro." I started to point to it on the map but as I lifted my arm the pain jerked it back down and I let out a short yell. "OK. OK."

He said. He reached into his pocket, pulled out some coins and deposited then into the ticket machine. Then he walked me through the gate, saying something to the ticket puncher, probably because he had only one ticket. We walked up the concrete stairs to the platform. The lines were backed up at each door marker. One train had already stopped and the passengers were pouring out. Then the loud, raunchy, high-pitched warning sounded that meant the doors were about to close and everyone better get on. A few years later that ugly warning was replaced with a smooth melodic chime. We moved up in line but could not get on the train, which was filled over capacity. "We wait." He then shifted my backpack off his shoulder onto the concrete platform.

Six minutes later another train arrived. After the arrivals got off, he walked up onto the train with my backpack and motioned for me to follow. He looked around, found a group of what looked like school children, and said something that caused the three of them to jump up off the bench seat, "*Doozo*." One of the girls said. "Thank you very much." I replied. The three started to giggle.

"Hai. You OK?" The warning music again started. He clearly wanted to get off the train and finish his babysitting assignment. "Hai, OK." I said. "Thank you very much."

"Hai, OK." He jumped off the train just as the doors were closing.

The next eight stops were spent entertaining the three girls who wanted to practice their English. "Excuse me. Where are you from?"

"Michigan" I said.

"American?" One of them asked.

"Where is …Michigan?" She asked.

"Um-It looks like this." As most Michigan people do, I held up my hand. There was no reaction so I called out the Great Lakes around my thumb, fingertips, and edges. "*Ah…Go kai do*." She said to the other girls. They all agreed.

And so it went for the next twenty minutes. They asked about my injury and why I came to Japan and how long I was going to stay. It wasn't much of a bother. They were cute and nice and just wanted to speak English. They kept my mind off the pain. Their English wasn't bad, and as I said, they were cute.

Chapter Three

I said goodbye to the high school girls at Ikebukuro station, walked down the stairs and headed for Kimi Ryokan. It was still only two o'clock. My ribs hurt from the weight of the heavy, sweat soaked gi that was in my backpack, which, no matter how I carried it, didn't help. It took a long time to walk from the station to Kimi. I kept taking wrong turns. Finally, I recognized a small shrine which was just down the street, looked up and there it was. Much like the day before, it seemed like nobody was there. I went up the steps, opened the wooden door, walked down the lobby past the hotel desk area and up the stairs to my room. All I wanted to do was lay down and sleep.

I put my backpack down on the floor outside the room and then realized that I didn't have my room key. "Shit." Leaving my backpack on the floor, I went back down to the desk area but no one was there. "Hello?" I shouted. I was in pain and could think of nothing more than lying down in my room. No answer. I shouted again with the same results. I was hurting, tired and not very patient. Reaching over the desk, pain again shooting all the way to my toes, I grabbed my key from the numbered slots where I saw Mr. Nemura put them, and headed back to my room. Opening the door, I dragged my backpack inside and stood in the center of the room. I couldn't believe how quiet it was. Outside, on the street it was so crowded with the noise of the people, the cars, and the music blaring from various stores. Inside my room, though I was aware of a kind of white noise, it was peaceful and felt like a retreat. I needed a retreat. This was just my first day and already I was injured and could not train. The Doctor had said no training for at least a week.

I looked around the room. There was no bed. It had been there in the morning. Now I started to worry. Maybe this was not my room. Had I grabbed the wrong key? At that moment the door opened and an old lady walked in. "*Konnichi wa, sumimasen* (hello, excuse me)." She seemed surprised to see me. "*Konnichi wa.*" I said. She said a few long sentences but I did not understand at all. "My room?" I said, gesturing to the room and then to me. Seeming to understand she said "Hai." Then she went back out to the hall and brought back a small wastebasket with a fresh plastic liner. She sat the wastebasket down next to the T.V. and started dusting off the flat surfaces. I watched as she glided around the room, paying no attention to me. "*Sumimasen*." I said when she looked to be finished. "Futon?"

"*Eh?*" She looked confused. "Futon…bed." I tried again.

"*Ahh, futon*" she said, pronouncing the fu almost silently and "ton" as "tone". My pronunciation was a hard "fu" and then "ton" with an "tah".

"*Kochira de gozaimasu*. (Here it is)" She walked over to the closet and slid open the shoji and pointed. I was failing fast and walked over to the closet, pulled out the futon and laid it on the floor. She quickly walked over, grabbed it and moved it over about six inches. Then, apparently understanding that I wanted to sleep, she went back to the closet, pulled out a blanket and pillow, carefully and neatly placed them on top of the futon, and patted the blanket to make it smooth. "*Hai, doozo*." She said. She picked up her cleaning tools and, with a bow, went through the still open door, closing it as she left.

I needed sleep so locked the door, pulled off my socks, squatted down next to the futon and rolled over onto it, trying not to lay on my ribcage. "Oh shit." I said out loud, and carefully rolled off the futon over to my backpack. Reaching into the front pocket, I pulled out the medicine the Doctor had given me, took the Pocari Sweat out of another pocket, and swallowed another four tablets, then rolled back over to the futon, stretched out and pulled up the blanket. That's all I remember.

Chapter Four

Loud voices and slamming doors woke me. Then I had to use the bathroom. It was down the hall from my room and just around the corner. As I turned that corner there were two women lined up outside the bathroom door and I took my place in line. They were both from Australia, they said, on a one year working holiday. Victoria was from Sidney. She was a lanky blond with an easy smile and much energy. She did most of the talking and seemed excited about every topic. Joanne was shorter and a little quieter although she was also very bubbly when she talked. Victoria and Joanne had already been in Japan for three months, most of it spent using Kimi Ryokan as a base but traveling by train to nearby areas for sightseeing. I was enjoying talking to them but my ribs hurt badly after the nearly four hours sleep, mostly on my side.

A couple came out of the bathroom. The young woman was still applying lipstick. "Sorry", she said. "No worries", Victoria replied. "We'll be out in a minute", she said, turning to me. Both of them went through the bathroom door which was being held open by the woman by one hand while not missing a beat with the lipstick. They were in the bathroom a couple of minutes when Victoria stuck her head out the door. "You can come in now if you want". I stood there, not knowing what she meant. "We're just cleaning up a little to go out tonight."

"Um, that's OK, I'll wait." Though I really had to go, I didn't know what else to do.

"There are stalls in here. Take a look. It's OK. All of us gaijin do it. This bathroom is way too small for the number of rooms here".

Anyway-I had to go. Opening the door, I walked past the two urinals which were right next to the sinks and mirrors where they stood. I walked to the farthest stall, saying "excuse me" like an idiot while closing the stall door behind me. Then I heard Victoria's voice. I was about mid-flow, squatting at the porcelain bowl which was Japanese style, sunk into the floor.

"There's just the two of us tonight. You want to go with us?" She was speaking a little louder than necessary, as if trying to conceal my bathroom noise.

"I don't know". I felt foolish squatting there towards them in conversation.

"This is your first night in Japan, right?" Joanne added.

"No, my second. I flew in yesterday."

"Have you been out at night yet?"

"No. I went to bed last night."

"Then you have to go out with us tonight."

I was finished and reached up to pull the flush string, feeling a little embarrassed. I was taking my time, hoping they would leave before I opened the stall door. They didn't though and kept trying to talk me into going with them.

"We have money, if that's a problem", Victoria said.

"No. I have money." I opened the door, walked over to the sink and stood there, holding my hands like a doctor prepped for surgery. Joanne moved over. She was putting on some kind of makeup. She bumped Victoria with her hips in a comical gesture to get her to make room. I reached to turn on the water and waited. "No hot water", Joanne said. "Have to get used to it. Showers are hot though."

I washed my hands, leaning down over the low sink, my ribs cracking at the angle. "Ou…I yelled and pulled back with a grimace.

"What's wrong?" Victoria asked. They were both looking at me. I told them the short version of my day at the dojo. "What are you going to do now?" Joanne was holding her makeup brush in her hand but had turned towards me. "I don't know. Wait and see what happens."

"Then you definitely need to go with us tonight. We're leaving at 8 PM. Meet us in the lobby.

"If I can, I will." I just wanted to get back to my room and go to bed. I left the bathroom to the two of them and returned to my room. It was time to take more of the pain medicine that the doctor had given to me. I reached for my almost empty bottle of Pocari Sweat, put all four of the pills into my mouth and swallowed hard. This time, because I took them with so little liquid, I could taste the herbal coating.

I found some crackers from my flight in my backpack and ate a couple to get the taste out of my mouth, sat down on the futon, rolled over to a laying down position, and closed my eyes.

But I couldn't sleep. The daylong attempt at a nap had left me groggy and dull. Besides, I realized I hadn't eaten all day and was starving. I looked at my watch. It was 7:45 PM. "What the hell," I said out loud, and got back up, changed into my one good pair of jeans and fresh shirt, combed my hair and left my room, grabbing my wallet and passport on my way out. I walked down the stairs and through the lobby area. No one was there so I opened the outside doors and stepped out onto the small porch that led down to the street. It was crowded, mothers with their children, school kids and lots of businessmen dressed in suits walking in small groups. I sat down on the porch and watched them. They seemed very happy and it looked like they were already quite drunk with their laughter, shouting and staggering. A small group of them noticed me and were walking towards the steps.

"Harro." Said the most boisterous one. "How are you?"

"Hello. I'm fine. How are you?" I returned his greeting.

"You American?"

"Yes. From Michigan."

"Ah, Michigan…nearby Detroit?"

I smiled and just said "Yes, that's right."

"Well, he's coming with us!" It was a voice behind me. I turned and saw Victoria and Joanne. Victoria wore jeans and a white blouse that was open a bit at the top. She had silver slivers hanging from her ears that shined when the light hit the right angle. Joanne wore a one-piece dress that was tied at the waist. There was a string of pearls around her neck. They both carried jackets. The businessmen were clearly stunned by this development and were openly starring at the two women.

"*Konban wa.* (Good evening)" Victoria spoke directly to them.

"*Ah... konban wa.*" It was the same guy that had been speaking to me. He and Victoria exchanged a few words. I have no idea what they talked about. But the group eventually continued down the street, all of them shouting out different versions of goodbye in English.

"See you later"

"See you next time"

"Nice to meet you"

When they had finally moved on down the street, Victoria grabbed my right arm and Joanne took my left. "Ou…" I cried out. "Take it easy." "Sorry love." Joanne said. Shall we go?"

"Where are we going?"

"We'll start at an Izakaya. Have you been yet?" said Victoria.

"No. A what?"

"An Izakaya" said Joanne. "They have a huge selection of food. And it's all good."

"And lots of drinks to choose from" added Victoria. I could see her priorities clearly.

They were pushing me along at a healthy pace, dodging more businessmen who couldn't resist saying "*harro*". Victoria and Joanne would smile sweetly, look directly at them and return the greeting.

They walked me further down the street, turned a corner and entered a vestibule that led to an elevator, to me indistinguishable from any other bar or restaurant on the street. Up to the fifteenth floor we went. The elevator had just enough room for the three of us, but at the last minute a group of five crammed themselves in beside us. We were then standing so close to each other that I had to pull my shoulders inward and put my arms in front of my chest. The pain hit me again. I could smell the alcohol and cigarettes on our hijackers. I could also smell the perfume and shower freshness of Victoria and Joanne who were giggling at the event.

Finally, we arrived and I noticed it was the roof. We squeezed out as one mass, the five strangers walking away towards another restaurant. They dragged me towards a set of double doors. Then we had to choose between inside or outside seating. Joanne made the choice. We veered to the right towards the roof-top open-air bar. "Inside is always smoky," she said. "And it's a perfect night for outside." "Outside is good", I said, looking to the left and seeing smoke rolling out of the door which was left ajar.

A young woman approached us with a concerned look. "*Nan nin sama desuka*? (How many?)" Victoria answered in Japanese, "*san nin desu*. (three)" The woman's face relaxed and she smiled. She said something else that I could not understand but had to mean "follow me". She led us through the front of the bar towards the back, where it opened up into a much larger space. Along the right side there were simple tables lined up against a concrete berm that served as a kind of half wall. It was only about four feet high and I could see a lot of the city. On the left was nothing but a wall with alternating sections of concrete and glass. Against the wall was a bar-like structure that held the cash register, plastic cups, assorted utensils, napkins, menus and a row of four beer kegs with their colorful taps proudly displayed.

We kept on walking. Then the hostess turned to the left and immediately again to the right. She pulled three chairs from under a table next to the outside berm. From the table we could see in two directions. The city sparkled. It was the most beautiful view of my life.

The hostess did not ask if the table was OK. She quickly left and returned with menus.

"*Onomimono wa*?"

"What would you like to drink?" Victoria asked.

"Japanese draft beer." I answered without hesitation. Victoria ordered for all of us. Joanne stood up and leaned over the wall. "You have to look at this!" She was talking to me. I stood up, Victoria right behind me. I could see everywhere, nothing but neon lights on the horizon, shielded only by higher buildings. "What do you think?" Joanne turned to me.

"It's gorgeous. Nothing like this in Michigan."

"See that red sign, the one with Rod Steiger 'I am a man'?"

"Yes. I see it."

"Look directly below it. See the small building? It's a *koban*. Just next to it is Kimi Ryokan." Victoria added, "if you look straight down that street, just follow the curve to the right, you can see part of Ikebukuro station." They pointed out other buildings and parks, clearly enjoying sharing their knowledge of this city.

"*O matta sei*. (Sorry for the wait)" The voice was almost singing. It was our waitress, another young woman who could have been the twin sister of our hostess, except that she was wearing a mini skirt and white blouse. She sat three large draft beers on the table. We took our seats, thanked her and reached for the beers. "*Kanpai*" we all said together. I was drinking my first beer in Japan on a rooftop overlooking a fantastic skyline on a cool night in April with two new female friends.

We talked about everything. They taught me much about Japan and its language, places to visit and most of all, its amazing public transportation system. They raved about how safe Japan was, giving examples of walking alone after midnight almost anywhere without any sign of trouble.

Joanne was a graduate student studying psychology. She was taking a year off her studies to travel with Victoria, her friend since childhood. She was studying child psychology with the intention of getting a PhD and opening her own practice. Recently she was re-thinking her career path and was quick to agree when Victoria asked her to take a year off. Victoria just wanted to take advantage of the one-year reciprocal agreement called working holiday between Australia and Japan that allowed a visa for one year for cultural exchange. She had finished her four-year degree in art history and just wanted to travel and see the world.

We talked into the night. The beer kept coming. I don't remember ordering anything. It was hours later that I realized that the pain in my rib cage was almost gone. Large quantities of beer will do that. More than likely I needed to relax. This was the first time since arriving in Japan that I could sit back and laugh and enjoy.

We ate much food. Victoria took the lead in that department. She was having fun ordering squid, octopus and other dishes just to see my reaction. But I was never a finicky eater and tried it all with no hesitation. I mentioned to them that my pain had almost gone away.

"Excellent. You just needed some time out with good company", Victoria said.

"And lots of beer. That probably helped the most", Joanne added.

"Let me see the bruise." Joanne said and scooted her chair around the table, close to me. Victoria also moved closer.

"Nah, that would be weird." But they insisted. Victoria reached over and pulled my shirt up. We sat there at the table, the two of them examining my third and fourth ribs. The waitress didn't seem to mind and bent down to take a look on her way back to the kitchen with a tray full of empty dishes.

"Do you think it's broken?" Joanne said.

"Don't know for sure but probably not. I think if it was broken, I wouldn't be able to even move without a heavy wrap."

"What will you do now?" said Victoria.

"I'll skip training tomorrow…um, today." I said, looking at my watch.

"I'll walk around, stretch, sleep and get ready for training the next day."

Joanne gently pulled my shirt down and started to tuck it in, but I stopped her. "That's OK, I can do that." I was full of food and beer and was ready to move on. We received the bill from our waitress, stood up from the table and started for the door where the cash register was. The place was still busy although it was close to 3 a.m. and we had to weave our way between the tables and the people who were milling around laughing and shouting. I wanted to pay the entire bill but they wouldn't let me. "No-let's share. We'll do this again", Joanne said.

We walked out and down the narrow hallway to the elevator which was sitting with its doors open. A minute later we were walking down the street again, heading towards Kimi Ryokan. The street looked different now, almost empty. Of course - there were no children or families, but it was quiet and almost secretive. I could sense this was an adult world now and could see in corners and at elevators the hostesses and small groups of salarymen saying goodbye to each other with much flirting and, what I assumed was promises of future meetings. Taxis were lined up to take the men home. I was to learn that thirty minutes later the same taxis would return to carry the hostess's home. I was to also learn much more about this world a couple of years later and become a part of it in a limited way.

We were at Kimi in no time. The street, being nearly empty, allowed us to simply walk straight without stopping or dodging groups of people, bicycles or cars. It was so quiet that we started to whisper as we walked.

Back at Kimi, we climbed the steps to the entrance. Victoria pulled at the door. Nothing happened. "It's locked", she said.

"What do we do now?" I said. "Can we knock?"

"No. That would make Nemura san angry!" she answered. "Let's just sit here for a while. It's almost morning. I think the cleaning ladies will be here in another hour?"

"Wait. Let's get some coffee." Joanne said. She led us back down the steps and another hundred feet down the road to a row of vending machines.

I was surprised at the type of drinks that were available. The normal sodas, coffee and other drinks, but also just about anything alcoholic, sake and shochu, in a variety of sizes and brands. We all chose coffee. Joanne stuck a five-thousand-yen note into the slot, pushed a button next to a picture of the coffee she wanted, and out came a cold can of coffee. She hit the button another two times with the same results. Then she hit the change button and out came the correct change. I remember being impressed that the machine actually worked, let alone gave back change.

We walked back across to Kimi, sat on the steps, popped open the coffees and stretched out our legs. It was quiet and cool. I was tired and sleepy. Joanne and Victoria still had some energy left but were ready to call it a day. We talked for little over an hour. It was close to five a.m. when the first cleaning lady appeared. "*Ohaiyogozaimasu* (Good morning)", she looked surprised to see the three of us sitting there.

"*Ohaiyogozaimsu*", we all said in unison. Victoria then explained why we were there and they both laughed. The cleaning lady had a high-pitched laugh that showed her sparkling gold teeth and I thought she would wake everyone up. She unlocked the door and held it open for us. We marched quietly into the lobby, up the stairs and down the hallway to our rooms. Inserting the key, the cleaning lady gave me into the lock and closing the door behind me, I fell into my futon and slept long and well.

Chapter Five

I awoke to a soft knocking on my door. Struggling up and off my futon, I got to the door just as another cleaning lady was opening the door. "*Ah, Sumimasen.* (Excuse me)", she said, clearly surprised I was there. Probably I looked like a wild man. At that time, I had long hair and a full beard and was standing in my underwear.

"Ah. OK. *Doozo*". Struggling into my jeans, I walked down the hallway to the bathroom. Kimi seemed empty. There was no one in line for the bathroom and no one inside. I examined myself in the mirror and shrugged. No wonder she looked a little scared.

I used the bathroom, cleaned up as best I could and walked back to my room. The cleaning lady was still there. Entering the room, I excused myself and headed for the closet, grabbed my backpack, reached into the pocket and removed my book and my wallet, dressed and left. Walking down the steps I noticed it had started to rain. I could smell the wet, dustiness of the new rain. It was a smell I had liked since childhood. There were crowds of people, some already popping open their umbrellas, the colors standing out against the blandness of the grey sky and buildings. I walked back up the steps, opened the door and reached into the umbrella stand just inside, pulled out a large one and turned back down the steps. I had always liked rainy days. Especially when it was possible to walk leisurely, not having to be anywhere. Turning right at the bottom of the steps, I started to walk towards the train station, vaguely looking for something to eat and some coffee.

I found a place called MosBurger and ordered two burgers and coffee. It hit the spot and I immediately felt better. In fact, my ribs were not hurting all the time now, only when I raised my arms or twisted the wrong way. I swallowed four more pain pills anyway, then pulled out my book, *The Lonely Planet Guidebook* to Japan, and sat back with one foot resting on the chair next to me. I was a long way from home and liked the idea that every movement I made, every decision as to what to do next, would be mine alone, not my work, not my family or friends, just mine. It was almost four P.M. on my second full day in Japan. I had bruised ribs, but all in all everything was pretty good. I had done OK at my first training. I had expected rough treatment and had even assumed that the level was higher here. I was not disappointed. This was going to be a month to remember, if I survived.

I left the burger joint and walked back to Kimi Ryokan. On the left, just a ten-minute walk from MosBurger was a small park. Back-tracking, I bought another coffee and made my way to the park. It was empty and I placed my backpack on one of the benches, sat down and again opened my guidebook and started to read and slowly drink my coffee. The rain had stopped. Feeling good, I rose from the bench and went over to a grassy spot next to the edge of the park, near the entrance. I did a few stretches and then stood at kata kamae and started slowly and lightly doing Jion. It felt OK. My ribs hurt with almost every move but not unbearably. I did the kata several times, each time increasing the power and speed. Same result. No more and no less pain. I tried other katas with varying success in terms of pain free performance. And then came Empi, by this time no longer doing them slowly. I started out with the turn sharply to the left side while blocking a kick from the front with my right arm. Then back up, right fist on top of left fist. Then I stepped to the right with a down block, then into a quick kibadachi facing front with right hand pulled back and left hand performing a hook punch across the front of my chest, then stepping to the front with a strong left-hand down block. I was getting into it and now threw a strong right hand rising reverse punch. The pain shot through my body and I yelled loudly, grabbing for my ribs. That was foolish. I should have rested all day and maybe then stretched a little, instead overdoing it. I felt the rib cage area, no idea what to look for but just seeing if there was anything different or noticeable. There wasn't, just extreme pain.

I walked back to the park bench and sat down, thinking "just relax", and, reaching for my coffee and book, sat there another hour reading. It was nearly six P.M. and I was hungry again. While reading I had stretched and moved around a bit to make sure there was no damage.

Back in Ann Arbor I had tasted soba. The waitress, a middle-aged Japanese woman, told me then that theirs was good but nothing compared to the real thing. I wanted soba. Mr. Nemura had pointed out a soba shop the day I arrived. The problem was finding it. I walked towards Kimi, hoping to be able to find it if I started from there. Arriving at Kimi, I glanced around, having no idea where the restaurant was and walked up and down the street in front of Kimi, finally seeing a display with noodle dishes. "This is not the restaurant he told me about", I mumbled to myself, opening the door. But it looked good and I was hungrier than ever.

"*Irashaimase* (Welcome)", came the shout from a young woman. "*Nannin sama*? (How many)" I signed my index finger.

"*Hai. Hitori sama* (one person)", she shouted to someone back in the kitchen. "*Hai. Hitori sama*" came the reply.

She led me to a counter, a kind of bar style counter with high stools and jars of strange condiments placed every two stools. I sat where she directed me. She gave me a menu and placed a set of chopsticks and a glass of water in front of me. Then she stood waiting.

I looked at the menu. I had studied Japanese menus a little in Michigan but could not understand any of this. "*Soba arimasuka*? (Do you have soba?)"

She looked at me a little puzzled but politely said, "*soba*?"

"*Hai. Soba.*"

"*Ah Sumimasen okyakusama*… (Um Sorry but…)", the rest I couldn't understand.

"*Soba, nai*? (No soba?)"

"*Sumimasen* (Sorry)", she said. "*Kochira no mise wa ramen-yasan desuyo* (This is a ramen shop*)*".

I did catch ramen. "*Hai. Ramen OK* (Ramen is OK)". I was a little embarrassed.

She smiled and asked a few more questions that went past me. I looked at the menu which had pictures of each selection and pointed at what I wanted. She smiled again. "*Kashikomarimashita*. (Ok-got it)"

I smiled back and shriveled into my stool. I was to learn the difference between soba and ramen over the next couple of weeks. To this day I love eating both.

"*Onomimono wa*? (How about something to drink?)" She was still looking at me and waiting for my drink order. "*Beeru kudasai*. (Beer please.)"

"*Hai*" she said, with a long extension of the "i".

I again pulled out my guide book and read. There was a section about Kamakura. My plan was to visit there my first weekend. I had memorized the language necessary to make the trip and did not fell it would be that difficult to go on my own. After last night though, I thought I might be able to convince Victoria or Joanne or both to go along. It would be great to go with someone.

My smiling waitress was back with a huge beer. She sat a glass on the counter and then poured the beer into it. "Arigato", I said. She smiled again.

I sat for a few minutes more. Then she returned with my ramen set, which consisted of a bowl of noodles, a small *cha-han* and a very small dish of vegetables. "*Doozo*", she said.

"Domo arigato", I said, already reaching for a pair of chopsticks from the lacquered box that sat on the counter. But she did not leave. She sat down on the stool next to me.

"Are you American?"

"Yes"

"Why are you in Japan?"

"I'm a tourist", I said, having decided before I came not to publicize the fact that I would be training in karate.

"A tourist?" She said. Her English was good.

"Yes. I want to visit tourist places, like Kamakura."

"Ah. But now you are in Tokyo."

"Um-I just arrived in Tokyo two days ago. I'm resting so I can visit many different places."

"Where will you go first?"

"I think maybe Kamakura."

"Oh. I love Kamakura." She went back to the kitchen.

I'm a little slow sometimes but this time I understood. Maybe it was because I was alone and, as I felt back in the park, free to do anything I wanted. My mind drifted back to my hometown where I had made friends with a woman who lived around the corner from my house. We would wave to each other and occasionally I would run into her at the bagel shop. Then suddenly her sister moved in with her and they started sitting on the front porch. I started to talk to them and became good friends with the sister, who was a little younger than me.

One day I stopped by to see the sister but was told she had moved out. My neighbor invited me in and made some coffee. We talked awhile and she said she had to get ready for a party. I started to leave but she told me to stay and that she would get ready while we talked.

She pulled off her shorts and blouse and walked into the bathroom to put on makeup. I was stunned but kept talking to her. Then she removed the rest of her clothes and walked out into the living room. She sat on the couch and talked as if nothing odd was happening. I just talked, not wanting to insult her by making a pass. Eventually she changed into a dress and was ready for the party. I left and walked back around the corner to my house. I told my friends about it that night and they all laughed at me. "You're an idiot!" My best friend's wife shouted.

"What?"

"She wanted you to make a move."

"You think so?"

"Oh God…." The whole room exploded with laughter.

I was not about to make the same mistake. I was just getting settled into my book when the waitress returned. She reached for my bottle and slowly refilled my glass.

"What are you reading?"

"It's a guide book."

"Oh" She did not move.

"I'm reading about Kamakura."

"Why do you have interest in Kamakura?"

"It's Japanese history. And I want to see the Big Buddha."

"*Ah. Dai Butsu*?"

"Yes. I had already read the Japanese name for Big Buddha. She still did not move.

"Why do you like Kamakura?" I said.

She took my bottle and again filled my glass.

"As you say, it is Japanese history. And my parents are living there."

"Oh. So-you go there often?"

"No. I work here in Tokyo and have two other part-time jobs also. I don't have time to visit my parents.

Silence. She went back to the kitchen again. I drank my beer and continued to read. It was very comfortable and I had nowhere to go.

"What is your name?" She was back and had another bottle of beer in her hand.

"Michael"

"My name is Yumiko. This is free." She tapped the bottle after she sat it on the counter.

"Really, thanks" I was ready to order another one anyway.

We talked a few minutes. She had just returned from a one-year home-stay program in Seattle. Before that she had studied English conversation for a few years. The topic eventually returned to Kamakura.

"Um…I'm planning to go to Kamakura this weekend. Would you like to go?" I was not going to blow it this time.

"Oh…Yes. I have to change my schedule but…sure. When will you go?"

"I'm thinking Friday night"

"Yes. I will go with you." The personal note of her answer struck me.

I told her I would see her on Friday to make plans. I did not really think she would go. The restaurant was getting crowded and she had a difficult time talking to me after that. I continued to read my book. It was now 9 PM and I felt tired and ready for bed and signaled to Yumiko. She came over and apologized for not talking to me.

"It's OK. I know you're busy."

"I am looking forward to Kamakura."

"Me too." She said as she handed me the bill. I took it, walked to the cash register with her, paid, and said goodbye. "I'll see you on Friday."

"That's great." She handed me a piece of paper with her phone number written on it.

I walked back to my room at Kimi, took off my clothes and fell into the futon, closing my eyes, but immediately I forced myself to get back up, walk out into the hallway, go to the bathroom with my toilet kit and prepare for a good night's sleep. When I returned to my room, I reached for my alarm which I had placed on the T.V. stand, set it for 7 AM, and again nestled into the futon, falling asleep with a very large grin on my face. I was going to the dojo tomorrow.

Chapter Six

Jumping out of the futon quickly when the alarm sounded, I went down the hall to the bathroom and was packed and ready to go at 7:30 AM and found my way to Ikebukuro station. It was crowded so I waited for a second train, which was no less crowded. Twenty-five minutes later I was walking down the platform at Ebisu station. I had roughly one hour to find a restaurant and have some breakfast and be at the dojo by 10 AM.

I walked by a Wendy's, a MosBurger and another place that looked like a fast food restaurant. I wanted to find an old-style restaurant, a place that was a bar at night but served breakfast in the morning, a place where the waitress and the clientele would be the same every day. Jim had told me their breakfasts were good and I could meet people. This was only for one month and I didn't want to spend every morning eating fast food and sitting on plastic chairs.

Walking down the main street that cuts ninety degrees from and goes under the Yamanote line at Ebisu station, concentrating on a few block's radius from the dojo, I saw a display on the outside of a restaurant. The sign read ham and eggs set in *kata kana* (Japanese script used for borrowed words). There was a piece of ham on a plate, covered with an egg and a small salad on the side. Lying on top was a slice of bread that looked like Texas toast. A cup of coffee rounded out the set. The price was 450 yen. I walked in.

It was smokier than I liked. But the tables were heavy wood - oak, I think, and the chairs were upholstered, old but with character. There were large, commercial photos of Paris, Madrid, New York on the walls with snapshots of the same cities pinned to the wall beneath each. Obviously, someone was a world traveler.

"*Irashai*! (Welcome)" came a greeting from somewhere in the back. Then something else I could not understand.

"Ah…please." He said when he saw me standing there. He motioned for me to choose a table and sit down. He was carrying an order which looked like the ham-egg set to another table in an inside corner.

I walked over to the opposite corner and sat down at a table looking out on the street.

"*Omatasei* (Sorry to keep you waiting)", the waiter was at my table already. He sat a glass of water down.

"*Ham-egg set kudasai.*" I tried to pronounce it in the kata kana manner.

"*Ah…ham-egg setto. Koohii de* (With Coffee?)"

"Hai." He disappeared into the kitchen. I watched the people walk up and down the sidewalks, amazed at the sheer numbers, having never seen these kinds of crowds before. I pulled open my backpack, sat it on the chair next to me, reached into a pocket and grabbed for the Advil, passing on the pills the doctor had given to me. I could still feel the pain most of the time but, either I was used to it or it was less than before. But I knew I would be moving my body in class and that there was a big chance of tearing or stretching the same area again. I took three.

"*Hai…Omatasei.*" The waiter was back with my breakfast and sat it on my table. It was a large plate with a section for everything, a large section for the slice of ham and the egg, a half section for a small salad, and another half-size section that held a small cup of coffee. The toast was placed on top of the ham. It looked great even if the coffee was small, pretty much the way it was depicted on the display out front.

"Karate"? He was looking at my open backpack where my gi and belt were sticking out from rummaging for my pain medicine.

"*Hai. Nihon Karate Kyokai.* (Yes-Japan Karate Association)"

"*Ah, wakatta. (*Oh-I see)" he said. "*Nihongo hanaseru*? (Do you speak Japanese?)"

"*Sukoshi dake*. (Only a little)" I replied.

"May I talk in English?"

"Of course. Please do."

"But please eat first." He said. "I will be back later to talk about karate." He left and walked over to a table where two young men had just sat down.

I gorged on the ham and eggs and put a spoonful of jam on the toast and sat back to drink the coffee. Outside a small group had formed. They greeted each and then opened the door, marched in and walked to the side of the shop to a long table and sat down. The waiter was there quickly with a jovial "*irashai*" and greeted them as friends. They seemed to know him also and joked with each other and patted backs. The waiter pointed towards my table. They all looked my direction, a few of them nodding their heads in a shortened bow. I nodded back, wondering what was happening. There was still a little time before I had to go, so I reached for my book. A few minutes later the waiter was back at my table.

"Was it good?"

"Yes. It was very good. The coffee was excellent too."

"Everyone comes here for the coffee, especially in the afternoon. These tables are all full."

"Really? Full of businessmen?"

"Yes. We say salarymen. They come here to have a break from their office. Some of them have much stress. Of course, some of them have nothing to do." We both laughed.

"At night, some of the same customers are here drinking."

"So-this is a bar too?"

"Well, I say this is a jazz bar. I play jazz music at night. I bought many jazz albums from all over the world."

"You like to travel?"

"Very much. You see the photos?" He pointed to the walls.

"I noticed them. Very nice."

"I took each of them myself."

"You went to all those places?"

"I go once or twice a year. Each time a different country."

Then it dawned on me. "Then, this is your place?"

"Yes. For many years. Maybe twenty years."

"That's great. It's a really nice bar-I mean jazz bar."

Looking at my watch, "Sorry, I have to go to the dojo. I would like to talk to you more sometime. Can I come again?"

"Of course. Please try the evening also. The mood is much different, and you can hear the music better. The customers don't like music in the morning so I play it very softly in the kitchen only."

"I will. I'm here for a month so I will have a chance to come at night. I look forward to it."

"Good. What is your name?"

"Michael."

"My name is Watanabe."

We chatted a few more minutes and I had to go. I paid the 450-yen bill and started for the door. He walked me out and thanked me for the business.

"They will stay another thirty minutes and then go to the dojo too." He motioned towards the group at the long table.

"Oh. They do karate too?"

"Yes. The same *ryu*, ah style. I think maybe the same dojo?"

I looked back at the group. They were watching me. A couple of them again nodded to me. I nodded back. "So, that means they are instructor trainees." I thought.

"Well, see you again Watanabe san."

"Have a good training."

I walked out the door and into the street. It was just ten minutes to the dojo, a few minutes back towards the station and then cut to the left and down another street. I found the metal stairway that led to the dojo and hiked upwards, stepped into the dojo entryway and up to the administration window.

The lady who had helped me with the doctor was sitting there.

"*Ohaiyogozaimasu* (good morning)" I said.

"*Ara. Ohaiyogozaimsu. Daijobu* (good morning, are you OK*)*?"

"*Hai. Daijobu desu* (yes-I'm fine)." I answered.

I had already paid tuition for the entire month. This was apparently known to her.

"Thank you very much for your help." I bowed.

"*Iie, tondemonai* (no problem-it's nothing*)*." She bowed in return.

With another short bow, I walked back into the dojo area, took off my shoes, stored them on a shelf, stepped up onto the dojo floor and walked back to the locker rooms. I was the only person there and changed quickly, went back out onto the floor and started to stretch in the warm-up area. It was another ten minutes before other karate students started to arrive. It was already twenty after ten. In the future

I would also not arrive so early in an attempt to copy the others. Today I was nervous and concerned about my rib injuries.

Soon there were around thirty students on the floor. Others were still arriving and would run up to the shelving area, kick off their shoes, run onto the dojo floor and back to the locker room with a short bow, much less reverently than me. It was ten-thirty on the clock in the break area. One of the senior students barked orders. We all ran to the line and stood at attention. We were there in less than a minute. It was Tanaka Sensei again. Someone called out commands, none of which I understood so I just copied the others in line.

We sat in seiza position, then came the command to meditate. There was total silence for about three minutes, then the senior shouted the regular commands to start the class. Tanaka Sensei turned one-hundred-eighty degrees towards us. Another command, and we all bowed to him as our teacher for today. Tanaka Sensei then jumped up from seiza position to a standing position, landing on both feet. I still do this occasionally today and it raises eyebrows.

Another command and the senior led us through warm-ups. Then it was time for class. The senior turned towards Tanaka Sensei and bowed. Then he ran to the back group with the rest of the senior students who had joined the class as a warm-up before instructor's class.

Sensei started immediately. "Heian Shodan!" He instructed us to go by his count. His count was extremely slow. At the end of each move we were to make perfect form. He waited until each of us had that perfect form before shouting out the next move. I was shaking and my muscles were crying out for mercy. It took almost a full ten minutes before he finally said, "*Hai yame.* (Ok stop)" Then he shouted, "*Hai...moo ichido...* (One more time)"

We started again. This time Sensei counted faster. But he still wanted every move to be perfect. And, at certain moves, he stalled the count, waiting for everyone to adjust, shouting at some of us for taking so much time. I was using every muscle in my body trying to make perfect stances and techniques. Sweat was already running down my forehead. "This is only the second kata", I thought to myself.

"Lower!" It was Tanaka Sensei. He had come up from behind while I was in the first back stance at the end of the kata. He grabbed my shoulders, moved my back knee out with his foot and pushed down with both hands. Then he counted for the next move.

"Lower…! He said it again. I moved as fast as I could, still trying to stay low, snapping into the next back stance-knife hand block. Sensei was there. He swept my right leg and down I went.

I jumped up into the third back stance move. Sensei pulled me to the front of the class, had me take stance as he took stance, becoming my attacker for the second to last move of the kata. Sensei then told me to block his attack. He stepped in with his left leg and punched high *chudan* level. He told me to turn from the second back stance-knife hand position to the third, blocking his punch. He had me practice it three times. The whole class was watching. I tried to turn into each block fast and strong while Sensei held his attack for me.

Then Sensei backed up and had me do the same while he stepped in with the same attack. We did this another three-times. The third time he stepped in, I turned and blocked his punch, and he immediately shifted his left leg, sweeping me down to the floor. I got up quickly. He then began to demonstrate the difference between the amount of weight on each leg of the technique. If I had twenty to thirty percent of my weight on the front leg, he explained, and was foot swept, as he demonstrated, I was less likely to lose my balance and be thrown to the floor. In other words, the foot sweep would not have as much effect on me since most of my weight was on my back leg. I may be thrown off balance, but probably not to the ground.

Sensei then called two senior students to the front of the class. He had one of them fall to the floor. The other was told to attack from above as soon as he landed. He did this three-times. In all cases, the fight would have been over with injury or death the result.

"Defense. Cannot do good from ground." He repeated it in Japanese. Then Sensei had the seniors demonstrate just being off balance but not to the ground. The results clearly showed the benefits of staying off the floor. Although each senior, when switching from offense to defense, was knocked off balance, each could defend himself as long as they didn't go to the ground.

Sensei then had the two seniors demonstrate the same techniques that he had performed with me. The lesson was clear. When turning into the back stance-knife hand block, we were to keep our weight on the rear leg. This would help prevent us from losing our balance and landing in a heap on the floor if a foot sweep was used. Sensei had the class pair-up and practice this one technique from the first kata everyone learns when they begin studying karate. We were told to do the techniques both ways, shifting our weight from the back leg to the front leg to understand the difference. This we did at medium speed ten times each. Then Sensei shouted for speed and power. What followed was an entire class, focused on this one technique, taking turns attacking with the left leg and step-in punch, then shifting the left leg over with a sweep as the opponent turned to block with his back-stance knife hand.

My partner was a young Japanese. He was intent on getting it right and attacked fiercely when it was his turn. He also defended strongly while I attacked him. We did this practice over and over again. My left leg was cramping from the constant contraction and expansion. My right forearm was aching from blocking my partner's punch, and my right ankle was hurting from the foot sweeps.

But I had learned a good lesson. I was able to stay on my feet now, even though being strongly swept. And I was having fun with my partner. I was exhausted and sweating heavily. But something else was happening as well. The techniques were flowing and working for me. I was becoming more relaxed even though my speed and power and technique was improving. I remember noticing that my training partner was getting tired and me feeling just the opposite. I was having fun.

"*Hai, yame*!" Sensei had us spread out again. "Hai...Heian Shodan, no count." We did the kata another five times with Sensei walking around, correcting form. I had more energy now than at the start of class. It was a new experience for me. I could have trained forever.

"*Hai, yame. Seiritsu.* (Ok stop and line up)" We all ran to the back and lined up. A senior student called out the formal ending of the class. I was finished. My ribs had hurt pretty much the entire class but I could stand it. And Tanaka Sensei had not taken it easy on me. I felt good as I walked back to the locker room.

Chapter Seven

After a quick shower I headed back across the dojo floor. We only had thirty minutes until the instructor's class started and they did not like stragglers lumbering across the floor after their class was in session. I hustled across the floor, put my shoes on and headed out the door, through the entrance and down the stairs. I could still smell the bakery next door as I hit the bottom of the stairs. It was noon. I had until 4 P.M. to do whatever I wanted. It felt great to have complete control of my life.

But what could I do for three and a half hours? Walking back towards Ebisu station I passed a noodle shop. I hadn't thought of eating but the pictures in the display of the various noodle dishes caught my eye. Backing up, I went through the door and sat down at a table.

"*Irashai*," came the usual greeting. I nodded at the person behind the counter.

"*Okyakusama*," she pointed towards the front corner where there was a single vending machine in the front corner of the shop.

"*Shokken*. (Ticket)"

I stood up and walked over to the machine. It was a regular vending machine with pictures of each ramen dish and its associated selection number. I still could not read very well but the pictures were clear enough. There were perhaps twenty different types of ramen dishes, all of them starting with the basic ramen noodle. There were many tempting choices ranging from the shio base, miso base and shoyu base. Ingredients varied with the base and included *negi* (onion), *nori* (seaweed), *tamago* (egg), pork and more.

I chose miso ramen with pork (*chashu miso ramen*). I had eaten it in Ann Arbor a few times and liked it very much. I put a thousand-yen note into the slot and pushed the button. Out came a ticket about the same size as a movie ticket. I waited for the change which should have been six hundred and fifty yen. Nothing came. I stood there for a few minutes probably looking pretty stupid.

"*Okyakusama-otsuri butan oshite.* (Customer-push the change button)" I looked at her but had no idea what she said. She repeated it but it didn't matter. She even added "*pushu…pushu*". Finally - another customer sitting at the counter walked over, pointed at the change button and pushed it. Out came the proper change.

"*Arigato gozaimasu.*" I said to him.

"*Iie.* (no problem)". He walked back to his seat.

"Hai" said the woman, as she motioned to put the ticket on the counter.

I sat back down at a high table and pulled my book from the backpack and relaxed.

Not much later I heard "Hai…*chashu miso ramen no okyakusama.* (the customer who ordered the pork ramen)" I looked over to the counter and she motioned that it was my order so I walked to the counter and picked up the tray.

"*Okyakusama…mizu*! (Sir-water)" She pointed to the back corner to a water cooler and a stack of glasses.

"*Arigato.*" I helped myself to a glass of very cold water.

The noodles were delicious, even better than those in Ann Arbor. Of course, that made sense. I was not in a hurry but gulped them down in just minutes, picking up the tray and placing it on the end of the counter as I had seen other customers do, thanking the lady as I walked out.

"*Hai, maido.*" She smiled.

I walked to a small park I had seen on my first day. There was no one there. It was about the size of a football field. Finding a bench, I opened my book, started to read, and fell fast asleep.

I awoke to the voices of school children playing games in the middle of the park. School was apparently out for the day and they were letting off some steam. It was almost four P.M. The next class was at four-thirty. Standing up and stretching the kinks out, I picked my book up from beneath the bench where it had fallen, stuffed it into my backpack and headed for the dojo.

There were a few Japanese students already on the floor using the makiwara as I walked back to the locker room, bowing to them as I passed. Five minutes later I was on the dojo floor warming up, and another five minutes later was invited to free spar with a middle-aged Japanese.

"Here we go again." I thought. We bowed and he attacked fast and hard, landing his fist on my chin. I had moved quickly to my right, but the punch had come too fast. It didn't hurt that much though, and I immediately planted a cutting round house kick to his mid-section with my left leg. It was a good kick. I knew he felt it. "Osu", he said, as he took kamae again. I just looked at him, trying to keep soft eyes.

He attacked again with a *mae geri, oi tsuki* (front kick and punch) combination which I blocked. But I was not ready for the sweep and went down hard. "Osu", I said, and jumped back up.

We sparred a few minutes more, exchanging good, strong techniques. The class was called to order. The teacher was one of the junior instructors from the morning class, and one of the guys that nodded at me at breakfast. We went through a short warm-up with my sparring partner leading the group. Then we started the class. The theme was kihon. We did basic punches and kicks up and down the floor, with the instructor yelling always for more speed and power. He was showing us how to bend the front knee to initiate the movement in stance. Then we were to transfer the weight and push off with the same leg when it became the back leg. He told us to keep our hips forward and stay low, demonstrating clearly.

I did what he said and could feel the difference. That's all we did for the hour, back and forth across the bowling alley floor. It was an excellent training and I learned some good pointers about moving fast and, more importantly, initiating the move quickly.

It was six o'clock when I walked down the stairs from the dojo and out onto the street. The sun was still shining but was lower in the sky. The air was cool and I felt relaxed and light, almost wanting to skip down the street. At Ebisu station, I put a hundred and twenty-yen into the ticket machine, grabbed the ticket from the cup at the bottom, walked to the gate, handed it to the ticket puncher, and stuck it into my pocket. My legs were cramping as I hiked the long stairs up to the train platform. Another three minutes later and I was inside the train, bound for Ikebukuro.

At Ikebukuro station, I started the fifteen-minute walk back to Kimi, just wanting to go back to the hotel and go to bed, but was also hungry again. Maybe not just hungry, but I found that Japanese food was so delicious that I wanted to try everything. Outside the station, I noticed a small bar. It was a stand-up bar with the words "Shot Bar", in English, on the window. It was only half full, but then it was still early evening. Walking into the bar, I found myself at one of the tall tables, not knowing how to order, just standing there. A business man in a dark suit moved over from the next table.

"You have to say your order, loudly, to the master." He pointed to the back of the bar.

"OK. Thank you." I looked around and saw that others were drinking whisky but some had beer.

"*Nama beeru kudasai*! (Draft beer please)" I shouted in the direction he had indicated.

"Oh, you're Japanese is very good." He said.

"Just when talking about food and drink," I said with a smile.

"Ah, but that is most important thing", he replied.

"Is there any food to order?" I asked him.

"You can order some yakitori. It is very good here. Please order when he brings your beer."

"OK, thanks." With that he moved back to his table where his friends started to interrogate him about his encounter.

The beer came and I ordered the yakitori, took a huge gulp from the mug and again pulled out my book. A few minutes later a small plate of yakitori appeared along with another plate that had salt, pepper, and other unknown spices, presumably for dipping.

Biting into the chicken, I found it was crisp on the outside and had a kind of mild salty taste and a seasoning I could not distinguish. It was hot and delicious. I followed it with another gulp of beer. This was truly heaven. My new friend was watching me.

"OK?" He shouted from his table.

"*Oishii*. (Delicious)" I replied. His friends laughed and raised their glasses to me. I raised mine to them.

I alternated between smaller gulps of the beer and bites of the yakitori. Soon, the beer was gone.

"*Moo ippai kudasai*! (One more please)" I shouted.

"*Hai!*" Came the reply.

I drank the next beer slowly and watched the T.V. which was on at low volume on the wall in the corner. It was eight o'clock. Tomorrow was another dojo day so I paid my bill, thanked the businessman for his help and started towards the hotel. I could feel the tiredness creeping up on me. It was time to go to bed. Though I had had only two beers, it felt like I had drunk many more. It was a little tricky to even walk straight down the street. I remembered that I had not eaten that much and had also sweat a lot. My cells had soaked up the alcohol.

Climbing up the stairs to Kimi, I walked to my room, opened the closet door and pulled my futon out. I pulled off my clothes, hit the futon and was almost asleep, but jumped up after remembering my wet gi, took it out of my backpack and hung it on a door hanger. Hopefully it would dry. Back to bed I went, checking my alarm quickly as my head hit the small pillow with yet another smile and then drifting off.

Chapter Eight

I was on the floor at ten o'clock, all alone, practicing kata. It had been hard to push myself out of the futon. It was still cold in the morning and it would have been great to just go back to sleep when the alarm sounded. But I didn't. It felt good to be the only person there. Looking around at the huge dojo, I thought about the many karate students that had trained here, and about the famous instructors that had trained on this same floor.

"Osu!" It was Antonio. I had met him the day before. Behind him came three other foreigners. I nodded hello to them and continued my kata practice.

When Antonio came back onto the dojo floor, he walked directly up to me.

"Good morning." He said.

"Good morning." I replied.

"Where are you from?" This was to be the usual first question when meeting another foreigner in Tokyo. I learned a few years later that being a foreigner, though in the dojo meant just another target for upper level Japanese, was also a kind of badge that we could display to each other. It meant that we were "outsiders" in this country but that we too, had a kind of secret, or exclusive club all to ourselves. Our foreignness made us special. Sometimes, I would find out, that was all we had.

Antonio squatted down onto the floor and started to stretch.

"Oh shit!" He said, pronouncing it as 'sheeet'.

"What?"

"My legs. They are still hurting from this morning's class."

"What class?"

"At the Hoitsugan." He said, pushing his head down to touch his left knee. He was spread eagle on the floor.

"What is that?"

"It is Nakayama Sensei's private dojo. It is not far from here, just down the street.

"But this is the JKA headquarters, right?" I was thinking I had come to the wrong dojo.

"Yes, yes. But Nakayama Sensei has his own dojo here too. It is a small one but very good feeling. And very hard training.

"So, you come to both dojos to train?"

"Yes. We train at seven-thirty at the Hoitsugan and then many of us come here for this class. This class is also very good, very hard."

"Can anyone go to the Hoistugan?"

"Yes, of course. You have to ask Kawawada Sensei. He will be here today. At least he said so."

"Will you introduce me?" I already knew enough not to approach a high-ranking Japanese Sensei without an introduction.

"If there is a chance, yes."

There were almost ten of us on the floor now, stretching and warming up. Some were doing light sparring.

"Great, thanks." I jumped backed up and started doing some basic punches and kicks.

"Osu. Good morning. You want to practice?" It was the same Japanese guy who had asked me to spar the day before. Only this time with perfect English.

"Osu. Hai, OK"

We sparred for a few minutes, trading punches and kicks. I enjoyed fighting with him the day before and now it was also a good session. We fought hard but not to win, just to explore the limits of our skills. I tried techniques that I hadn't dared until now.

In one exchange, as he was coming in strong with a front kick, I shifted a little back and to the left to escape. When his front leg came down from the kick attempt, I followed it down with my front foot and swept it forward. He was on the floor. I had felt no resistance and it had taken no effort at all. It was all timing and positioning. I helped him up and we started back at it.

After just a minute, he came in with the same kicking attack as before. I foolishly tried to do the same evasion and sweep. It was a fake. As I shifted, he kept his knee high in the air but he had no intention of front kicking me. He simply changed the kick into a reverse round-house which landed perfectly, his heel struck on the right side of my neck. It was controlled but it still hurt.

He immediately apologized. But I just said "Osu."

One of the seniors called the class to attention so I bowed to my fighting partner and ran to get in line.

The teacher today was Imura Sensei. He had been training with us in the back of the group. I could hear him when we did partner work and occasionally see him. I did not want to be his partner. He started the class immediately with no warm-up and took us through basic drills and then started adding techniques of increasing complexity. All basics were done up and down the floor. There was no stopping at each end of the floor, just turn and go back. He called out rapid-fire orders, yelling for more speed and more power. This we did for a full thirty minutes.

Then Sensei had us all form a tight circle and take natural stance. On his count we were to raise our right leg and thrust kick the person to our right. Then we had to set the same leg down, pivot on it to round-house kick the same person with our left leg.

The problem was, of course, that the person on our right was also doing the same to the person on his right, so we were attacking a moving target. The thrust kick was not that difficult, simply do it. The only variable was whether the person on the right leaned forward or backwards during their own kick. The second kick, the round-house, was a different story. After setting my right leg down from the thrust kick, I picked up my left leg, pivoted on my right and aimed for the mid-section of the person on my right. But since he was doing the same thing to his partner on the right, it was hard to make contact.

Sensei was strict and shouted at us to make contact with both the thrust kick and the round-house kick. We all strained to comply. In addition, while I was concentrating on making contact with the person on my right, the person on my left was nailing me hard with his two kicks, knocking me off balance.

Sensei kept shouting, "Bend your legs to make yourself stable. Grip the floor. Tense your body."

I was doing all that but was still losing my balance. I kept trying to do it correctly though and was not the only one struggling. After about ten minutes of doing it by Sensei's count, he told us to continue with no count.

It was a disaster. Though the entire class had been able to at least go through the motions when he counted, we lost it without his cadence. It was remarkable though, we were all trying as hard as we could to do it right, but even when we failed, it was still an enjoyable training. I heard laughs and saw smiles on many of the students.

Sensei shouted, "*Yame! Hai, hantai.* (Ok stop-reverse)"

We now had to start all over going to the left side, first by the count. It seemed like a completely different drill, as if we had never done anything like this before. But we did know about the moving target part of the drill, so caught on much quicker.

Within minutes we were doing it fairly well. Then Sensei shouted "no count". Again, we started out looking like amateurs. But soon enough we were giving our all to do it perfectly and with speed and power, Sensei still shouting at us. It was wonderfully hard and fun at the same time. The class was over. We all lined up, sat in seiza, shouted the dojo kun, and bowed out.

We ran across the floor to the locker rom. The instructor class trainees were already filing in and were warming up. I changed quickly, as always chatting with the other students about what we had just done. I was walking from the locker room towards the front when Antonio caught up with me.

"Wait a minute." He lightly grabbed my arm. "I will introduce you to Kawawada Sensei."

We walked to the makiwara area where a stocky Japanese was pounding away. I immediately recognized him as he had participated in the back of the class my first day.

"Sensei. *Shitsurei desu ga, daijobu desu ka*? (sorry to bother you-is it ok?)"

"*Hai. Nani*? (Ok-what is it?)"

"*Sensei, kono hito wa Michael to iu hito. (This is Michael). Kare wa Hoitsugan dojo de renshu shitain desu.* (He wants to practice at the Hoitsugan dojo.)"

"*Ah so*?" Sensei looked at me.

"*Hai Sensei.*" I replied.

"*Kuni wa, dochira*? (What country are you from?)"

"America."

"America...*doko*? (Where in America?)"

"Michigan Sensei."

"Ah, Michigan. *Sore...doko*? (Where is that?)"

I motioned with my hands while saying California and then New York. Then, in the middle, I showed my hand and said "Michigan" and pointed to the approximate location in mid-air. Then I raised my left hand to show the shape of my home state, again like all Michiganders, and indicated the five lakes that surround the state.

"Ah, *go kai ko*? (Ah, the five great lakes?)" he said.

"Hai."

"Why practice Hoitsugan?" He asked, in English.

"It is a strong dojo." I answered.

"How long train?" This was the same question I was asked at the Honbu window my first day.

"Five years Sensei."

"Mmmm. You come tomorrow."

"Hai Sensei. Thank you very much."

Sensei immediately turned to continue his makiwara practice.

I bowed and walked off the floor and down the stairs with Antonio.

"I will show you where the Hoitsugan is. "

We walked down the same street that went to Ebisu station that I took every day. But this time in the opposite direction. Soon we turned right and then curved left. We continued for another few minutes.

"Here we are!" Antonio was pointing to a very plain apartment building of about six floors. Nothing showed itself as being a karate dojo except a very small JKA sign just beneath the entrance to the basement floor of the building and a small Hoitsugan sign.

"Want to go inside?"

"Is it OK?"

"No problem."

We walked down a flight of stairs and then came to the end which led out to a long hallway lined with karate gis. A couple of pots with small trees also lined the hallway. I could smell the gis and could tell they were still wet from sweat and not from washing.

We turned to the right and walked past the showers and a small utility room. Then we walked onto the dojo floor. I will always remember the smell. It was a combination of the old wood floor and walls, the years of sweat condensed on the floor and the feeling of having finally found the place I had traveled all this way for.

We walked through the doorway and into the dojo. To the left and at Shomen was a small shrine and some pictures of Funakoshi, with fresh offerings by Nakayama Sensei's wife.

At the right was the locker room. It was very narrow with a line of lockers on the dojo side and just enough space to change. I stood with Antonio outside the locker room and looked around.

"This is excellent!"

"Yes. It is very good."

"Can I really train here?"

"Of course. You must come tomorrow. Sensei told you."

"Tomorrow?"

"You asked Sensei. He said yes. You must come tomorrow."

"OK. I will be here."

"Want to see where I live?"

"Live?"

"There is a room with beds that foreigners can stay in. Come on."

We walked back up the stairs and came to a small apartment style space that had bunk-beds. Antonio showed me his bunk. It consisted of a single bed and two small chests.

"It is very small but we all live together and it is a good feeling."

"It's great." I will be here tomorrow morning."

Antonio walked me back upstairs and out onto the street.

"I'm going to work in a couple of hours."

"OK. Thanks for your help. I'm looking forward to tomorrow."

With that, I walked back down the street, found the main road and made it to Ebisu station. I had a few hours until the four-thirty class but wanted to visit Tokaido, a company that made and repaired martial art uniforms. They also sold accessories, weapons, belts and all things martial. Jim had told me about the place and that I should take a look. I wanted to buy an extra karate gi. Also, I wanted to have a new black belt with the words "*Nihon Karate Kyokai* (Japan Karate Association)" embroidered on it along with my name in katakana.

I made it to Tokaido, which at that time was in a small, old building. When I walked in, an old gentleman was sitting behind a counter at a stitching machine. He was working on an old, beat up gi. I waited.

He did not notice me for a while so I called out to him.

"*Sumimasen*. (Excuse me)"

"*Hai. Matte kudasai*. (Please wait.)" He did not look my way.

I waited a few more minutes. Then I started to get impatient. He kept working. I was ready to leave and picked up my backpack from the floor and threw it over my shoulder.

Then he stood up, slowly, stretching upwards and twisting from right to left. He held the gi top he had been working on by the shoulders, first looking at the front, then turning it to look at the back. Seeming satisfied, he laid the gi across a work table and turned towards me.

"*Hai. Nan desho*? (How can I help you?)"

My anger was gone. He had to be over eighty-years old. His face was dark and wrinkled and marked with dark spots along with about a four-day beard. But he smiled at me and his eyes seemed to say that now it was my turn to receive his attention.

I explained in bad Japanese with lots of English thrown in. "*Atarashi karate gi kaitai*. (I want to buy a new karate gi.) And *atarashi kuro obi kaitai*. (and a new black belt.)"

"*Hai. Donna dogi hoshin desu ka*? (Ok-what kind of go do you want?)"

I understood the question but could not answer because I didn't know what gis were available.

"*Wakarimasen*. (I don't know.)" I said. Not knowing how else to indicate that I didn't know.

"*Eh? Wakarimasen*? (Huh-you don't know?) He looked puzzled. Then he must have realized that my Japanese was severely limited.

"Hai hai." He walked over to the display on the wall which held several styles of gis. He pointed at the different brands, naming them and indicating to me their respective qualities, most of which I could not understand. But one of them he called Tokaido.

"*Kore kudasai*. (This one please.)" I reached to feel the quality of the material. It was exactly what I wanted. It was a strong canvas gi and felt good between my fingers. The seams looked and felt strong and seemed to be of superior quality than the others.

"Ah. Tokaido." He smiled. "*Nani ryu*? (What style?)"

"*Nihon Karate Kyokai* in Ebisu." I replied, mixing Japanese with English.

"*Ah, hai hai, naruhodo. Tokaido no ho ga ii desune*. (Ah yes. Tokaido is best for you then.)" He was smiling again.

When he asked for my size, I told him a size five for the pants and a size six for the top. Jim had told me that I could split sizes here, something that couldn't be done in the States at that time.

I smiled. "*Soshite, obi mo hoshi desu*. (Also-I want a belt.)" I had learned the word "*shusu*" from Jim and indicated to him that type of belt. He understood and said the belt would take one week for the embroidery. He gave me a piece of paper and told me to write my name on it. Then he read it and asked me to pronounce it. I did and he wrote something in Japanese below my name.

I arranged to pick the belt up the following week but asked to take the gi with me that day. I paid for everything, tried to put the new gi in my backpack, then decided against it since there was not enough space. The old man found a paper bag with "Tokaido" written on the sides. He placed the gi inside and handed it to me. I said thank you and turned towards the door. He shouted after me, "*obi.... wasurenai de*! (Don't forget to come back for the belt)"

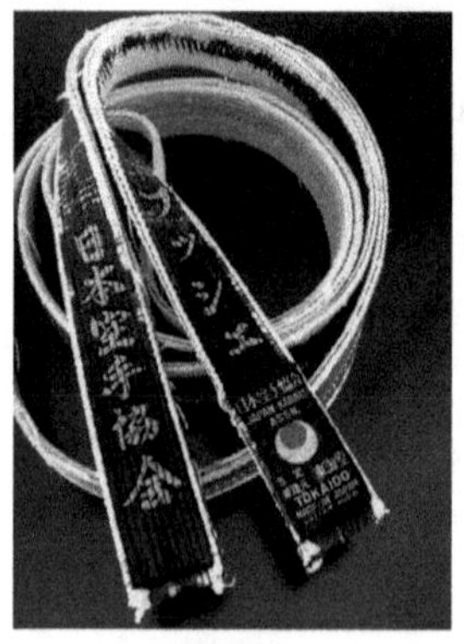

"*Hai. Arigato gozaimasu*."

The whole experience, which had started out with me being frustrated, had ended very pleasantly. This would be repeated many times in my first month in Japan, and again in the future. I would eventually learn to be more patient and slow down a little, values that would help me immensely with my personal life and business life.

Chapter Nine

It had not been that far to Tokaido but it still was almost time for the four-thirty class. I was in Ebisu and found a ramen shop next to the station, ordered my ramen and pulled out my book.

Thirty minutes later I was back in the Honbu dojo, trying to warm up with a series of basic punches and kicks. It looked like it would be a small class since only six students were on the floor. I felt a little tired and had a difficult time getting psyched for class this time. The fast pace of the last few days was catching up to me. My ribs had hurt pretty much all week, not enough to cause much trouble during training, but because of the constant tensing and manipulating for positions during drills so as not to get hit there again, I was exhausted. I would feel better after a good night's sleep, I thought.

The Sensei was again one of the instructor trainees from the noon class. He was also a previous sparring partner from one of the drills. He was good and he was tough. He led the class through the Heian katas and then started on the more advanced katas. Apparently, this was just for warm-up. The six of us were then paired up and he shouted, "*Jyu kumite*".

What followed was thirty minutes of free sparring. Three-minute rounds, a quick rotate to a new partner, and another three minutes. This lasted until the end of class. Sensei walked around and was very active in calling out mistakes in our techniques and even showed me a trick he used to fake out an opponent. He took position opposite me and told me to stand in basic free sparring stance. Then, we started lightly to free spar. Suddenly, he came at me with a right mae geri to my stomach. I instinctively dropped my lead hand to block it. But then his right hand shot out and caught me perfectly, splitting my bottom lip. My block to his kick found only air. He had not snapped it out, only raised his knee as if to throw it. I had been completely fooled. It was so simple and effective. It cost me a bloody lip but was worth it. I would use it often in the future.

The class ended. We had sparred for half of it and I was spent and regretting that I had to wake up so early the next morning to go to the Hoitsugan dojo. Taking a quick shower, I dressed and headed out across the floor. Arriving at the front of the dojo, I saw the vending machines. Instead of leaving right away, I dropped a hundred-yen coin into the slot of the machine and punched the button for a Pocari Sweat, took it over to the seating area, sat down and popped it open. It was relaxing to sit there, not a care in the world, watching as the rest of the small class left, saying "Osu" to each of them. I sat there for fifteen minutes, then grabbed my bag and walked out and down the stairs, dropping my empty can into the bin next to the vending machine.

Arriving in Ikebukuro, I stopped at the first yakitori restaurant I could find, ordered some chicken, a tomato salad and a beer. I wanted to get to bed early and sleep. Tomorrow would be an interesting day and yet another new experience.

The next morning, I was up at five. Antonio had told me not to be late so I wanted to have plenty of time. I walked down the stairs and went through the door to the dojo. No one was there but it was still early. I bowed toward the picture of Funakoshi. Then I walked over to the locker room and changed into my new gi. It fit well. "This is going to be a good class." I smiled.

I was on the floor and stretching when Antonio and three others arrived. They had stumbled out of the dorm, hair matted in areas and still sleepy-eyed. Another group walked in from outside the dojo, also quiet and obviously not quite awake yet. So far, all were Gaijin. There was little talking, just a few introductions and greetings.

Kawawada Sensei walked in. Everyone greeted him with a strong "Osu". He took off his jacket, hung it on the wall, and started stretching. He seemed to not notice me. I was to learn that he most certainly did, but it was just his personality to not show it, waiting to see me train and, more importantly, see if I came back.

It was just a few minutes later that he called the class to order. We all lined up, with Sensei in front of course, facing Shomen. A senior student, named Richard, called out the commands to start the class. We all bowed towards the front. Sensei turned to face us, then we bowed towards him. My first class at the Hoitsugan dojo was about to begin.

There were twelve students. We were told to line up and take kamae. From free sparring stance, left leg forward, Sensei walked past all of us, adjusting hands, feet and bodies. He told us to switch to right leg forward, and he did the same.

Back in left leg forward stance, he had us slowly move into a left jab position, turning into a deep hanmi, stretching out the left jab and pulling the right hand as far back as we could. Sensei came by and told me to pull my front foot back. This jab drill was to be in place, just pushing forward with the front knee a little, not moving the front foot.

We all did the jab technique slowly, at Sensei's count, while he adjusted us again. It was a simple jab and return to free sparring kamae. But Sensei changed almost every aspect of how I was performing it. I was leaning forward, he said. My left jabbing hand was not direct enough to the target. I was turning my left fist over too soon. Even my eyes were focused in the wrong in the direction.

All were positive improvements though. This simple jab technique was to become a favorite of mine and would also become a great feign for various combinations that would help me in the future. He was adjusting others also and I could hear numerous shouts of "Osu" throughout this part of the training.

Sensei told us to switch legs and warned us to remember what we had just learned. This time he was less gentle as he walked among us, batting an arm in place, kicking a back leg that was locked and straight. Next, he let us step out with our front foot with the jab, which was more natural to me. Still, he wanted the front knee deeper and the rear leg to be flexed, not straight. He would slam his arm into anyone who did not have a good withdraw hand, giving them a subtle reminder. Altogether we spent half the one-hour class on this basic technique. I was to learn that Kawawada Sensei would often teach with this kind of detail.

Then we were told to make partners. I was slow to find a partner but one found me. He was a tall, lanky, blond-haired Brit. He lived at the Hoitsugan. We were to practice the jab techniques we had just drilled. I stood across from the Brit. By Sensei's count we took turns at our partner, first at close range with no foot movement. Then we made more distance and stepped out a little with the front foot.

My partner's arms were as long as his legs and he kept nailing me in the face with every jab. I was trying to control mine. But with every painful shot, I started to do the same with him. Sensei shouted at both of us to control our punches. Both of us turned his direction, bowed, and shouted a loud "Osu." We rotated to get a new partner. Sensei added a reverse punch to the drill. He wanted us to step out with the jab and then push off with our rear leg to drive forward with the reverse punch, allowing the rear foot to move forward naturally. This we did a number of times with our new partner.

Sensei yelled at us to make more distance with the driving reverse punch. He told us to push off with the rear leg by kicking at the ground, then to twist the hips forward out of *hanmi* (hips back), to front facing stance. Again, he scolded us for not making a strong withdraw hand to improve the reverse punch. We did this basic drill for the rest of the class. The only variation was when Sensei showed us how we could go in low with the reverse punch and penetrate the opponent's defense by bending the rear leg, lifting the heel off the floor just after pushing off with it, something that would not be allowed by another Sensei in the very near future.

The skin on both my left and right toe was hanging off when we were told to line up at the end of class. As usual, it started to hurt just as soon as the class was over. I limped into the locker room and pulled off my gi. Everyone just wrapped their towel around themselves and stood around talking while waiting for their turn outside the showers. I did the same. This practice was suddenly outlawed when the first female students started coming regularly. When my turn came the hot water was gone, replaced by a cold, powerful stream that nonetheless felt great, except for my toes that were raw and very aware of the cold water on the cold concrete. I made the trip back to the locker room, finished toweling off and reached into my first aid kit for the anti-bacterial foam to spray on each toe and wrapped bandages around them.

The Hoitsugan folks had invited me to go with them for breakfast. We had an hour and a half until the Honbu class. The Brit with the long arms that I had such a fierce battle with was adamant that I go with them. "Come on. We go every day. It's a custom." He said this directly to me and meant it sincerely. I gladly accepted. We went to a coffee shop just a few blocks from the Hoitsugan. It was apparent that they frequented the shop often as the waiter greeted them with a cherry "*Irashai*!" We all ordered about the same thing, my favorite, ham egg set. Thus, started my every day routine for the rest of the month.

Although the rest of the Hoitsugan guys tended to skip the evening classes, I vowed to keep on going since it was only for one month. They would spend the afternoon and evening hours teaching English to pay for the luxury of staying in Japan. We talked about a variety of topics, generally not related to karate. Roger asked me where I was staying. I told him Kimi Ryokan.

"That's in Ikebukuro, right?"

"Yes. About thirty minutes by Yamanote line."

Half of the group had stayed there at least once. They all agreed it was a nice place and a good experience.

"But this is even better." Roger said. "Have you seen the living area at the Hoits?"

I told him I had seen it.

"You should think about it. You eat, sleep and dream karate. And there's no train ride required."

"Sounds great." I said. "But how is it arranged?"

"You just have to be approved by Kawawada Sensei. It helps if one of us recommends you."

"I'll definitely think about it."

Before I knew it, the break was over and it was dojo time again. We all paid our bills, four-hundred-fifty yen each, everything seemed to be four-hundred and fifty yen, and filed out the door and onto the street. Once all of us were out of the shop, a couple of the guys decided they would not go to the next class for some reason. The rest of us trudged down the street towards the Honbu dojo. "This is where it gets difficult." Roger said. "After you're all cooled off and having relaxed for an hour. It's tough to get going again."

But get going we did. We all marched up the stairs to the dojo, changed into wet gis and warmed up as well as we could. The next class would start in fifteen minutes. And it was once again Tanaka Sensei.

"That's why the other two are skipping." Roger said. "Bad experience, I guess."

Although I feared the worst, the class was excellent with Sensei having us go through all the Heian and many of the advanced katas, slowly the first time and normal speed the second time. Sensei walked around and corrected our technique. The last fifteen-minutes we did one-minute free sparring drills. Sensei shouted "*Hajime*" and we sparred one partner for one minute. Then we rotated to new partners and did another one-minute session.

Sensei shouted "relax" and I tried my best to comply. I was almost out of gas when the class was over. It was an exhausting training but not at all something to be afraid of. I was glad I came.

While in the locker room I asked the rest of the guys if there was a laundromat near the dojo. Roger laughed and said to just stick with them because that's where they were going. We all walked down the street to an old building. It took just ten-minutes. The coin laundry was attached to the side of a sento. The bath portion did not seem to be open. We washed our gis in the small coin operated washing machines and drank canned coffee from a vending machine on the street in front of the sento. It was only my second canned coffee. It tasted a little sweet and though I never put sugar in my coffee in the States, it was delicious.

We talked, the four of us, for an hour while the gis thrashed around in the quiet, slow moving machines. Roger, Antonio and Peter, a Belgian who was staying at the Hoitsugan for two weeks, collected their gis as soon as the spin cycle finished. They would hang them outside the dorm at the Hoitsugan to dry. I needed to dry mine so said goodbye to them and pulled out my book. I stuck my wet gi into the dryer, dropped in a couple of one hundred-yen coins, and sat back into an uncomfortably small, plastic chair. It took an extra two-hundred yen to thoroughly dry the gi and by that time I had taken a good nap, waking up several times with my head nearly touching my lap. It was almost three o'clock when my gi came out of the dryer. I folded it, stuck it into my backpack, bought one more Pocari Sweat from the machine and headed for the Honbu dojo for the evening class.

Walking down the side roads between the Hoitsugan and the Honbu dojos, I felt the cool breeze that still lingered in Tokyo's spring. The sun was warm also and the combination made me feel good and happy and free. I still had another three weeks to go.

The nearer I got to the Honbu and my next class, the more I started to talk to myself. The weekend was to be for site seeing. I had to stop by and talk to Yumiko and make arrangements for traveling to Kamakura. The girls had been bugging me about going out with them again. I walked past the Honbu and turned towards Ebisu station to see Yumiko in Ikebukuro. In fact, despite my vow, this would be my new training pattern for the rest of the month, take the first class at the Hoitsugan, have a small breakfast, then attend the ten-thirty class at the Honbu. The rest of the day would be free. I would still go to an evening class once in a while, but the main schedule had been set.

Chapter Ten

With a quick smile Yumiko motioned me to a table. Ten minutes later she came over and brought with her a tall mug of draft beer which she sat in front of me.

"Hi Michael." Another nice smile.

"Hi Yumiko." You look busy tonight."

"Yes. Every Friday night it is busy like this. Japanese salary men finally relax. They start here and then go to an Izakaya or a night club later. Usually they will get very drunk and catch the last train home.

"Sounds like fun to me."

"Maybe. But sometimes it is very hard. Employees must go out with their boss. Even though they might want to go home instead. They have to waste many hours and drink too much."

"I see what you mean. It would be fun if you did all that because you wanted to, not because you had to."

"Ah. You understand very well."

New customers arrived and she had to seat them, take their orders and bring their drinks. She was gone another fifteen minutes and then returned to my table.

"Do you want ramen?"

"Yes. Can you bring me the same thing I had last time?"

"*Kashikomarimashita.*" She smiled and left.

I sat and sipped my beer. Customers came and went quickly. I could see them and certainly hear them slurping their noodles in huge, noisy bursts. I was to learn the correct technique finally and continue to slurp, Japanese style, to this day, even if there are no Japanese around. It just feels good.

Yumiko was back with my ramen set. It looked and smelled delicious. She sat it on the table and then left again. "I will be back and we can talk more." I knew she was working hard and I was content to sit and enjoy my ramen and beer.

"I can sit for five minutes." She was again at my table and slid into a chair next to me.

"OK. Well, I wondered if you still wanted to go to Kamakura this weekend."

"Oh yes, of course. I told my parents that I would visit them. Will you go with me to their house?"

"Um, are you sure it's OK?"

"Sure, it is." She said this in an almost slang, American manner, stretching out the "sure".

"OK then. Can we meet tomorrow morning?"

"Sure, how about seven AM? We can meet here, outside the shop." She pointed to the sidewalk beyond the door.

"Great. I'll be here at seven. I don't know exactly how to get there though."

"It is no problem. I know the way very well."

OK. I'll leave it to you then."

"Oh. I'm very sorry but I have to go back to work." Customers were pouring into the shop now.

"Great. Go ahead. I will see you at seven AM." I smiled at her and she returned it with a huge grin as she hurried off to greet the new customers. I sat a while longer, finishing my noodles and sipping my beer. I was content and looking forward to the weekend. After another twenty minutes, I got up from the table and walked to the front of the restaurant to pay my bill. An additional person was added and was tending the cash register, presumably because the next few hours would be too busy for Yumiko to handle by herself. I paid and looked around for Yumiko to say goodbye. She was at the back table but looked up and waved.

Walking down the side streets towards Kimi, I saw many interesting looking shops tucked away in the little nooks and crannies just off the street, most of which I had no idea what their purpose was. It all seemed so foreign, exotic, and tempting, so full of secrets and possibilities.

Back on the main street I noticed how much more crowded it was. It was Friday and similar to the USA, the Japanese were ready to let loose. But while through the week the mix was about equal between mothers with their children shopping, teenagers going to or returning from *Juku* (after school tutoring), and business men, the street was now owned by loud and already drunk men of all ages. The moms and kids were nowhere to be seen. I continued towards Kimi, responding to "harro" from almost every large group. My goal was to catch the girls before they left the hotel for the evening. As I had hoped, I met them at Kimi just as they were getting ready to go out. As soon as they saw me walking down the hallway to my room, they invited me out with them. We were now just inside the Izakaya, the equivalent of a British pub in atmosphere. In the USA, there is no equivalent.

The Izakaya was already crowded when we arrived. I looked around and saw no empty spots. Customers were sitting at low tables on the floor. No one was wearing shoes, which were placed in small, mailbox size, wooden cubbyholes as we entered.

I was ready to tell the girls that we should try to find somewhere else. But then the young guy at the entrance shouted something, a waitress appeared and ushered us to a wooden, rectangular table near the back. She talked to the three people sitting there. They didn't seem to mind at all as they slid around to one side to make room for us. She motioned for us to sit on the other side, wrapped around the end. It was perfect for conversation. Before we had even sat down, she had our drink orders.

"So. What's the deal with your new girlfriend?" I had mentioned her as we walked to the Izakaya. Victoria was almost laughing.

"Her name is Yumiko. Not a girlfriend. I just met her this week."

"And you met her in a bar?" Joanne added her voice to the harassment.

"No. It was a ramen shop."

"Do you know her, anything about her?" said Victoria.

"I know she studied English in Seattle last year."

"How did you get her to go with you?" Joanne again.

"We just started talking and the subject came up. Her parents live in Kamakura." I left off the part about visiting her parents.

"Are you staying overnight?" Victoria had a cunning look on her face.

"I think it's a day trip. According to my guidebook it's only two hours from here."

"That's right. We went there a few months ago. It's not that far." Joanne said.

"I don't think it's anything at all. I asked her and she said yes. She said she would show me the city."

"Yes. I'm sure that's all she wants to show you." Joanne was smiling at Victoria.

"I think so. Do you think differently?"

Victoria laughed out loud. "Of course, we think differently. You meet the girl for the first time, ask her to go to Kamakura with you, maybe overnight, and she says yes. Most definitely she has the hots for you.

"Absolutely." Joanne added.

"I'm not so sure."

"But that's OK. Enjoy yourself with this new girlfriend. By the way, how old is she?" Victoria looked out over her glasses which forced her to tilt her head downward. She looked every bit like the stern school teacher.

"I don't know, maybe kind of young."

They both groaned and looked up at the waitress who was back with our beers and waiting for our food order. We opened the menus. Everything looked delicious and I could have eaten half of what was on the menu. But we all made our selections and the waitress hurried back to the kitchen.

"So, when are you leaving?" It was the stern teacher again.

"I'm meeting her at seven in the morning at the ramen shop.

"And when are you getting back?"

"We didn't discuss that. I'm guessing late Saturday night."

"Or Sunday night." Joanne suggested.

"If that's what happens." I said.

"OK. Well, enjoy the weekend." Victoria again looked over her glasses.

We talked about the week's events, mostly mine, telling them about my discovery of the Hoitsugan dojo and that there was a possibility of living there.

"You're going to leave Kimi?" Joanne asked.

"Not sure. It's tempting. The dojo and the dorm are in the same building. It has showers and toilets. The Honbu dojo is right around the corner. There's a lot of pluses."

"Yeah, but you would miss us." Joanne said.

"True enough." I replied.

Both of them had been hired for one month to teach English conversation at a local trading company. They had to teach from eight in the morning until five in the afternoon. The company provided free lunch and paid them ten thousand yen an hour. A month's work would earn them a million and a half yen, the equivalent of almost six thousand US dollars at that time. They were both planning a trip to Paris. The one-month job would pay for all of it. Such was the life during the bubble era in Japan.

At that time in Japan, it was easy to find good paying teaching jobs. It was well known that to travel all over the world, one could spend a month or two teaching in Japan and then use the money to pay for airplane fare, hotels, food and other expenses for up to six months. Many foreigners were doing it. This would last into the early nineties.

We sat and drank a few more beers and ate lots of Izakaya food, still my favorite in Japan. It was getting late, almost ten PM, and I wanted to get up at five to get ready for my trip, so convinced them to leave with me. We paid our bill and walked out onto the street. There were far fewer people on the street but they were much drunker. After numerous interruptions by groups of men wanting to speak English but mostly wanting to hang around with two good looking foreign women, we arrived at Kimi. I said good night to the girls and headed off to my room. Five AM would come soon.

Chapter Eleven

The alarm rang and I jumped up from the futon, wrapped a towel around me, walked down the hall to the bathroom for a quick shower and shave, and walked back to my room. Turning the corner, I almost ran into Joanne and Victoria.

"Looking good!" Victoria was still in her pajamas. I was wearing just the towel.

"Sorry. Didn't think anybody would be awake this early."

"It's OK. We wanted to see your girlfriend." Joanne said.

"No no, don't do that. I don't think she would like it."

"Don't worry. She won't see us. Victoria pinched me in the stomach and then poked me in the chest, clearly teasing me. I never found out if they followed me to the ramen shop. Victoria said they did but Joanne said they didn't.

I dressed and filled my backpack with maps, camera gear, cash, traveler's checks, and anything else that might be needed, including my tooth brush. Then I was off. As I got closer to the ramen shop where Yumiko worked, I could see her sitting on a bench, ten feet away from the front door, her own backpack on the bench beside her.

"Good morning Michael!" She was waving and looked happy to see me.

"Good morning Yumiko."

"It's a beautiful day, isn't it?"

I hadn't noticed but she was right. The air was cool and clear and there was almost no breeze, a great day to travel.

We made our way to the Yokosuka line from Ikebukuro. This early in the morning on Saturday, I was surprised to see so many small groups of middle to older Japanese, both men and women, with their backpacks and hiking equipment. It looked like they all had top of the line boots, hiking pants, walking sticks and hats.

"Every weekend they go hiking. Most of them are still working. They have stressful jobs but hike so they can relax."

"Where do they hike?"

"If they go this way, probably at Okutama or Mitakeyama or some other close mountains.

"I'd like to go sometime, but I don't have hiking equipment, especially boots."

"You really do not need professional equipment. They go every week so they buy all the good stuff. Just a backpack and some tennis shoes are good enough, unless you go to the high mountains. Maybe we will go sometime."

"Maybe next week?" I suggested.

"Maybe." She replied.

We were at Kita-Kamakura station. I noticed quite a few of the hiking groups got off the train with us.

"Are they going hiking here?"

"Mostly they will walk from here to Kamakura. Then there are some local trails they can hike."

We got off the train and walked along the platform to where the railroad crossing bars were. Then she guided me down a pedestrian walk until we reached the front entrance of a huge temple grounds. "This is Enkakuji." She announced.

We walked up the steps and passed through the front gate, paid the hundred-fifty-yen fee and walked into the beautiful temple area. This was my first cultural trip since arriving in Japan. What I saw before me was stunning. Many large, old temple buildings were scattered over a gravel carpet that flowed upward and rolled itself out to reveal distinct sections that seemed to have their own stories.

We walked onward and I glanced to my left and saw a small building that had a kind of wooden, open porch in back. Assembled on the porch were a group of men, wearing loose fitting, black hakama. They were holding on to wooden bows. I stopped to watch.

"This is Kyudo. Shall we enter?"

"Is it OK?"

"Yes. We cannot talk though. It is something like zen."

Walking through the open gate, we sat down on a gravel patch between two tree-planted areas. It looked like the group was practicing and the Sensei was softly speaking to them. The Sensei would say something and the students would take aim at straw targets positioned ninety feet back and at a right angle from the entrance. They took turns slowly raising their bows, first almost above their head, stretching out their left arm straight, then lowering the bow, pulling back the string with their right arm slowly and purposefully. When everything was right, they let the arrow go. I watched as most students hit the target, some in the center, some at the edge. After releasing the arrow, the students did not simply let the bow drop. They slowly lowered it back to the starting position, much like our *yoi* position at the end of a kata. The entire movement was performed in a thoughtful, controlled manner. It did indeed look like zen to me.

We watched for a few minutes more. Then we pushed ourselves up from the gravel, wiped the stones off our jeans, and walked back out of the training area, continuing up the sloped grounds. Not more than a hundred feet from the Kyudo training area Yumiko stopped me.

"Here is your Sensei's memorial site." I had asked her on the train to watch out for Funakoshi's memorial site. Antonio told me just a few days before that it was here.

Kamakura – Funakoshi Sensei Memorial

We walked up to the markers. There were two of them, one had the famous quote from Funakoshi "*karate ni sente nashi.* (There is no first attack in karate.)" Yumiko pointed it out to me. I had read extensively about Funakoshi and knew the quote well. She went over the characters one by one, pronouncing each for me to repeat. I stood with my feet together and bowed.

"*Sugoi!* (great!). You look just like Japanese."

"Can I touch it? I want to wipe away some of this dirt."

"No problem. I will help."

We cleaned off the two marble stones and I told her a little of the history of Funakoshi Sensei, how he was born in Okinawa, became a student of both Azato and Matsumura, gave a demo to Hirohito, before he was Emperor and then was invited a few years later to demonstrate karate at Master Kano's judo dojo in Tokyo. Then I explained how Nakayama Sensei trained under Funakoshi and that I am now training under Nakayama at the Hoitsugan dojo.

"So-you know Nakayama Sensei?"

"Not yet. Probably I will meet him next week."

"*Omoshiroi*... interesting." She replied. We walked further. Yumiko pointed out a Zendo. It was an old temple style building that had an open front. When we walked through, I could see that there were sliding doors for rainy, snowy or windy days. There were two people sitting seiza on the tatami mat floor.

"Do you sit?" She asked.

"Yes." We took off our shoes and placed them in shelves lined up at the entrance. She led me to the front. I copied her as she bowed first, sat down on the tatami in seiza position, put her hands, palms up, on her thighs, and straightened her spine. She shifted the back of her head upwards, then tilted her chin slightly downwards.

"It is important to sit erect, with your back straight. My father always says "back straight, chin down". I followed her instructions. "Now move slowly to the right and then to the left, gradually stop moving." I did as she said.

"Now close your eyes almost tight and try to lose thinking."

We sat for a while. I don't know for how long because time stopped for me. It was quiet and there was a slight breeze and my body was alert and she was sitting next to me and everything was so perfect. I could have stayed there forever but we eventually stood up, bowed to the front, and walked out to the temple grounds.

Looking out across to the other side, I saw another old building. It was surrounded by a rambling garden. We walked over and crossed the small bridge leading to the entrance then walked among varying clusters of flowers, trees, rocks and many barren areas that consisted only of white pea gravel accented by irregular shaped stones. There were bamboo groupings that towered above the other garden elements and even competed with the two-story building behind the garden for sunshine.

We walked over another small, red, wooden bridge then turned right and followed a footpath along a tiny creek that meandered through the entire garden, seeing from the inside what we had already viewed from the perimeter. Each change of flora imposed on me a slightly different feeling. I felt relaxed, fresh and full of energy.

Passing the clean, simple gravel and larger stone areas, I could feel the clarity that started first in the Zendo where we had just sat a half-hour before. Coming to the bamboo, very green stocks about four inches in diameter, with the sun twinkling through their leaves, I could imagine the swordsmen testing their skills (and their blade) against the tough, outer bark of the mature bamboo. We walked, not talking much. It was time for reflection, not idle chatting.

After another thirty minutes we found ourselves out of the garden, across another bridge and into the temple grounds once more. The garden was at the top and, looking down, we could see all the other temple buildings, gardens, and many more people. We had arrived early when there were few visitors. Now we could see a mass of people streaming upwards from the entrance into the grounds, trying to decide where to go first.

"The people will keep coming now. It will become more and more crowded. It is easy to come here from Tokyo."

"It's quite a change from Tokyo." I felt calm now and did not look forward to walking downwards into the crowd.

But we did. We walked down the hill, on the left side, avoiding most of the people who were still starting up the hill. We walked towards the temple entrance, out the gate and down the steps to the sidewalk, then down a short street, crossing over the railroad. We were heading to Kamakura, just a short distance, Yumiko told me, from where we now stood. A short walk perhaps, but down a street already filled with cars and small trucks, spewing exhaust gas and noise, making for a very dangerous and shockingly different environment then we had just experienced. We arrived at Kamakura from the back side, through the neighborhoods.

Suddenly the road was a little wider and the shops and buildings gave way to well-kept homes. The sidewalks also became wider, making me feel a little more relaxed, not having to worry as much about the narrow sidewalks and the cars that were passing so closely. We kept walking and came to an intersection that widened even more. Yumiko took my hand.

"Close your eyes." I closed them.

She walked me slowly a little further down the sidewalk, turned me to the left and then straight for another few feet.

"Don't open." She said. I could feel gravel now.

She put both her hands on my shoulders, turned me another direction and then stopped me.

"OK. Open your eyes."

Before me was the *Dai Butsu* (Big Buddha), looking out over the city and bay. To say it dominated the temple grounds would be a huge understatement. The temple *was* the Dai Butsu and the Dai Butsu *was* the temple. I stared at the face. His eyes were mostly closed, his head fairly level. His robe was over the shoulders, drooping at the neck downwards to the navel. His hands were placed together, palms up, elbows on his thighs. There was a small jewel in the middle of his forehead. He was sitting on a raised concrete stage. I could see the hills that separated the temple from the neighborhoods behind him, a green and contrasting background to the bluish gray color of the Buddha.

Kamakura Dai Butsu (Big Buddha)

"I don't know what to say." That was my intelligent reply.

"I always feel the same. I have been here many times but I always feel his spiritual power."

We walked closer. Like Engakuji, the temple grounds contained other, smaller temple buildings and gardens, but the grounds were far sparser. The gravel stretched on forever in front of us. We walked up several short steps closer to the Buddha.

"This is so much better than the pictures I have seen."

"You like it?"

It's amazing. I can't believe how powerful, how imposing he is."

"Imposing?"

"Yes. Ah…imposing means overpowering, taking over all our feelings and senses."

"Oh. Yes, I agree."

We walked around the Dai Butsu. I saw the back where one could enter and climb up to the head level. I did not want to do that. What I wanted to do was sit in Zazen and meditate in front of him. There was no place nearby that would allow for that, other than in the middle of the gravel where all the other people stood and walked. Yumiko told me that would not be a good idea. She did not say why. We walked back down towards the entrance.

"Are you hungry?" Yumiko asked.

"Very hungry"

"Let's go to a soba shop. It is ten minutes from here."

We walked out the gate and onto the street. There were small shops everywhere selling souvenirs, mostly related to Dai Butsu but also including other, typical stuff such as salt & pepper shakers, spoons, plaques, T-shirts and lots of lacquer ware boxes, samurai swords, maps, jewelry and bins of dried goods such as bonita flakes, small fish and even dried soba and ramen. We kept on walking, stopping now and then when we saw something interesting. The ten-minute walk took thirty-minutes, but we finally arrived at the soba shop. There was already a short line though it was only 11 AM, so we waited. The shop had not yet opened so we would be able to get a seat quickly. From the front of the shop we could see Sagami Bay with its mixture of small fishing boats and some larger sail boats.

“We can go to the beach after lunch, if you want.” She said.

“That would be great.”

As we stood in line, I was surprised to see so many foreigners, that is, Westerners, passing by. Many of them smiled and said hello. But some turned their heads the other way as they approached and started speaking Japanese loudly. I would see this again and again, especially a few years later. Foreigners living in Japan sometimes liked to put down tourists, as if they were a stray animal that wondered into their yard, insinuating that there was not enough room for ‘newbies’, and tried to show their Japanese-ness, thereby excluding the tourist. I remember that later I found it easier to assimilate to the Japanese than to the expats.

The door opened, we walked in, found a table and sat down. The menu was on the wall, but it was all in Japanese so it was hopeless for me.

“Can you read the Japanese?”

“I’m afraid not. Would you mind ordering for me? Whatever you like will be good for me. The waiter appeared and Yumiko ordered, glancing over to me while he waited.

“Do you want beer?”

“Do you?” I answered.

“Sure. It is good with soba.” She relayed our beer order to the waiter who then walked straight to the back wall, opened a large, glass cooler, and withdrew two bottles of beer. He was back at our table in seconds, opening the bottles as he walked across the floor. They were huge bottles, what the Japanese call O-Bin, short for *ookii bin* (large bottle). O-Bin would become a standard phrase for me when I entered a restaurant over the next few years. He sat the beers and two glasses on the table, excused himself and went to the kitchen to turn in our order. The shop was now packed and I could see the line outside slowly growing and now stretching further down the sidewalk.

“I come to this shop when I am here visiting my parents. The soba is delicious. The owner is a friend of my father’s.”

“Oh. What does your father do?”

“He works in Tokyo, in Nihonbashi, at a trading company. What does your father do?”

"He is a judge in district court in Michigan."

"Does he judge for murders?"

"No. He handles traffic violations, minor offenses, marriages and things like that."

"Marriages? Is he a minister?"

"No. In the US, a judge can also perform marriages, not just ministers."

"Does he perform a lot of marriages?"

"Not really, just occasionally. But years ago, during the Vietnam war, he did many of them in one year. The US government instituted a draft to get enough soldiers. As time to report for duty came closer, more couples decided to marry because it was a way to avoid being drafted. In the last couple of weeks, I remember cars lined up outside our house, waiting to get married in time to beat the draft. I also remember how much it interrupted our television watching with people standing in our living room all evening long."

"I don't remember Vietnam much. My father says there were many Americans in Japan at that time."

"Yes. Japan was a main staging area and also an R&R port."

"R&R?" She laughed at her own pronunciation. "It is hard to say for Japanese. But what is it?"

"Rest and relaxation - a break from serving in the war."

The waiter was back with our soba. But instead of a hot, steaming bowl of noodles, he sat down a large dish with a bamboo insert, covered with a mountain of green noodles. Then he sat down a brownish sauce, along with an even smaller dish of pickled vegetables.

"This is called '*zaru soba*'. It is served cold. We have to dip like this." She picked up a rather large portion of noodles, dipped them into the sauce with a kind of swirling motion, and stuck them into her mouth, rather seductively, at least to me at the time. I copied her, minus the seductive part. They were cool. The flavor, with the *nori* (dry seaweed) and soy sauce and wasabi, exploded inside my mouth. Yumiko could see that I liked it.

"What do you think?"

"It's one of the best things I've ever eaten."

It was not an exaggeration. Once more, after just a week in Japan, I experienced another unique food. It was to happen often over the next few weeks, but I still remember that first taste of cold soba.

We ate and talked, drank our beer and talked and even touched hands a few times across the table. It was only one beer but we both were feeling the effects.

"We should go. Others are waiting." It was another typical Japanese idea, always thinking about the welfare of others, their comfort, and social courtesies in general. I paid our bill and we walked out into bright sunshine.

"Whoa" throwing my hand up to cover my eyes.

"Yes. It is *mabushi*, yes?"

"Mabushi?"

"Bright.

She pointed in the direction of the bay and we started walking, quickly leaving the city streets for the neighborhoods. We walked through the side streets, the houses well-kept with manicured gardens and concrete walls surrounding each.

"This is a beautiful area." I said.

"Do you think so?"

"Everything is so clean, so simple."

"Yes." She paused. "And this is my house."

"Really?" It was a little larger than the others. There were three old men standing on ladders, trimming trees. "Are we going to visit?"

"We can. But my parents are not at home today."

"Oh, that's too bad." But actually, I was glad to not have to meet them. I was having a good time just being with her.

"We can visit another day, if you want." She replied.

We continued down a hilly path that eventually led to the beach. It was still early in the year. There were shells and seaweed everywhere along with jagged twigs and larger logs half floating at the water's edge, not a pretty site. The sand was dark, the color of volcanic ash. There were a few people mingling in small groups. One group was all teenagers, a mix of boys and girls. The boys wore wet suits with the tops pulled down to their waists, revealing either a dark tank top or a bare chest. The girls all wore bikinis, despite the early season, and were laughing and flirting, much like any beach scene in the States.

Another group down the beach a little was clustered around a small fire. They had tables and chairs set up and were cooking something on a stick.

Seeing me looking their way, she explained. "They are barbecuing shrimp and sausages and squid.

"Looks great. I bet it is delicious."

Further down the beach, partially hidden by an old concrete dock, was a small group of all boys. They were listening to music and joking around with each other, occasionally tossing a Frisbee.

"In another few weeks, they will clean the beach for the summer season. Then they will build huts and people will sell food and drinks and jewelry and other things. It will become very noisy and crowded.

"Do you join them?"

"I used to. I used to wear a bikini like those girls." She pointed to the closest group of girls. "Now I only come here a couple of times in the summer because I live in Tokyo."

"But it's not so far. We got here in less than two hours."

"Yes. But I have friends in Tokyo. I do things with them."

We walked further down the beach. I wanted to hold her hand and get closer, but I didn't know the custom and I was afraid of making a typical American mistake of assuming it would be the right thing to do. She solved the problem by taking my hand and leading me to some rocks that stood near a path that led upwards into another neighborhood. She sat on one and I sat on another, facing her. She pushed her left knee between my bent legs and used her right knee to squeeze my left. She leaned forward slowly and kissed me stiffly. It was not very well done but I didn't argue or complain. We sat for ten minutes, embracing and watching the ocean.

I felt strange. There didn't seem to be enough real passion. It was as though she initiated the contact because she thought she had to, that it was expected by me. It was pleasant, but I eventually suggested that we get back to town. She was, I think, disappointed and a little perturbed. We climbed off the rocks and walked over to the path.

She led the way up but did not hold my hand. We walked through the neighborhood and reached the main street.

"You do not like me?" She suddenly asked.

"No. I really like you."

"OK OK." She grabbed hold of my hand and started swinging it, happy again, acting a lot like one of the teenage girls we saw on the beach.

We walked down the street for fifteen minutes and arrived at the train station. It was four o'clock. Although I had enjoyed the day, I was also eager to get back to Tokyo. I had skipped Saturday training to make this trip and I felt strangely guilty.

"Shall we go?" Yumiko asked.

"I think so. We can have dinner when we get back."

We bought tickets, walked up to the platform and waited for the train which was there in less than five minutes. It was an express train and we were back in Ikebukuro in less than an hour and a half. Though we talked a lot as the train rumbled through the towns, we were both tired and struggled to stay awake. As we left Ikebukuro station, we started looking for a restaurant. Yumiko took the lead and I followed her to a side street just outside the station but on the opposite side from where the ramen shop was located.

"I go here with friends sometimes. They have great Yakitori."

We entered the Yakitori restaurant and Yumiko said hello to a couple of the waitresses. We sat down at a small table near the front. One of the waitresses, Yumiko's friend, was soon at the table. Yumiko introduced us. We gave her our order and sat back to relax. I was glad to be back and looked forward to a cold tall Sappori beer. It was Saturday night. The restaurant was full but the crowd was a little younger and consisted less of businessmen. In fact, there were many couples.

Yumiko's friend came back with our beers. I had let her order for me again so did not know what would be coming. On the way to the table, just inside the door, was a large display case showing off their menu items. They had great looking fish, pork and beef. The scallops looked especially delicious. But this restaurant was famous for its skewed chicken. That's what Yumiko ordered for us.

"Keiko visited me when I was in America. She stayed two weeks and we drove to Carmel and stayed at a small hotel. The hotel was close to the ocean and we could hear the waves all night. It was wonderful."

"I went to Carmel a couple of years ago. The view is beautiful. I remember having breakfast at a restaurant called "*The Broken Egg*." It was known for its omelets."

"Ah. We had breakfast there too!" She replied.

"Really? It is close to the ocean and you can watch the boats going by as you eat."

"Yes. We did that too." She replied.

"I had a huge omelet, vegetarian I think, and lots of homemade fried potatoes. But I remember it because of the view. Some of the windows were open and I could feel the breeze off the ocean."

"Yes-hai hai, I remember that too!" She was bouncing off her chair with excitement.

Keiko brought our yakitori, two large plates fitted with skewered things. There were a couple of beautiful looking roasted vegetable sticks, some of the scallops I had seen in the display case, huge mushrooms, and even some tempura. And then there was the chicken. It all looked delicious. It had sear marks from being grilled over the charcoal. Some of it was flavored with salt, some soy sauce, and some with a wonderful sesame topping. Since it was cooked over the fire there was almost no fat, just the natural juices and the seasoning.

I didn't know I was so hungry. Yumiko also ate more than she thought she would. We ordered more beers and sat and talked. Suddenly I noticed it was almost midnight.

"Whoa…it's late!" I said to Yumiko.

"Oh yes. I forgot about time. Want to go?"

We got up from the table and I paid the bill that Keiko brought to us. Yumiko had to say goodbye to Keiki, another waitress and the guy who was standing at the hibachi grilling more chicken. Outside it was fairly quiet. We walked towards the ramen shop where Yumiko worked.

"*Kyoo…arigato ne*! (thanks for today)" She was smiling.

I was at a loss as to what should come next. Fortunately, she took over, grabbed my hand and led me away from the ramen shop. "I live fifteen minutes from here!" She was still smiling.

***

"I know you didn't stay here last night." Victoria had just stepped outside. I was sitting on the steps at Kimi writing in my journal. It was five pm.

"Things went well, I guess?"

"Yes. Things went well."

"Good for you. Are you going out with her tonight?"

"No. Starting tomorrow I have an early karate class every morning."

"I see. Are you up for some dinner then?"

"With you guys?"

"Nah. Just me. Joanne went to Osaka for a few days. She has a friend living there."

"Sure. What would you like to have?"

"Let's go to a small Izakaya in Shinjuku. It's called Tengu. It's a chain but they have great food and it's not so expensive."

"OK. Do you want to leave now?"

"No. Give me a half hour to get ready."

"How about we leave at six-thirty? I'll get my karate stuff packed for tomorrow."

Victoria hopped up the steps and disappeared into Kimi. I sat there for a while and continued writing, then went back to my room, packed up my training stuff, setting it next to the door and made my way to the front steps to meet her.

She was waiting and we walked to the station. The ride to Shinjuku was only four stops. The train was not very crowded which surprised me after being jammed into the cars all week long. We actually sat down. We passed Mejiro, Takadanobaba, Shin Okubo, and then rumbled into Shinjuku. It was much bigger than any of the other stations and had many exits. Victoria knew where she was going though and we found our way out of the station and onto the street at a place where everyone called Studio Alta, a huge building with many shops.

Whereas the train was empty, Studio Alta was packed. It was a spot used by hordes of Japanese to wait for and meet friends. It was also perfect for people watching or girl and boy hunting. We plowed through the crowd and headed down the street to the next corner and then under the tracks for about five hundred feet. Then she took me down a side street that led to another main street. "There it is!" She pointed to a sign which was on the second floor of a ten-story building. We walked another few hundred-feet and then climbed up a metal stairway to the Izakaya.

It was an excellent, lively establishment. The waiters all said hello to Victoria. "Been here before?" I said this with a big grin. Within minutes we were sitting at a *zashiki* with a cold glass of beer. "This will be an early night for me. OK?" I thought this would be fair warning.

"No problem. I could use some extra sleep tonight."

Chapter Twelve

Week Two

I had set my alarm for five-thirty but a crash of thunder shook me out of sleep a half hour earlier. Still in my futon, I listened to the thunder and could see lightening which seemed to slip through the cracks in the old hotel structure. It was a perfect morning to turn over and go back to sleep. "It's only one day." I thought. "And I'm on vacation." I closed my eyes.

The alarm sounded and I slammed at the off button, but lingered there with my eyes closed.

"What are you doing?" I said out loud, jumping out of the futon and starting to the bathroom to get ready to go. Fifteen minutes later I headed out the door with my hundred-yen umbrella from my first day.

The lightening was still active and I battled the high winds and driving rain along with the hordes of businessmen and women as we struggled our way to Ikebukuro station. I learned by watching them how to tip my umbrella just right to pass slower groups while being careful not to spill rain water on them. I found myself looking out for the lightning bolts, as if I could dodge one when it came.

Making it to the station, I collapsed my umbrella and bounded up the steps to the platform. Glancing behind me I saw a sea of people, their umbrellas still open, entering the station. Most of the umbrellas were black, but some bright colors popped out. In fact, watching the bright colored umbrellas was the only way I could tell the mass was moving. Otherwise it looked like just a black blob, going nowhere. I watched them enter just so far and then, at the same point, lower the umbrellas. For some reason I thought about sea lions jumping off the cliffs.

My science teacher back in tenth grade said that when it rained, the humidity in the air between the drops could often approach zero. This was, presumably, because all the moisture had some way become the drops. But the humidity on the platform which was covered overhead but otherwise exposed was close to one hundred percent and there was steam everywhere. The train arrived and I stepped up onto it. Whether it was too early in the morning or too early in the year, the air conditioning was not turned on. I had already started to sweat. Now it was dripping off my face and I could feel it running down my legs.

When the train arrived at Takadanobaba and another huge crowd boarded, the air was finally turned on. I sucked it in and tried to maneuver to be directly beneath the overhead vents, fighting to move an extra inch or so, finally giving up when I saw that an old lady occupied the best spot. It was a miserable trip and when I got off the train at Ebisu I was soaked in sweat. I had thirty minutes to walk to the Hoitsugan dojo, more than enough. Looking ahead I saw Antonio and ran to catch up with him.

"OSU. Good morning. I thought you stayed at the Hoitsugan."

"OSU. You made it." He replied. "I spent the weekend with my girlfriend."

"I will be here every morning from now on." I said.

"That is good. Nakayama Sensei will be here today."

"Really? Excellent. Do I need special permission to train?"

"No. I will introduce you. He will ask a few questions. Then you just train."

We walked together the rest of the way. It was seven-fifteen when we arrived. Antonio went into his dorm room to change. I went to the locker room. Other students arrived. We all stretched and warmed up, but I did not see Nakayama Sensei yet. Antonio introduced me to the others, a couple of them I knew from the Honbu dojo. In all there were fifteen of us in the Hoitsugan dojo that morning. We chatted a little while continuing to warm up.

I happened to be facing the entrance to the dojo area when Nakayama Sensei walked in. He walked slowly and deliberately. Someone shouted attention and we all stopped what we were doing, some struggling to get quickly up from the floor. We stood straight and at the next command bowed to Sensei who bowed back with a smile. Sensei walked further into the dojo. He took off a light, black jacket, hung it on a hook in the corner, walked to the middle of the floor and started doing some light stretches. We had already lined up and stood silent, facing Sensei, who then nodded at the senior student. We bowed to Sensei and sat in seiza until he rose and motioned for us to do the same.

Sensei told the class to spread out. He then took us through a short series of basic punches and strikes, just for a warm-up. The pace was not fast but there was very little time between sets. Basics over, Sensei had us stagger the lines for kata, Kankudai. Sensei started the lesson by telling us to perform the kata to his count. We did what he said and he observed our techniques as we progressed through the moves.

The second and third moves of the kata, after the opening hands to the sky, were the topic of Sensei's first lesson. Sensei stood in front of us in kamae. He raised his hands up and then back down, paused a second, then quickly changed into left kokutsu dachi with the two blocks. Then he just as quickly shifted stance to face to the right in another kokutsu dachi with the same blocks. He pointed out that some of us were blocking too low and told us to look through the open hand and that the block was to protect against mawashi geri or punch to the head, coming from the side. We practiced those two moves a few times. Then Sensei did the move from the beginning one more time, stopping when he reached the third move again. He dropped his blocking hands and addressed us still in the right hand kokutsu dachi.

Sensei said something I could not quite understand. Others did though and started responding, some in English which Antonio translated quickly into Japanese for Sensei. One of the answers must have been correct. Sensei stood up from the stance and started explaining the difference in how he performed the second and third moves of the kata. He explained, partially translated by Antonio, that not long ago the kokutsu dachi was much higher than how we perform it now. The stance became lower in order to both improve the balance of the two moves and to strengthen and train the leg muscles.

Sensei went on to tell us that most stances these days are performed lower than in the past for the same reasons. He showed us zen kutsu dachi, kiba dachi, fudo dachi, neko dachi and ended with kokutsu dachi again. He performed each stance twice, emphasizing the difference in height and how that difference changed the muscle groups that did the work, often raising his gi pants up to his knee to show the muscles. I remember having the brief thought of how lucky I was to have the chief instructor of the JKA, Funakoshi's direct student, standing there teaching me.

Sensei told us to go through all of the stances, one by one, at his command. We were to do both high and low versions, stopping after each to feel the leg muscles in order to understand how they changed according to the different height. It was a great lesson. I could feel the difference easily.

In the middle of the kata, there is a point where the karateka turns from the front, raises the knee and both arms, left supporting the right, and strikes to the chin towards the rear, then lands low to the ground on both hands and turns immediately back to the front in a low kokutsu dachi.

Sensei had us all do the move. Then he walked around and adjusted us as we waited in position, hands still on the floor. He told us to look out at approximately three meters, made sure our hands were facing inwards a little, and that we did not have our backsides up in the air, pushing us gently down when necessary. Then Sensei had us repeat the move a few times. He was not happy with our progress though and soon walked over to the corner of the dojo where the weights were kept, grabbed a bo staff from the rack, and then came back.

"*Hai. Moo ikkai*! (Ok. One more time!)" He shouted.

We complied. Sensei waited until we turned into the move from the front to the rear, then swung the bo directly at Antonio, hitting him cleanly but lightly in the upper body. He walked around and did the same to almost all of us, including me.

"*Minna osoi*. (Every one is slow.)" He said. Then he set the stick onto the floor, got into position and performed the same technique. He was about seventy-one years old at the time, but he turned with the upward strike to the rear and smoothly dropped to the floor, back straight as a board. Then he stood up, grabbed the bo again, handed it to Antonio and told him to stand about three feet away and swing the bo at him. Sensei again did the technique. Antonio swung the bo at him-but Sensei was already on the floor, ramrod straight. We all looked at each other.

Sensei told Antonio to distribute the rest of the bo staffs to the group. We were to practice that move. Sensei walked around and showed us how to perform the move better. The trick, he said, was to use the momentum from turning into the strike to help with the fall to the ground. Then he told us we had to completely relax the muscles for an instant in order to fall quickly with the natural help of gravity. Then, just as quickly, we had to catch ourselves before we hit the floor by using the same muscles we had just relaxed. We all took turns with partners. I was having a hard time and was getting clobbered in the head, stomach and chest every time. Sensei walked up. He had me get into augmented strike position without the turn. Then he told me to perform the move without pushing forward into the full technique. I did this over and over until I could totally and instantly relax my body and then catch myself. After about ten repetitions, Sensei told me to now do the correct move. I did as he said and, although it did not feel perfect, was able to control my muscles more effectively and after a few more times with Sensei watching, I was performing it quite well. "*Soo yu fune*! (That's the way to do it!)" Sensei said. A private lesson by Nakayama Sensei.

The group went through the entire kata two more times with Sensei watching intently, stopping us a few more times to correct a hand position or adjust a technique here and there. He was always patient and relaxed. But he still carried the stick! Never did he walk away and relax while we did mindless repetitions.

Class was over. We bowed out and most of the class went to the locker room to change or headed for the showers. Antonio grabbed me. "I will introduce you." He walked me over to where Sensei was standing and talking to another student. Antonio bowed. I followed his lead.

"Sensei…*kochira wa* Michael Busha. America *kara kimashita. Ikkagetsu kan renshu suru tame ni kimashita.*"

"*Ah so desuka? Nani shu*?"

"What state are you from?" Antonio translated.

"Michigan Sensei.

"*Ah so? Doku ni tomatte irun desuka*?"

"Where are you staying?

In Ikebukuro. Kimi Ryokan."

"Ah. Kimi." He seemed to recognize the name but I couldn't tell for sure.

"*Nandan desuka*?"

I quickly answered without translation. "*Nidan* Sensei."

"*Ja. Nihon ni itteiru aida, tanoshinde kudasai.*" I looked at Antonio.

"Please enjoy your stay in Japan."

"Hai. Arigato gozaimasu." I bowed.

Antonio and I said goodbye to Sensei and walked across the dojo floor to the locker room. We both pulled off our gis and wrapped towels around our waists. I walked to the door.

"Wait." He said, and took a peek through the door by slowly opening it just a crack. "OK. Sensei is gone. We don't walk with just towels when Sensei is still on the floor.

"I will remember that." I felt stupid for not even thinking of it. We showered, dressed and walked out onto the street. It was already warm and very humid from the rain which had now stopped. We walked to the same café I had visited the previous week. As we entered, Watanabe san said hello to Antonio and then to me. "Ah. Good to see you again." He smiled and patted my shoulder as if we were old friends.

There were several others from the morning class already sitting at a table and half way into their morning breakfast sets. Antonio and I joined them and ordered our breakfasts. Introductions were made and we all started to discuss the morning training. Then the topic turned to life in Japan. Three of the students actually lived at the Hoitsugan, including Antonio.

Richard was an American. He was the senior student and therefore taught class when Nakayama Sensei was traveling or when Kawawada Sensei did not teach. I knew him from one class the previous week at the Honbu dojo. He seemed tough enough. He also did not seem to be able to control his punches very well, or he didn't try, which was a respect issue. Kevin was totally different. He was more reserved and very soft spoken. I had seen him warm up that morning with some light kumite. Soft spoken but fast and powerful as well.

Then there was Juan. He was currently living at the Hoitsugan but sometimes moved into a small apartment. Antonio had told me stories about him already. He and Juan had a complicated relationship. Both spoke excellent Japanese and both were from South America, Juan from Columbia and Antonio from Argentina. Perhaps they were competing to represent South America. Or maybe it was that Juan had been in Japan a shorter time but felt he was more senior. He was, after all, a Yondan, Antonio was a Nidan.

Antonio told me a story about how a British karateka had broken his leg in class one day. He was taken to the hospital and the leg was set into a cast. The Brit was out for three months and then finally came back to class. Juan was teaching that day. He had gone through basics to warm up the class. Then he assigned the class to partner training.

The partner training consisted of a drill where one person stepped in with a punch and the other person simply moved to the outside, blocked the punch and swept the front leg as the attacker was still settling into his stance. The Brit had rotated through half the class, always telling his partner that his leg was still healing and to not sweep hard. Most of his partners did not even do the sweep, stopping just short of his leg.

He said the same thing to Juan when finally facing him for the drill. But instead of taking it easy, Juan swept his leg hard and sent him reeling to the floor in severe pain. The leg was re-broken and led to another four months in a cast.

It was said that Nakayama Sensei heard about it and told Kawawada Sensei. Kawawada Sensei apparently had a conversation with Juan that, according to witnesses, had Juan bowing deeply over and over while absorbing the screaming from Kawawada Sensei, who was shouting directly into Juan's face.

Antonio said he ran into the Brit a year later and that he was back training but at a different dojo somewhere in Ueno. Also, said Antonio, he was only training twice a week and not six days a week anymore. I was to meet and get to know the Brit another year later and this story was confirmed.

Jacque was also living at the Hoits, as they called it. He was a tall Belgian and from what I saw of his kata that morning, he was very good, sharp and powerful. Nakayama Sensei had corrected a technique and he had immediately adjusted and bowed deeply with a loud "arigato gozaimasu".

Olaf was Iranian. He was shorter than me but was also fast and powerful. I had seen him sparring at the Honbu on several occasions and, although he found himself on the floor a few times, he also was able to return the favor frequently.

We talked for about half an hour. It was relaxing sitting there with these karateka, drinking coffee, telling stories and listening to their complaints about life in Japan. My experience with things Japanese was limited to just one week so I had more questions than complaints or stories. I learned many things at these breakfasts which repeated almost daily for the rest of the month I was to be in Japan. I got to know these guys well, except for maybe Richard, who did not like to talk about his personal life much, preferring to just talk karate.

It was time to leave. We were all going to the Honbu for the ten-thirty class. Kevin and Richard and Jacque had to return to the Hoits to get their second gi. I was carrying my second gi in my backpack. Antonio, Olaf and I started to walk down the street after paying the bill.

"You should move closer to the dojo." Antonio said.

"Why?"

"You will spend most of your time here in Ebisu, right?"

"Yes. That's true."

"Sometimes you also go to the evening class?"

"Yes. I'm not sure I will always go."

"It would be better to live in Ebisu. How about living at the Hoits?"

"What? Is that a possibility?"

"Yes. There are two bunks available."

"How is that arranged? How much does it cost?" I was very surprised by this possibility.

"Kawawada Sensei must approve it. But he usually will if you are a serious student."

"Is this something you could help me with?"

"I would have to talk to Kawawada Sensei. He just left for a clinic in Kyushu."

"Oh. Then it might not work out for me. I'm here for only this month."

"We can try. Please wait a couple days, he will be back."

Chapter Thirteen

We were at the Honbu dojo and walking up the steps. It was time for the second class of the day. The teacher would be Asai Sensei, at least that's what Antonio said, who seemed to know everything that happened in Ebisu. We were in the locker room changing when in came a group of Japanese. I recognized some of them as the instructor's class students who had trained in the back of my class. Some of them I knew only because they were on the floor between the end of my ten-thirty class and noon, stretching and warming up for the instructor's class. But I had not yet seen them come in as a group and they seemed rather serious and quiet.

Antonio greeted a couple of them with "OSU" but there was no conversation. They changed quickly and started for the floor. The three of us changed slowly and stayed in the back of the locker room until they all had left.

"This looks like it will be a tough class." Antonio whispered.

"Really, why?"

"These guys usually just go to the noon class, the instructor's class."

"But I see some of them in this class."

"Yes. But they just sneak in after the class starts to get warmed up."

"So, what's going on?"

"Asai Sensei is teaching. I think there will be much sparring. Do you know Yahara?" Antonio described him as being one of the group that just left the locker room.

"No."

"He is very fast and powerful and does not like to lose. He is a kind of favorite of Asai's. Also, he loves to spar. There will be much sparring today." Antonio repeated. I felt like putting my street clothes back on and heading for the door. But it was not possible, of course.

"We had better get out on the floor. He said.

We quickly finished changing. As I opened the door to the back of the dojo and walked out onto the floor, I saw that there were already a couple of students sparring. Several others were getting warmed up, but they were in pairs and it was obvious that they too, would be sparring soon. "Here we go." Antonio whispered to me as we crossed the floor. Richard, Kevin and Jacque had just started across the floor to the locker room. It seemed they also sensed something serious.

Antonio told me to quickly warm up and that we then also had to start doing some slow free sparring. "We have to do what they do." He said. They will ask you to spar. You cannot say no." "OSU." I replied. I could see he was not in a happy mood.

Our three breakfast buddies were also warming up. The whole class seemed to be totally focused and there was not the usual chatting or quiet talk going on. My stomach hurt and I had to go to the bathroom. But there was nothing I could do. Antonio and I started slow free sparring. It soon became regular speed though as we matched the pace of the other students, who were gradually increasing their speed.

Though Antonio and I were supposed to be warming up, he started tagging me hard in the chest and stomach. My ribs were still sore, and it hurt. I started to block harder but that just made him come on stronger.

Yahara was there in a second. "*Yame* (stop)." He said. Then he started shouting at us. I did not understand a word. But Antonio did and bowed and replied with what I could tell was contrite language. I knew he was apologizing. Yahara left and went back to slow sparring with another Japanese.

"He said to slow down and not hit each other so hard."

"OSU" I was glad to hear it. Class had not started yet and I was already sore and sweaty.

"*Seiritsu*! (Line up!)" It was Yahara again, calling class to order. We lined up just as Asai Sensei stepped onto the floor. Asai Sensei shouted something and Yahara ran to the front to lead warm-ups, though we were all soaked in sweat. Asai Sensei strolled over to the makiwaras and began to whack away. My eyes strayed as I watched him alternate reverse punches by shifting from right to left. It was smooth and practiced. I made a mental note to do the same.

Yahara's warm-up was more of a stretching drill. He had us do slow, easy stretches that felt good and relaxed my muscles which were tense from the sparring. I was enjoying it very much.

Suddenly Asai Sensei, apparently finished with the makiwara training, shouted out another command and Yahara told us to line up with a partner. One of the Japanese, who often trained in the back of my class as a prelude to the instructor's class, stood across from me. I really had to use the bathroom.

Asai Sensei walked to the middle of the class where Yahara stood with his training partner. The partner stepped aside as Asai Sensei took his place to demonstrate the first drill to the class. It was a simple drill. Yahara was told to step in with a jodan punch. Then Asai Sensei shifted forward and to the left with right hand *nagashi ude uke* while raising the left hand to grab the upper part of Yahara's punching arm. Asai Sensei then showed us that the defender's left hand could also grab the shoulders, neck and almost anywhere else. He explained that we should enter the attack, not escape from it, while using both arms at the same time. He had Yahara attack several times and showed us the different possibilities. He also stressed that timing and commitment was important to do the technique successfully.

He had Yahara attack half speed and showed how incorrect timing could result in catastrophe, as Yahara's punch came within millimeters of Sensei's face. Also, when Sensei moved too fast, Yahara simply changed direction and again pulled his punch just short of Sensei's face. Sensei explained again through body movement how either too slow or too fast was not good. We had to time the technique perfectly. It was a clear explanation. Sensei told us to work the drill, slowly at first, then picking up the speed.

I was the attacker first and stepped in at medium speed with a *jodan* punch. My partner entered smoothly and brushed it aside with his right hand while grabbing my upper arm with his left hand. Sensei was there watching. "*Hai hai. Soo yu fune*. (Yes-that's right)"

I attacked a few more times and my partner practiced his timing and varied the grab. Sensei told us to switch. My partner stepped in with his lunge punch and I shifted forward a little to the left, guiding his punch away while reaching for his upper arm, just as my partner had done to me. "*Soo ja nakutte*. (No-not that way)" Sensei was still watching us. He motioned for me to step aside and took my place. My partner stepped in with the same *oizuki*. Sensei attempted to copy me by shifting too far out to the left, forcing him too far to effectively utilize his left hand, which caused a lack of balance and total disconnect of lower and upper body. He dramatized this by reaching over and pretending to stumble, showing how ineffective my technique was. Then Sensei had my partner again attack, slow speed. Sensei shifted much less outside, in fact just barely missing the punch, but still blocking it with his right hand. This time though, as he demonstrated, his left hand did not have to travel far to grab my partner's striking arm. He showed how much stronger and connected the body was simply by not shifting as much. Also, he explained, the attacker could not follow the shift as well if it was performed at the last second.

I understood clearly. Sensei had me step back into the drill and instructed my partner to step in again. I shifted just slightly outside, parrying the punch and grabbing it with my left hand. I could feel the punch go by my face. Sensei had us all do the drill a few more times, fine tuning our stances and ordering more speed. Satisfied, Sensei then moved me aside again and had my partner step in with the same attack. This time he continued the defense by also grabbing the punching arm with the blocking hand, pushing downward with his blocking hands, while pivoting on his left leg a hundred and eighty degrees. My partner was quickly and completely on the floor, his face wrenching against the hard dojo wood. Sensei demonstrated the technique a couple of times. Then he told me to try it.

My partner stepped in. I shifted in, slightly to the left with my block, grabbed his arm in two places as instructed and tried to pull him down. Instead he just stumbled forward a little. Sensei then showed how we had to pivot on an axis with no lateral movement until the last second, again, timing was important. We had to shift in, block and grab, and then pivot using good timing. Sensei had my partner attack several more times. Finally, I started doing the technique as he wanted. He told the class to practice it ten times.

Then it was my turn to be the attacker. I stepped in with what I thought was a fast enough jodan punch. My partner didn't even defend.

He just stood there. “More speed!” He shouted. I recovered and then stepped in again. This time he shifted in but showed what he thought of me by not even blocking, instead dropping his arms to show his disgust. “More speed!” He repeated, his voice louder than before.

I started again, this time concentrating on bending my front knee, pushing off with my back leg and then transferring the drive to my other leg at about the halfway point. I let out a loud kiai, yanked my withdraw hand back and threw my jodan punch at him. He shifted in again, this time parrying my block and grabbing my upper arm. With the prescribed drill done, he pulled his right leg forward and then quickly back again, taking out both of my legs. I fell to the floor with no control at all, ending up in a pile at his feet. He urged me up with a jerk of my arm. “OSU, good.” He said. “*Moo ikkai*. (One more time.)”

I got back in attack stance, again pushing off and concentrating on every part of my attack. This time he stepped in with a clean *nagashi uke*, grabbing my arm, holding it while pivoting, and then placing his right leg in a position to again sweep. He didn’t though. He just made contact with my back leg, applying another twisting motion that would have broken my balance had he followed through. Pulling back, he did the last part of the technique slowly. He was showing me how to do it. After two more times, the last time again sweeping me to the floor, he indicated that he would attack and came forward slowly. I shifted, blocked, grabbed his arm and pivoted, then reached my right leg around to his back leg, applying pressure to try to sweep.

“*Dame*! (No good)” He had me take the sweep position, my left hand holding on to his punching arm. Then he showed me how to twist with my hips, keeping a good connection between my upper and lower body, pushing his upper body one way simultaneously sweeping his leg the opposite way, to the front. I attempted the technique a few times, finally understanding it. “*Pointo wa, taimingu*. (The point is-timing)” He explained. “Not try sweep leg then twist hips reverse direction. *Soshite* (and) not do other way, try same time. He took the attack position. “*Mo ikkai*.” I was ready though.

Or so I thought. He stepped in fast and I started to enter into his attack but was far too slow and he nailed me hard. Blood started to flow.

"*Daijobu?*"

"Hai."

He pointed towards the back where there were rolls of toilet paper on a shelf near the heavy bag in the corner. He motioned with his fingers to grab some and stick it in my nose. With a wave he sent me off. Running to the front, I grabbed a small wad from the roll and stuffed it into my nose, then ran back and stood opposite him. He was smiling.

"*Mo ikkai.*" He repeated. "*Kyotsukete.* (Be careful)"

He stepped in fast, pushed off to the left and entered, using the same concentrated effort as a few minutes before. His punched just missed. I'm quite sure I was faster to enter into his attack but I'm also sure that he pulled his punch a little. He worked with me for a few more minutes until Asai Sensei shouted for us to stop.

Sensei told us to get back in line. He then explained that we would do *jyu ippon kumite*. He told us not to announce where we would attack. It could be anything, a punch, a kick, at any target. We were to do this for three minutes and then stop. Then rotate to get a new partner and do it again. "Ah, excellent." I thought, "controlled sparring." It was one of my favorite drills. You could go hard and fast either as attacker or defender. But it would be just one technique and then stop, a minimum risk of injury.

We all bowed to our partners, took free stance and started the drill. My side had to attack first so I stepped in with speed and power, attempting a front kick to the stomach. My partner stepped to the side, blocked my kick and returned it with a round house kick that landed hard on my rib cage. Grimacing, I quickly got back into sparring stance. He attacked with another round house kick which I blocked, but then caught his follow-up punch on the chin. I ended up on the floor four times in that one minute. Asai Sensei called time and we all rotated to new partners. After another two rounds, I was face to face with Yahara.

It was a long three minutes. Yahara was not in a teaching mood. I tried attacking as fast as I could. He would bat my punches and kicks away as if they were gnats that were pestering him. His counters found their mark every time with a mixture of face and body contact.

I blocked high, he punched low. I blocked low, he punched or kicked high. If I was not able to block fast enough, he came straight in, holding back just enough to not break any bones. I was physically and mentally exhausted and could hardly stand up. Yahara shouted at me. "Make strong!"

I was light-headed and could feel myself ready to pass out. "Don't". I willed myself up and continued the drill, trying to attack harder. Yahara just played with me, clearly disgusted. Asai Sensei shouted and as we lined up to bow out, I bowed to Yahara and he just barely nodded his head and looked away. I stood in line and forced myself to not fall into a heap onto the floor as we ended the class.

Back in the locker room I sat down on a bench and struggled to catch my breath. Antonio was breathing hard but did not seem as overwhelmed. Yahara was nowhere to be seen.

"He will go to the next class," sensing what I was thinking.

"Another class? You're kidding!"

"No. He is in the instructor's class. It looks like Asai Sensei will teach it also."

We changed clothes quickly, me working hard just to move my body which hurt everywhere. We walked out of the locker room and headed for the front. I was always able to see a few of the instructors warming up but this time I saw much more.

Asai Sensei and Yahara were sparing. Yahara was not doing well. He was in the front corner of the dojo on the floor. As he stood up, Asai Sensei jumped around him and attacked him from the other side with a very smooth front kick and reverse combination which I assumed was yet another foot sweep since he landed on the floor three times. Yahara seemed slow and sloppy, but he kept getting up.

"That's the key. I thought. "Just keep getting up."

"*Hayaku dette*! (Hurry up and leave!)" The shout came from one of the instructor trainees. I had stopped and was watching them spar. We were supposed to quickly walk off the floor and leave.

"Hai." I answered, then bowed off the floor and limped down the stairs. Antonio was waiting for me. He had not stayed to watch, probably because he knew the consequences. He wanted to buy some pastries at the bakery next door. I couldn't resist and bought two cream cheese filled beauties. We left the bakery and walked to the park just a couple of minutes from the dojo, the same park in which I had fallen asleep the previous week.

"What was that all about?" I asked, as we sat down on a patch of grass near a metal swing set.

"I told you there would be sparring."

"Who was the guy I was with when Asai demonstrated the technique, the one before *jyu ippon kumite*?"

"That was Imura. He is a good teacher and sometimes comes to the Honbu in the evening."

"He is fast. I could not defend against his step-in punch until he slowed it down for me"

"I have seen him and Yahara spar together. It is a beautiful thing." Antonio grinned.

"I would like to see that. Speaking of Yahara, what's up with him? He treated me like I was less than low class."

"He is like that. Everyone says the same. I have talked to him a few times and he seems OK. But on the dojo floor he is always serious and tough."

"He didn't seem so tough with Asai Sensei." I told him what I had seen.

"Asai Sensei is not human. Everyone knows this." He was grinning again.

We ate our pastries and talked until Antonio had to leave. He was teaching Spanish and had to prepare a lesson. "Keep thinking about staying at the Hoits. You will enjoy it."

"Will do. Thanks."

Antonio headed for his dorm room at the Hoits. I walked to Ebisu station. Victoria was going to meet me at Takadanobaba station to look at another hotel which would be two stops closer to Ebisu. But it would be a lot closer from this hotel to the station, which would save me almost twenty minutes every morning, so in all it would mean my morning commute would be thirty minutes shorter. I trudged up the stairs to the platform, got on the train that arrived a minute later and surprisingly found a seat.

I hurt everywhere and was tired and fell asleep immediately, waking at the melodic announcement in a nasal voice, "Takadanobaba…*Takadanobaba de gozaimusu.*" Jerking my head up, I checked the sign. It seemed like I had just sat down, but it was indeed Takadanobaba. Victoria was standing on the platform, waving to me as I stepped through the doors of the train.

"*Ohaiyogozaimasu*. She had a nice smile.

"Hi there." I tried to be as cheery as she was.

"You look like shit. Bad day at the dojo?"

"Very bad. My body is mush."

"Want to get some coffee?"

"Nah. Let's go see the hotel." We walked down the steps and out onto the street as she led me across a small intersection and down Waseda dori. Passing a second street, she pointed to a building on the corner.

"There's a good bookstore, on the fourth floor. You can go there and relax and read anything you want without buying it. Their English language section is huge."

We kept walking another five minutes and turned right as she pointed to the left and indicated a Wendy's Hamburger restaurant. "We'll go there after seeing the hotel. You need to relax a little."

After another minute we came to an old, wooden building with concrete steps in front. Over the door was a sign that read "Taioso". We walked up the steps and through the door, took off our shoes, placed them in a wooden compartment along with another twenty pair. Then we stepped up onto the main floor. I looked to the right where there was a fairly large kitchen area. To the left was a small window which appeared to be the office. It looked very much like the Honbu dojo window. Junko was sitting at the window on the other side of the wall.

"Konnichi wa."

"Konnichi wa." Victoria answered.

"Konnichi wa", I parroted.

Victoria was doing very well in Japanese. I let her do the talking although it was obvious Junko spoke good English. We followed Junko around to look at the kitchen which was connected to a small dining room. I would be able to buy and prepare any food I wanted. We went upstairs and Junko showed us the rooms, which were six tatami-mat, and then the toilets, which were communal and unisex. They were larger than Kimi's.

Victoria and Junko were already discussing move-in dates. They looked at me and Junko said in English, "Is tomorrow OK?"

I said yes. That was it. I would be moving all my worldly goods into this hotel. The price we would pay would include one sento ticket a day. There was no shower. To me it did not matter so much since I showered at the dojo.

We said our goodbyes and Victoria and I walked back down the street towards Wendy's, crossing Waseda dori, turning left and entering the restaurant on the right side. We both ordered coffee with me also ordering a cheeseburger, taking a seat in the no-smoking section on the right-hand side next to the front window.

"I've talked to Junko many times. She's wonderful and really likes foreigners."

"How did you find out about this place?"

"From some of the teachers I work with. This is close to many of the teaching jobs you can find here. The Tozai line takes you straight into Tokyo. Also, it is only two stops to Shinjuku."

"How about Joanne? Will she move here too?"

"Yes. I think so. I'll talk to her tonight. Maybe we can move her stuff along with mine. Can we do it tomorrow afternoon?"

"Sure, right after my karate class. I'll be home around this time."

"Great."

We talked for a while and then she had to go to Shinjuku to teach a class. I walked around Takadanobaba for a few minutes and came upon an old movie theater on Waseda Dori that advertised two movies for six-hundred yen. They were old movies, 'Fistful of Dollars' and 'For a Few Dollars More'.

It was exactly what I wanted to do. Paying for the ticket and buying some popcorn, I went in to find a seat. It was nearly empty. This was the matinee and there was still twenty minutes before it started. I relaxed into my seat ten rows back and in the middle. It was cool and quiet, with Japanese music playing, and I fell asleep.

The start of the first movie woke me with a jolt. I couldn't believe it. The movie was not dubbed in Japanese. Instead it had Japanese subtitles with the original English voice track.

I sat through both movies completely relaxed and at peace. Though my body certainly hurt, I was still doing OK and was training every day. I'm not sure I saw all of either movie, drifting off for much of the time into some much-needed sleep.

When I walked out of the theater, it was getting dark. Locating a coin laundry I had seen near the station, I threw my sweaty gis in along with a couple of towels. Across the small street there was a row of vending machines. Putting two-hundred yen in the slot, I punched a button and an ice-cold Sapporo beer dropped into the chute at the bottom. I sat in the laundry room, read my guidebook and sipped the beer and was again getting tired. Before long I was on the train back to Ikebukuro and Kimi Ryokan, walking up the steps, saying hello to a few foreigners who were sitting and smoking and heading up to my room. I barely got the futon out of the closet before passing out on it.

Chapter Fourteen

It was Tuesday morning and the Hoitsugan class was huge. We were lined up with Nakayama Sensei in the front. He had entered the dojo a few minutes earlier than usual to chat with us. According to Antonio, he did this a few times every couple of months. He would single out one or two students, always foreigners, and ask them where they were from and how long they had been training. It was never a deep conversation, just idle talk. But it meant a lot to the students.

Today's class would again be kata, this time Jitte. Sensei had us do the kata twice to his count. Then he started to point out a few of the movements that he said needed work. In the end it turned out to be nearly every move.

The first movement, from kamae position, was to be done quickly at first and then immediately change to slow and dynamic. He demonstrated, changing speed flawlessly from beginning to end of the move, at the end twisting his hips back just a little from hanmi position to a more front facing position. He had us do the same and walked around the class, reaching under the *tekubi chudan osae uke* and pushing up, checking for proper muscle tension and blocking effectiveness. The next move he focused on was the shift to the right with *chudan kake uke* in kibadachi stance. He told us to look first before shifting. Also, the shift should be only about six inches with no bouncing. To do this Sensei said to push off with the left leg and demonstrated that the left leg should push off at a low angle so as not to hop, simply shift. If we move just the short distance, enough to create a lateral force, there need not be a change in height.

Sensei went to the corner and returned with a wooden bo. He again walked among us and had us do the technique several times on our own as he lightly tapped us on the top of the head if we hopped up during the shift.

"*Motto hikui*. (Deeper.)" He said to me as I felt the bo staff.

"OSU." I tried again as Sensei left the stick sitting on top of my head.

"So so." He went over to another student.

Satisfied with our progress, Sensei then told us to continue from that move by his count. We pivoted on our left leg into the first *migi teisho chudan yoko uchi*, then continued with the next two moves. He stopped us and had us go back to the first of the three moves. Then he told us to be sure to let the left foot face forward with the first move by bending the left knee as we let the foot turn to the front. From there, it would be the same as the previous shift technique but without the shift, just feeling the correct angle with the left leg and pushing out. He demonstrated how the move could also be to the front, depending on the situation.

The other two moves in this set were to be performed the same way. Sensei showed us how to twist the hips simultaneously as we moved to increase the power of the block. The block was to the side, not to the front, he reminded us. We progressed through the kata, Sensei instructing both basic and very detailed points. Then we came to the *migi shuto jodan uke*, followed by the *ryo sho koko bo uke* designed to block and then grab a stick. Sensei again grabbed the bo and called Antonio to the front. He had Antonio assume the both fists thrust downwards position in preparation. As Antonio turned into the first part of the technique, Sensei slowly swung the stick in a downward path from high to low at Antonio's head. The stick made contact with Antonio's right sword hand block. Then Sensei showed that the left hand could then grasp the stick, using the elbow as a kind of lever, twist it out of the attacker's hands, ending up with control of the stick, the right and left hands changing position.

Sensei gave the wooden stick to Antonio and told him to swing it at him slowly. When the stick landed onto Sensei's open right hand, Sensei performed the next move cleanly and jammed it solidly but with control into Antonio's stomach. Antonio was clearly surprised, as were all of us. Muffled laughter was heard as Sensei just smiled. "*Yatte mitte.* (Try it.)" We paired up, retrieved more sticks from the corner, and started practicing the technique, Sensei walking around again to make corrections. When he was satisfied, Sensei had us move on to the next move which is almost the mirror image of the same technique. We all fumbled with the switch but after a few minutes again became comfortable. We finished the rest of the kata with Sensei focusing on quick hip rotation on both the high/low blocks and the last rising block combinations.

Sensei then had us pair up and grab the sticks again. He told us to work with our partner to understand defense against the stick. We were told to attack our partner from different angles. The defender would then have to block or deflect the strike.

My partner and I started the drill. He attacked from overhead, from the side, and straight out from his center. I blocked the stick well except for the straight thrust. When we did the thrusts, my partner had to stop the stick every time to avoid burying it in my stomach. I was trying to use *soto uke* and *gedan barai* but was having no success. Sensei stopped us, moved my partner out of the way, took his place, and told him to attack again. Sensei stepped back, quickly raising both hands to about shoulder height, then back down, neatly deflecting the stick. Then Sensei asked for more speed. Again, Sensei smoothly parried the thrust. Sensei then took the stick from my partner and motioned for me to join him as defender. He attacked a couple of times at medium speed. I copied his block, raising both hands quickly and bringing them downwards as I entered into the thrust, easily avoiding it. Sensei then thrust faster, making me move quicker to successfully block. I was getting it and felt good. Then Sensei thrust out again. I entered and raised my hands as before-but he withdrew the stick and then thrust it again, square into my mid-section. I had expected the same thrust path and was surprised at how badly my new defense technique had failed.

"You cannot preconceive the attack." Antonio was translating to all of us who were by then standing in a circle, watching and listening.

"You must block the real attack, not the attack your mind thinks will come. You must wait until the last second before you enter or move sideways or step back. It will take many years to perfect. But you must practice this idea. It is best to work with your partner in this way every day."

Antonio interrupted the explanation with a question to Sensei in Japanese about something he did not understand. They had a short conversation and then Antonio continued the translation.

"Sensei says the feeling will eventually become more natural if you practice not using your mind as much as trusting your feeling and keeping your eyes in soft focus. Sensei says you must, of course, practice the physical movements over and over to make them automatic. But you must also practice not thinking."

Sensei told us to make partners again with one person attacking, announcing the technique in advance. We did this a couple of times, just basic one step sparring. Then Sensei told the attackers to keep on announcing the attack, but one of every three times, perform a different attack. "In other words, lie!" Antonio said, probably not a direct translation.

We practiced that way back and forth for a few minutes. It was stressful at first, expecting a mid-level punch to the stomach but instead having to defend against a high-level kick. I had trouble changing from what was announced to what my partner actually did.

"Relax. Do not think so much. Relax your shoulders, your arms and your mind. You cannot focus on what the attacker says." Antonio was again translating. "The idea of announcing the technique is to set up an expectation in your partner's mind. Your partner's job is to deal with that expectation by keeping his mind open."

I did as Sensei said and was able to slowly grasp the idea. Though my partner announced the attack, I did not focus on what he said. Rather, I focused on defending any attack that came my way. I relaxed and tried to see the attack as it was, high, low, punch or kick. My defense was not pretty at all. But slowly I was able to protect myself. It was a great class and one of the best lessons in karate that I have ever had. To this day I do not pay attention to what my partner announces. I just block what comes my way. Oh sure, I do the drill as the instructor tells us. But I do not assume the announced attack is what will come at me.

Sensei stopped the class but had a few more words to say. Antonio again translated.

"You must practice this every day. Regular drills are very important because you have to learn specific attacks and defenses and body movement. This also trains the muscles to do what you want in a split second. But take the time to practice emptying your mind with this style of training as well. You must do the kata correctly, but a real fight is a different thing." Clearly, he was emphasizing one of Funakoshi Sensei's tenets.

Class was over. Sensei said we would continue with Jitte next class. We bowed out, cleaned the floor, showered and walked to the coffee shop for some breakfast.

The topic of conversation at breakfast was, of course, today's lesson. The general agreement was that if we practice the "lie" drill regularly, we would certainly get better and learn how to relax.

"It's the mind worrying about what the attack will be that makes me tense." Antonio said. Most of the group agreed with that. We discussed how best to ensure that we do, in fact, practice it regularly, with all of us vowing to do our best. Then the topic changed.

Kawawada Sensei was returning Friday. Antonio said that he would be teaching on Saturday morning. Then Antonio turned to me.

"Now you can ask about staying at the Hoits."

"Actually, I'm moving to Takadanobaba today."

"But you need to stay at the dojo for at least a short time. It is a different lifestyle."

"Just ask Sensei on Saturday!" Richard ordered me. He was not smiling.

"Hai. Osu."

Walking to the Honbu dojo, I thought about Richard's comment. Now I had a real dilemma. I had promised Victoria to move into Taio-so today and had even paid for the rest of the month in advance. But most of the students grudgingly did what Richard told them to do. He was the senior student and although had probably been hit on the head one too many times, it was still a requirement of the dojo to maintain Sensei/Kohai rules. "I'll think about it later." I told myself.

I walked upstairs and into the Honbu dojo, already knowing what was in store for today's training, "more sparring", Antonio had said. The class was hard and was over in a flash. We lined up for basic step-in techniques. After practicing the drills individually, we each got a partner and worked together. The attacker would step in with a punch, and then immediately step in again with another punch but add a twist of the hips and an outward move with the rear leg to end up at an angle to his partner. The partner was just a target and would move back while blocking. Then we added different punches and kicks into the drill, both partners switching to attack and defense. Imura Sensei explained how to quickly shift outside the line of attacks by twisting the hips hard and letting the rear leg move almost on its own. Then we were told to shorten the drill to just one attack and shift. We practiced, rotating to get new partners.

Then Sensei said to do the same two drills, but mix it up so that sometimes we did one step in and shift, then another time did two step-ins and shift. The defender had to relax and be ready for either attack. I was surprised that it was another drill that emphasized relaxation and not expecting a certain attack. I remember wondering if Imura Sensei had discussed this with Nakayama Sensei.

It felt good though and I was able to relax and flow with the attack much better than some of the other students because of the Hoitsugan training that morning. The last few minutes were spent doing *jyu kumite*, rotating to have a new partner every couple of minutes. We were told to use the new drills during sparring, but it seemed to be just free sparring with little attention being given to the previous drills.

The class was over. I showered quickly and hurried to Ebisu station. It was time to move my meager belongings to Takadanobaba, along with Victoria.

Chapter Fifteen

Victoria was waiting on the steps of Kimi Ryokan.

"Hi there. Ready?" She was in a good mood, as always.

"Ready."

I had packed my clothes that morning so it took just a few minutes to haul it down to the front of the hotel. There was only my backpack and my duffle bag. For Victoria it was a lot more. She had a stack that consisted of several duffle bags, two medium size suitcases and a dozen large department store plastic shopping bags.

"This is all yours?"

"No. Joanne says she wants to move too, so some of it is hers."

"How do we get all of this to Takadanobaba?"

"I called a taxi. He will be here any time now."

I was relieved that we didn't have to lug all the stuff on the train. The taxi pulled up to Kimi. We tried to load everything into the trunk but had to put some of it in the back seat with Victoria who gave the driver a map. We arrived at Taioso after a forty-five-minute ride through a maze of side streets so narrow I thought we would have to back out of them. The street in front of Taioso was one lane and very narrow. The taxi pulled up to the front steps and the driver was helping us unload. We placed all of it at the top of the steps. Junko had seen us arrive and came out to greet us.

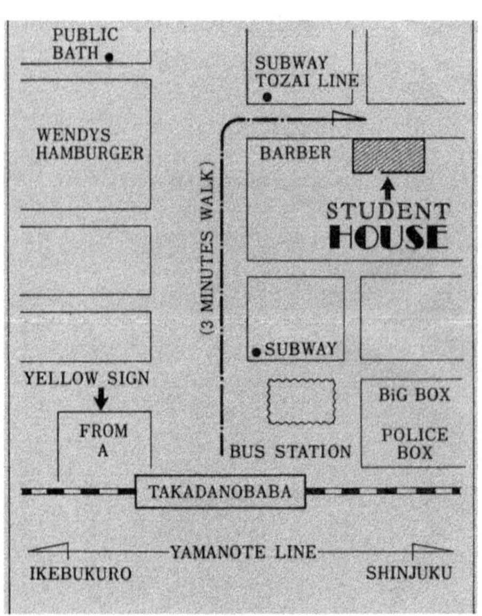

Map Of Taioso Student House (Author Residence Several Times in Japan)

"Konnichi wa."

"Konnichi wa." We both responded. Although Junko's English was good, I found that she wanted to speak Japanese to foreigners as much as possible. She was my first big step in starting to actually learn how to speak Japanese. I learned much-needed confidence from Junko over the next few days. In the future I would learn even more about the language and the culture due to her excellent personality and mentoring.

Victoria paid the taxi driver and had a short conversation with Junko.

"The rooms are ready."

"OK. Let's haul it inside." I replied.

We took her and Joanne's things to a room two rooms down from the bathrooms, to the right at the top of the stairs. They would be sharing the room. She helped me with my comparatively small stack. My room was to be at the top of the stairs, to the left and down one room. That meant I would have a view of the courtyard and also be two rooms down from the bathrooms. It was an excellent location. I sat my things down on the tatami mat after removing my slippers taken from the shoe box area just inside the front entrance. There were no personal slippers and you wore what was available, sharing with the other borders.

My room was very similar to the room at Kimi Ryokan, six tatami mats, a closet that ran the length of the side wall, and a T.V. and clock on the hallway side wall next the door. Also, at the hallway side wall was a small vase with a replica of a full-bloom cherry tree with a white, gravel landscape. All in all, it was a nice room. A year later I would be fortunate to spend another six months in the same room, Junko saving it for me per our letter correspondence.

I put away my bags and walked down to the bathroom. As I stood at the urinal, Victoria walked in. She glanced at me and immediately covered her eyes.

"No need to do that." I said.

"I guess not. We'll be meeting here a lot from now on." She laughed and hurried into a stall. I was also a little embarrassed and hurried to finish before I had to hear her using the toilet. Across from the bathroom there was a row of deep, stainless steel sinks. We met again as she joined me there and we laughed together.

"This is certainly different than back home."

"I don't care so much. It was the same at Kimi." I replied.

"Yeah, but it feels different this time. Maybe it's because only you and me are here. Before it was Joanne and me. So, what are your plans tonight?"

"No plans."

"Let's do something."

"Sure. What?" We both finished washing our hands. There was a small sink in the bathroom we both had already used, but apparently, we had the same idea of making a big deal out of washing again.

"Have you been to Sensō-Ji?"

"No, not yet. I've read about it though." In fact, it had been highlighted in my guidebook as a place to visit.

"Want to go?"

"Now?"

"Sure. It's only an hour away if we use the Tozai line."

"I had no argument and wanted to see it. "Let's go." I replied.

She hurried back to her room, disappeared for a few minutes and was at my door as I opened it after retrieving my back pack. We walked to Takadanobaba station and bought our tickets. From the Tozai line we transferred to the Ginza line and were there in forty-five minutes, after another short transfer to the Toei Asakusa line.

A trip to Asakusa provided the opportunity to see two major religious sites at one time. Not that rare in Japan but more unusual in the middle of Tokyo. There was Sensō-ji which is a Buddhist temple and Asakusa Jinja which is a Shinto shrine. The entire area was heavily damaged in the 1945 bombing raids. One of the gates leading to Asakusa Jinja is called Nitomen and was built in 1618 and used by the Tokugawa Shogun.

We walked down the old streets filled with souvenir shops and hundreds of people, both Japanese and foreigners. There were food stands everywhere and the smells were fantastic. I stopped Victoria a number of times to buy a small bowl of ramen, a yakitori stick, some nikuman and other Japanese goodies.

It was getting dark and the red lanterns were turned on, forming a beautiful border on the main street and the side streets where they gradually faded out after a few blocks, the atmosphere suddenly becoming more exotic and sensually charged.

Victoria and I stopped at a small shop that sold sake. We bought one cup each and sat down on cheap chairs to relax before getting any closer to the temple. We watched the people, all of them happy and excited, walking towards the main steps. We talked about Japanese culture, a little about ourselves and settled into a closeness that comes from similar personalities living far away from home. We bought one more cup of sake and started holding hands on top of the plastic table.

Drinking our sake for a few minutes, we just sat, watching the whole scene. The smells and lights and music and, of course, the sake, all cast their spell on us.

"Let's go inside." She finally said.

We stood up from our cafeteria style chairs, said thanks to the very kind old lady that served us, and continued to the temple, walking along with the mass of people, trying to hold hands but eventually giving up because of the crowd. As we walked up the steps I reached into my pockets and grabbed a couple of fifty-yen coins and gave one to Victoria. We both tossed the coins into the wood slatted box just in front of the main opening to the temple and stood with our feet together, bringing our hands together and clapping to awaken the Gods. We bowed and said a silent prayer. After a couple of minutes, we turned and walked down the steps.

After a rather quiet ride back we arrived at Takadanobaba at seven o'clock and stopped at a small Izakaya at the main intersection just outside the station. We found a table easily and ordered *kare* (flounder), some skewered vegetables, more yakitori and a couple of beers. We talked about the evening and how we were feeling, and that it was probably the isolation and loneliness and foreignness rather than pure attraction between us.

"It's not a problem." I said. "Let's just go back to our rooms and wait for another day."

"There will be another day, won't there?"

"Oh yeah, I'm sure of it."

"OK. Let's go."

We left, walked down Waseda dori and ten minutes later we turned onto the narrow street leading to our new home. We walked up the steps. Junko was there.

"*Daijobu* (Are you ok?)" She said, she noticed with a glance that we were holding hands.

"*Daijobu desu. Asakusa ni itte kimashita. Totemo tanoshikatta desu.* (We're ok. We went to Asakusa. It was very fun)" Victoria replied.

"*Ah so, yokatta desu ne? Ja-oyasumi nasai.* (Really? That's great, isn't it? Well-good night)" Junko was looking at both of us in a knowing manner. We both said good night to her, walked up the stairs, turned left, took off our slippers and stepped onto my tatami mat.

***

My alarm rang and I jumped out of the futon. It was five-thirty. Trying to be quiet, I walked out the door to the communal sink, washed my face, brushed my teeth and made a quick stop at the bathroom before heading back to the room.

"*Ohayo*. (Good morning)"

"*Ohayo*." I replied. "You can sleep more if you want. I have to go to the dojo."

"OK." With that she fell back onto the futon and was silent.

I packed what I needed and started for the door, thought briefly about writing a short note, decided against it, and left.

Wednesday and Thursday went quickly and I basked in the instruction from Ogura and Kurasako at the Honbu and Richard and Juan at the Hoitsugan while Victoria and I went out each night. Friday morning Antonio reminded me that Kawawada Sensei would be back and would be teaching Monday. He was happy.

"You have to ask him."

"But really I am still thinking about it." I replied.

"No. You have to ask him. Richard also told you to ask."

"I know. But the place I'm staying at is great."

"You came to practice karate, right?"

"Of course."

"Then you need to experience life at the Hoitsugan dojo."

"OK OK. I'll ask him." I gave up. Deep inside I knew I would be asking him.

Now what would I do, I thought. Victoria and I had become close and we were having a good time. I was sure that if I moved to Ebisu and stayed at the Hoitsugan, it would put a crimp on our time together. I still had a few days left before I had to ask Sensei. I decided again to think about it later.

The early Friday training was conducted by Juan instead of Nakayama Sensei. I was disappointed but in the end the class was very hard and quite fun. We did partner training, starting with one-step sparring and gradually working up to *jyu kumite*, rotating about every three minutes. We even had a five-minute water break. No one drank water-just got down on the floor and stretched. Juan liked to start out with no warm-up stretches. We all went out for breakfast as usual and then walked together to the Honbu. The weather was perfect, warm with a slight breeze that helped dry us out from the previous class. We were not to stay dry for long. The Honbu class was led by Ueki Sensei and consisted of Hangetsu kata for the first half and more free sparring for the second half, me being suspiciously lined up against the instructor trainees. Ueki Sensei had us perform the kata several times while he walked among us, tweaking as he went, especially the stance and the breathing, ensuring that we were breathing in on the block and out on the strike, staying aware of the connection to the floor in Hangetsu dachi, briefly putting us with partners to "test" the connection. At the end he explained that we do not always breathe in on the block. "You have to adjust depending on the situation, timing and your body. Please experiment." Apparently, he meant during the next kumite part of the class. We were to attack three times and then defend three times with our partner, then rotate and do it again, paying attention to our breathing patterns and deciding which worked best. Sensei called out several different combinations of strikes and blocks, mixing them up to give us ample examples with which to experiment. It was an enlightening training and I also found that my breathing rhythm changed proportionately to my state of exhaustion.

Chapter Sixteen

Joanne was back. We were all sitting in the dining area at Taioso. It was five P.M. on Saturday night and we had bought a couple of Sapporo beers from the vending machine across the street.

"So-what are we doing tonight?" Victoria was looking at me.

"How about Shinjuku?" Victoria looked excited at my suggestion.

"Shinjuku sounds great. I didn't have much time to relax in Osaka. Mostly I had to babysit a group of salary men."

"Then let's go." Victoria was already standing up and tugging at Joanne. We went back to our rooms to clean up. We met back in the dining area and walked to the station. It was only two stops to Shinjuku from Takadanobaba.

"Let's go to Kabuki-cho." Victoria said just as the train doors opened. I knew nothing at the time about Kabuki-cho's reputation as a rough neighborhood and as a hangout for young, up and coming Yakuza roaming the streets, enforcing local territorial rules, but mostly just acting out.

We found it and started looking at the store fronts and their wonderful displays of food and drink, finally coming to one restaurant that had an outside stall selling *ebi yaki* (grilled shrimp). The sign said two ebi and a *dai joki* (big draft beer) for one thousand yen. The shrimp were huge and were nicely charcoal grilled with what appeared to be course sea salt.

"*Irashaimase*!" It was a loud and clear welcome. "*Ikaga desu ka*? (How about it?)"

"*San nin bun kudasai*. (Three please)" Joanne replied.

"*Hai, kashiko marimashita*." He put six of the giant shrimps into one basket. "*Hai, doozo*." He motioned for us to enter. "*Irashai*!" Another greeting from inside as we walked through the door. "*Doozo. Okake kudasai*. (Please have a seat)" We took a table against the wall close to the door where we could still see some of the street traffic through the front door. Three draft beers were delivered in a flash and we clicked glasses, took a drink and dug into the shrimp that was also delivered quickly.

It was the best shrimp I had ever had, just the right combination of slightly burned soy flavored shell but soft inside with that salty taste. Mixed with the beer I was a very happy diner. All three of us gobbled the shrimp and then relaxed to enjoy the beer.

"This is so good!" Victoria was beaming.

"Should we get more?" I asked.

"No. Let's go find another Izakaya." Joanne replied.

We sat and talked for a while, mostly about Joanne's trip to Osaka and how bored she was for the whole week. "But I did make a lot of money. So- I guess it was worth it. By the way, thanks for moving my stuff to Taioso."

"Do you like your room?" I asked.

"Yeah, it's great. Plus, I have it all to myself." She grinned and elbowed Victoria in the ribs.

Victoria was ready to go. "I know a place."

We walked out of the restaurant, saying goodbye and thanks and stopping to tell the hawker outside how much we enjoyed the shrimp and beer. "*Maido*! (Come again!)" He answered.

We had just started walking down the street when a group of three young men stopped us.

"Where you go?" It was obviously the leader.

"We want to find an Izakaya." Victoria answered.

"You come us!" He said, motioning the opposite direction down the street away from the main part of Kabuki-cho.

"*Dooshite*? (Why?)" Joanne countered.

"You come! He repeated. Then he grabbed Joanne's arm.

"Wait a minute!" I said this in English, thinking they actually knew a few words. It had no effect though as the other two started to grab Victoria's arm and jerk her forward.

"Stop!" I shouted. Joanne and Victoria had already freed themselves and were standing a few feet away, arms flailing to avoid another controlling grasp.

"Back off! I said this also in English but with more forcefulness.

"*Nani itteiru wakaranai!* (I don't know what you are saying!)" The leader reached to push me away. I stepped back though and he stumbled forward. Taking advantage of his imbalance I slid into him with my right leg and swept him to the ground. The other two came to his rescue but had to step around him first to get to me. I shouted "stop" a few times and Victoria shouted it in Japanese "*yamete kudasai*". But they did not stop.

I positioned myself so as to only deal with one of them at a time. It was quite easy, a tap on the chin for the first one and a reverse punch to the sternum for the other. The leader did finally get back up but they had lost their confidence and though they shouted a lot, none of which I understood, they stayed their distance. I told the girls to start walking away. The guys kept shouting but did not follow.

"That was intense." Joanne said. "What was that all about?"

We were sitting at a table four floors up at another Tengu. We could see a large section of Shinjuku through the window. It was dusk and the lights were already illuminating their beautiful patterns that showed off the maze that made Shinjuku so popular with locals and foreigners.

"They were young Yakuza, I think. They had the punch perm hair and short sleeves showing their tattoos." Victoria replied.

"Why did they bother us?" I asked.

"Who knows? Maybe they wanted to have drinks with us." Victoria answered.

"At least with you girls." I was looking at both of them.

"But you convinced them that it was a bad idea."

"Yeah. Sorry about the trouble. I didn't know what was happening. Couldn't understand anything they said.

"It's OK. How did you do that? I saw the guy who grabbed me land on the ground a few seconds later."

"He was off balance." I replied.

"How about the other two?"

"They didn't have much spunk." I said. They gave up easily."

"Anyway, thanks."

"No problem. Didn't expect that though. Have you had trouble with them before?"

"Never, I've heard about them from my Japanese friends. But I thought they usually leave foreigners alone."

We drank way too many beers and ate enough for a couple of days. I'm not sure how we made it back to Taioso. I know we walked because the trains had stopped for the night and the line for the taxis was long.

We did eventually arrive and stumbled up the stairs. *Obaa san* had already unlocked the door. On the narrow street, just in front of the hotel, we foolishly bought two more five-hundred-milliliter cans of Sapporo beer to share. It's just something you do when all reason has left. We quietly opened my door and stepped in. Immediately Joanne and Victoria headed down the hall to the bathroom.

"I'll go to." I said.

"You can wait until we get back." Joanne said.

We had stopped once at a small children's park because we couldn't walk anymore without emptying our bladders. There was a concrete toilet in the corner of the park. Joanne went first and Victoria and I talked just outside until she finished. I told Victoria to go in while I waited with Joanne. I remember getting very antsy while she was inside, wondering if I could wait much longer. Finally, it was my turn and I brushed by Victoria nearly knocking her over as she came out. Finished, we all ran from the toilet, giggling like ten-year olds, on our way to Takadanobaba.

The girls were back in my room. I made a quick trip and when I returned, they had already opened the first can of beer. We sipped from it, passing it around like boys at a camp fire.

We talked until it became light outside and sometime after that we opened the second can of beer, our eyes getting heavy and the conversation slowing.

"I'd better get to bed." Joanne finally said, in the middle of a yawn.

Victoria was half asleep already. "No. Just crash here. It's alright." She didn't ask me.

Needing no convincing, Joanne went sleepily to the closet, pulled out the futon set, laid the bottom and top on the tatami floor, and fell onto the top, curling into a ball. Victoria straightened the bottom futon, pulled it away a bit from Joanne and motioned for me to join her. We all fell asleep.

Chapter Seventeen

I woke up around noon. The girls were still rustling around in the futons. I read through my training notes and thought about what to do about Richard's requirement that I ask Kawawada Sensei's permission to stay at the Hoitsugan dojo. Surely it would be a good experience for me. To stay at the Hoitsugan would make the one-month trip to Japan complete, living and breathing Shotokan karate.

Though I had already paid for the remaining two weeks at Taioso, it would not be that painful financially to lose it. Maybe I could get some kind of refund. Victoria might be a little upset about me moving to Ebisu but, I came here for the karate experience. I made the decision quickly. I would ask Kawawada Sensei as soon as possible, then move to Ebisu and stay at the Hoitsugan for my last two weeks in Japan.

Victoria and Joanne had slowly crawled out of the futons and were sitting up.

"I need coffee." Victoria mumbled through her yawn.

"Yes, please!" Joanne echoed.

They went down the hall to the bathroom to try to wake up, Joanne said. I wanted coffee also and was struggling to sit in the room while they slept, almost leaving a couple of times but thinking it would be rude. Eventually we all walked down the stairs and out onto the street. It was just five minutes to Wendy's. We all ordered coffee to go and continued down Waseda dori to the corner across from the station. There was a bakery there that sold excellent pastries. Japanese pastries are not as sugary as those in the USA. The flavor is much simpler and more recognizable as to the ingredients. Some of them had curry inside, some mayonnaise and some even had small cocktail wieners. We bought a couple pastries each and walked back to Taioso and sat in the dining room behind the kitchen and across from Junko's residence. It was a very sparse room with a calendar and a few pictures on the wall. The tables were standard issue high school cafeteria style, gray, with narrow legs and plastic seats and backs.

"What a night." Victoria hadn't said much until now.

"I'm going to need some solid food." Joanne mumbled.

"Let's go get some ramen." I suggested.

Putting the remaining pastries back in the bag, and placing the bag onto the shelf in the kitchen, we again walked outside, turned left at Waseda dori and headed for a ramen shop that Victoria knew. Joanne and I ordered miso ramen; Victoria decided on shio ramen.

It was a quiet lunch at first but as we ate, the lovely ingredients brought out smiles all around and soon worked its magic on our stomachs and on our attitudes.

"This is wonderful!" Victoria was still smiling.

"Ramen is always delicious." Joanne agreed.

I couldn't stop slurping the noodles but managed a sloppy "oh yeah!"

I was feeling a little crowded and wanted to have some time alone. "I have to go to the dojo for a meeting." I lied.

"What time will you be back?" Victoria asked.

"I'm not sure. Probably they will want to have dinner. We have many things to talk about."

"OK. I guess we're on our own tonight." Victoria was looking at Joanne.

It was 9 o'clock in the evening when I returned to Taioso. I hadn't gone to Ebisu. Instead I went back to Shinjuku and found one of the biggest bookstores in Japan, Kinokuniya. I spent a long and luxurious few hours roaming the English section on the fourth floor, chatting with other foreigners and also Japanese who hung out there just to strike up a conversation in English for practice. When Kinokuniya closed its doors for the evening, I walked across the street to Che Che. Their window displayed a great looking plate of curried rice, which I had tried once in Toronto. I sat on the second level which overlooked the first level in a sort of balcony/loft type design and took my time eating and reading the rest of my guide book. It was time to decide on a last side trip for my months' vacation.

My plan was to leave on Wednesday and travel around the main island, basically following directions right out of my *Lonely Planet* guidebook. But now I was locked into a strict schedule, at least at the Hoitsugan. Monday through Wednesday, Nakayama Sensei taught. Thursday through Saturday, Kawawada Sensei was the instructor. Normally that would be great but I felt I had not yet seen much of the country. I decided to leave right after the Saturday training at the Hoits over the next two weekends. That would give me from about nine o'clock on Saturday morning until late Sunday night to travel, two more times. That would have to suffice.

Now I just had to choose a destination. With such a short time, I decided to limit my trips to three hours away from Tokyo. I could arrive somewhere at noon, explore the rest of the day, have a few beers at night, then still have all day Sunday to explore. It was a good plan and I was quite happy. Finishing my curry rice, I left the restaurant, walking by the long, luscious display of pastries and candies on the first-floor level on the way to the front door. It was dark now. I walked for an hour through the side streets, stopping a couple of times at *yatais* (food stands) for a glass of sake and some yakitori. I opened the door to my room, expecting to see Victoria there, but she wasn't. So, I made my way to the bathroom and prepared for bed, hoping to start the week in good spirits.

Chapter Eighteen

The alarm startled me. It was already six-am and I had slept deeply. I found myself again at the sink brushing my teeth, feeling as if I had just performed this same action a few minutes before, but it had been a solid eight hours ago. I felt great, picked up my backpack, stopped for a few minutes to clean up the mess the three of us had made, and walked down the stairs and out the door for Takadanobaba station. My karate month was almost half over.

Richard was waiting for me at the Hoitsugan dojo.

"Kawawada Sensei will be at the Honbu this morning."

"Ah. OK. OSU."

"You have to talk to him then."

"What do I do?"

"Antonio will be here. You talk to him. He will walk up to him with you. You can talk in English, but speak slowly and use simple English."

"OSU. OK"

Nakayama Sensei walked into the dojo, pushed his chest out and drew his arms back into a great stretch. "*Samui desune*! (Cold, isn't it?)"

He was wearing a light jacket as usual which he pulled off as he walked further into the dojo, hanging it on the same hook as before. Antonio started us out slowly then increased the pace until we had a nice glow, again reducing the movements to long, slow stretches to bring the warm-up to a close.

Sensei worked us on kumite drills. With a partner, side A would step in with a jodan punch as side B stepped back with age uke and gyaku tsuki. But then side B would continue forward with a oi-tsuki, side A then moving backwards to block and counter Side B's attack. No shifting outwards or inwards was allowed. It was a controlled way to do free sparring. In fact, many exchanges during free sparring don't last any longer than what we were doing with that drill. We added a mid-level punch, a front kick and a round house kick to the drill and rotated to get new partners. It was a simple but excellent training and helped me understand the importance of quickly changing directions from moving backward to driving forward, without losing balance and having to waste time regaining that balance in order to effectively mount a strong forward attack.

***

The Honbu class was packed with a group from Belgium. They were going to be in Tokyo for one week, according to Tanaka Sensei. Tanaka Sensei had each member stand in front of the class and introduce themselves. There were twelve in their group. For them, it was a dream trip, as mentioned by the group's leader who went last in the introductions. They had held fundraisers for two years to be able to make the trip together. Ten of them were black belts and two were brown. All of them looked tough enough to me. Tanaka Sensei started to speak in English.

"This is example…international karate. I teach them in *Belgi*, now they come Japan." Sensei turned to the group leader. "You train very hard, study new technique, take back your country. Please enjoy Japan life."

Sensei motioned for the Belgians to get back in line. As usual he also led the warm-ups. Then we were told to line up with the Belgian group on one side and the rest of us on the other side. We started with ippon kumite, my favorite. We were told to just use the standard step-in punch face, punch stomach and kick stomach. The defender would be free to use any technique. My training partner was a strong looking tall Belgian with a shaved head. He looked like he had just been released from prison.

I bowed to him when we first paired up but he had barely acknowledged me. I knew that meant trouble. My side was first to attack. I stepped in with *jodan tsuki*. He didn't move so I pulled my punch, just barely touching his chin. He slapped away my punching hand. This was not going to be good. Stepping back for another attack to chudan level, I pushed off with my back leg and lept forward. Again, he did not move but pushed my hand away.

"What is wrong?" I said

"Is not strong punch. No need to block."

I started again. This time I pushed off even harder and faster and aimed my right foot towards his mid-section. He blocked but still did not move, simply batting my lower leg with his blocking arm. "Not strong!" He repeated.

"Not strong my ass", I thought as I returned to the attack position. We were supposed to do five sets of three different attacks and then the other person was to attack. I stepped in for the next *jodan* punch as hard as I could. The punch caught him on the chin and his head jerked back.

"Ah, OK. Strong punch."

I then attacked to his *chudan* level, burying my right fist into his stomach, holding back just enough to not be an asshole.

"Ah, strong too."

"This guy is a jerk", I thought. "Just get this one over with and then I'll have another partner."

I attacked full speed with a mae geri. He moved back quickly and cleanly to the side, blocking my kick strongly. We went through the rest of the set with him now stepping either back or to the side with his blocks and counters. And then it was his turn to attack.

He stepped in before announcing or bowing and slammed his fist into my nose. I couldn't see for the tears and then the blood. "Asshole!" I said this out loud while I ran over to the corner, grabbed a roll of toilet paper, tore off a long piece and stuck it into my nose. Coming back to the line, I bowed to him and stood in natural stance for his next attack. "Let's continue." I said.

He stepped in with his chudan attack. It was strong but I was ready and pissed. I stepped to the front and a little to the left, grabbing his punching arm, then shot a cutting kick into his rib cage, holding back very little. He bent over and started to gasp for air. I caught him as he slid to the floor.

Tanaka Sensei was there immediately. "*Daijobu*? (Are you ok?)", he asked the Belgian, who mumbled something I could not understand. Another instructor trainee who was in line came running over at Sensei's command. He sat the Belgian on the floor, pushed his feet outward and took a position behind him. He squatted down, put his knee gently into the middle of the Belgian's back, grabbed both of his shoulders and pulled back, making room for more air to enter his lungs. "Relax", said the trainee in good English, walking him through what he was doing. I remember this was the first time to hear him speak English. He had always ignored me before and I assumed it was because I could not speak Japanese and he could not speak English. This took about five minutes, the trainee finally massaging the Belgian with one palm on his sternum and one on his back. I remember it as a kind of movie clip; the four of us, Tanaka Sensei, me, the trainee and the Belgian all huddled in one spot while the rest of the class continued with their drills, all shouting at the top of their lungs as they attacked and countered. My head was aching from his punch, my nose was stuffed with toilet paper and it was hard to breathe. The Belgian was OK. He got up on his own. Sensei was lecturing us.

"Cannot better if both have bones break", he scolded. "More control!" Then Sensei shouted for the class to rotate to get a new partner. I bowed to the Belgian who bowed back, certainly only because Tanaka Sensei was standing there. The rest of the class went well. The other members of the Belgian group rotated through as my training partners and we had good drills together.

Class was over. The line at the showers was longer than usual because of the visitors. I found myself standing next to the shaved head Belgian.

"OSU!" I said to him.

"OSU." He replied.

"You OK?" I asked.

"OSU. You OK?"

"Hai, OK" I replied.

We then talked about ourselves as though we had met at a karate party for the first time, me asking him about his training, his dojo and home town, him asking me the same. He was next in line for one of the shower stalls when one of them became free.

"You go ahead." He said.

"No no. You go." I replied.

"OK." He said. He then reached out his hand. I shook it firmly, grabbing his shoulder at the same time.

"Good training." I said.

"OSU, good training." He replied.

I eventually found an empty stall, showered, and walked across the dojo floor a little after noon. There were lots of stares but no one said anything, probably because the lateness was caused by Tanaka Sensei's visitors.

"Kawawada Sensei is back." Antonio seemed almost solemn. "We will ask him now. He is in his office."

"Now?" I was not ready for this.

"Come on. We go now."

He led me over to the window, said something in Japanese, then walked me through the door into the office and towards Kawawada Sensei who was sitting at a desk with two senior instructors. Sensei looked up as we approached. Again, Antonio spoke in Japanese, which caused Sensei and the two instructors to turn their attention to me. I was not comfortable at all.

"Hai?" Sensei said.

"Ask in English." Antonio prodded.

"OSU Sensei. I would like to study karate and live at the Hoitsugan dojo for my last two weeks in Japan."

"Eh. Stay Hoits?" Sensei looked at Antonio, who translated and hopefully improved upon my request language.

"*Dooshite*? (Why?)" Sensei was looking at me again. Antonio just said "why?"

"I want to experience real dojo life."

Again, Antonio helped. His translation took much longer then I thought necessary and I knew he was elaborating on my behalf. Sensei looked at me.

"*Hai. Nishukan, doozo*. (Ok. Two weeks.)"

***

At the station I stopped for lunch at yet another ramen shop then boarded a train to Takadanobaba. On the way to Taioso I stopped at a coin laundry to wash my gis. There was blood all over the gi I used that morning and I needed bleach to clean it off. The coin laundry sold box detergent but I didn't see anything that looked like bleach. I picked up my back pack and headed for Taioso. Junko could tell me where to buy it. She was sitting at the window when I walked in, doing paperwork.

"*Konnichi wa*." She greeted me.

"*Konnichi wa*. Junko san, *doko de* bleach *o kaemasu ka* (Where can I buy bleach*)*? Not knowing the Japanese for bleach.

"*Arimasu yo* (I have some.)"

"*Honto*? (Really?)"

"*Chotto matte kudasai*. (Wait a minute.)"

She came back with a box of bleach about the same size as the detergent that was sold in the vending machine at the coin laundry.

"*Ikura desu ka*? (How much?)"

"*Iie, daijobu desu. Takusan arimasu kara*. (It's ok. There is plenty)"

"*Desu kedo. Okani o haraimasu, um…haraitai…*, I should pay."

"*Okani o harau beki, desu ka*?"

"*Harau beki*?"

"*Harau beki, iku beki, yaru beki…*should pay, should go, should do…"

"*Ah, wakarimashita. Arigato gozaimasu*. (Ah, I understand. Thank you)"

"*Iie. Dooshite* bleach *wa hoshin desu ka*? (No problem. Why do you need bleach?)"

I thought about it for a couple of seconds and then I understood. I reached into my back pack and pulled my gi partially out to show her the blood.

"*Ara. Taihen na renshu deshita ne. Daijobu desu ka*? (Ah. Tough practice. Are you ok?)"

"*Hai. Daijobu desu*. (I'm ok)"

"*Ja, kiyotsukette kudasai*. (Please be careful)"

"*Hai. Arigatogozaimasu*. (Thank you)"

I put the bleach into my back pack and again headed for the coin laundry. There was no one else but me so I put my clothes into the washer and placed the hundred-yen coins in the slot, stretched out on a chair, and grabbed a second chair to put my feet up. Leaning my head back against the wall, I was asleep in less than ten seconds. Forty-five minutes later the chime of the machine woke me. Transferring everything into the dryer, I sat back down, leaned back again but my neck cracked loudly and hurt like hell. Standing back up, I walked outside and across the street to a vending machine. After putting a five hundred-yen coin into the slot, I ran my fingers left and right, trying to decide what to drink, finally hitting a button and watching an ice cold can of Asahi Dry drop down through the chute, took it back to the coin laundry, popped the top and had a long swig. It tasted good and I waited for the dryer to finish. Back at Taioso I walked up to my room, pulled the futon out of the closet, laid down and fell fast asleep.

Victoria was shaking me awake. "Hey you-are you alright?"

I was not yet alert and mumbled a response.

"You OK?"

"Ah, yes. How are you?"

"Junko san said you were hurt at the dojo and that there was a lot of blood."

"Yeah. But I'm OK."

"Good. Want to get something to eat?"

"What time is it?"

"Just after seven."

"OK. But no alcohol tonight."

"Sounds good to me."

We walked out into a very quiet evening. The sun had just set but it was still light. The air was a little crisp but still the evening was pleasant. We walked down Waseda dori towards the station, found a small restaurant and walked in, was directed to a table, ordered and sat back to relax.

"I need to tell you something.

"Sure. Go ahead." She replied.

"I have decided to move into the Hoitsugan dojo for my last couple of weeks."

"Really? I thought you were going to stay at Taioso, with me." The last part of her reply was stressed.

"So did I. But I came here to do karate and staying at the Hoitsugan would be a kind of immersion."

"Training twice a day is not immersion?"

"Good point. Yes, it is. But staying at the Hoits will allow me to be around Sensei and the other students more. That way, I will be even more involved in dojo life."

"I see your point. Does that mean we won't get together anymore?"

"No. As a matter of fact, I also want to take a couple shorter trips. I thought we could go together."

"Where to?"

"Not sure. I would be able to leave right after Saturday morning class, about nine o'clock."

We talked about an hour. She was not as upset as I had imagined. I asked her to think about some possible places to go. We walked back to Taioso, pulled out the futon and went to bed.

Chapter Nineteen

We were all stretching and trying to get warmed up. It had been raining most of the morning and colder than usual. Nakayama Sensei walked into the dojo. Everyone turned to him and bowed. As usual, he took off his jacket, hooked it on the wall, and did a few warm-up stretches.

"*Samui desu ne*!" We all mumbled in agreement.

Antonio ordered the class to line up. I'm not sure how he knew when to do this. I was looking directly at Sensei and did not see anything, not a nod or gesture or anything. We bowed, did *makuso* and spread out into lines per Sensei's instructions.

"*Kyoo wa…kata Jitte*! (Today is kata Jitte)," true to his word from the previous class. And although this class (in my journal) includes some repetition of the previous Jitte instruction, I include it here to provide an example of Sensei's patience and humility.

We all staggered to make some distance. Sometimes this was hard to do. Today there were only ten of us, so not so crowded. Sensei counted the moves out. He instructed us to move slowly and do each technique to the best our ability. "*Hai…ich…* .

Sensei walked around and adjusted a few of us. I had learned to push the hips forward. Sensei told me to bring the hips back into hanmi position. He also raised my bent wrist so that it was a little higher.

Sensei demonstrated. His movement was precise and practiced. It was a smooth transition from yoi through to the block. The block was medium speed at first, then grew slower with more tension until the end. I could see the power coming from Sensei, his eyes seemed also to focus and grow intense. He repeated the move twice more, then told us to try it.

Then we continued with the next move, which is towards the left side at a forty-five-degree angle. Again, I had learned to draw my left arm back in order to make a more dynamic left-hand pressing block. Apparently so had others.

"*Hai, Yame*. (Stop)"

Sensei took the first stance and then moved slowly into the second, pointing out that the left hand moved from the hikite position directly into the pressing block, with no extra move. Then Sensei continued with the next move.

"*Yori ashi shinagara… Matte matte…soshite saigo ni te waza shite*. (As you slide to the right…wait until the very end to perform the hooking block.)"

Again, Sensei showed his ability to go from slow to fast, adding a dynamic level that impressed me.

"*Kore wa dame*! (This is no good!)" Sensei did the move again, hopping up as he did the yori ashi. He told us to start again and began counting out the moves with us performing the first three moves ten times. Finally, he seemed satisfied. "*Hai, soshite ...shi…* (Ok, now the fourth movement.)" This went on, move by move for the next hour. My favorite was when Sensei brought out the bo staff, as he had the previous class. From the last mountain posture block, the technique was to thrust the hands downward, across the chest, to a very dynamic kamae (posture). Then the bo stick would be swung towards the head by the opponent attacking from the front.

From kamae, it was necessary to strongly turn to the right with a rising, open hand block, slightly cupped to allow for catching the stick, and then grabbing it and pushing downward. At the same time, the left hand raised to also grab the stick. The idea was to eventually twist it enough to either break it away from the opponent or at least control it enough to use it on the opponent.

Sensei called Antonio to the front of the class, handed him the bo staff, and told him to swing it downward, aiming at Sensei's head. I remember so well that I was glad Antonio was chosen and not me. I would not want to swing the stick at Nakayama Sensei's head. Antonio did what Sensei said, first at slow speed per instruction. Then Sensei told him to swing fast. Sensei demonstrated that the first block, when turning to the right from the previous kamae, had to be fast, and had to have good timing. He did this several times. Sensei wanted to show what would happen if the timing and speed were not perfect. As the stick came towards Sensei's head, Sensei performed the rising block intentionally slow. Antonio, not realizing this, suddenly attempted to stop the stick in time so as not to make contact. He tried, but the stick struck Sensei on the top of the head, not full force, but enough to make a noisy thud. Antonio dropped the stick and rushed over to Sensei to check if he was OK. Then he bowed deeply, apologizing over and over and keeping the low bow. Sensei would have none of it and pulled Antonio up from his bow.

"*Dakara (therefore)* ... Sensei explained. Movement must be strong and with good timing."

Sensei was beaming, clearly enjoying the clarity of his lesson. He reached over and patted Antonio on the back, smiled and motioned him back in line. Antonio bowed deeply again and joined the rest of us. Sensei had us practice the technique for another ten minutes.

Class was over. We showered and walked to the café for breakfast. Antonio was quiet. Richard spoke up. "Don't feel so bad. Sensei did that on purpose."

"I know, but I didn't stop the stick." I should have stopped the stick, pronouncing it as "steek" both times which was slightly comical, but no one said anything. Antonio was embarrassed.

"Sensei wasn't angry. In fact, he seemed to enjoy himself." I said.

"Is not important. I fucked it up."

"Don't worry about it. Some of the senior students at the Honbu will hear about it and make you feel better." Richard was always happy to add charm to the conversation.

"Is OK. Also-is not important. Important thing is hitting Nakayama Sensei."

Antonio was not going to be cheered up. But it was time to head over to the Honbu. We all walked together, still trying to make Antonio feel better. The Honbu class was one hour of *jyu kumite*. Iida Sensei was the instructor. There was a ten-minute warm-up first and then Sensei announced sparring drills. We would be in groups of three. Two students would spar for one minute, the third would referee and call points. I remember thinking I was going to pass out. The only break every two minutes was to judge, and we were told to watch carefully "judging is also training."

When class was over, I staggered into the shower, dressed and started for the stairs. Antonio was waiting for me. He was always faster than me. Sometimes I think he just did a quick rinse off.

Chapter Twenty

Antonio and I walked down the steps and out onto the street.

"You will move in today, yes?"

"Yes. But I'm going on a trip this weekend"

"Is OK. Is your vacation."

He said goodbye and headed back to the Hoitsugan. I walked the few blocks to Ebisu station, bought a ticket and started off for Tokaido. I had almost forgotten to pick up my new belt. The old man had been right to warn me.

Belt safely in my backpack, I decided to walk around for awhile. I was starving and found a little *yakitori ya* (grilled chicken shop) not far from Tokaido and had a delicious lunch. After a couple of hours of walking, I was totally lost and started asking people on the street how to get to a train station. A group of high school girls volunteered to escort me. They giggled and spoke in English for the ten minutes it took to get to the station. It was quite fun and we talked a few minutes longer at the station before I left.

Back at Taioso I met Victoria. She was sitting on the steps with another Australian woman who had just arrived. She introduced us. We talked for a few minutes until Junko called the new boarder into the lobby to give a tour of the hotel.

"So, are you going to move out of Taioso?" Victoria grabbed my arm lightly.

"Yeah. I just got permission from Kawawada Sensei yesterday."

"Will that be for the entire week?"

"For both weeks, until I leave."

"In that case I'm going to make a quick trip home. I don't expect to see you much anymore so now is a good time."

"But we can try to meet." I said this meekly and she didn't buy it.

"I think you want to hang out with your karate friends."

I did not have a good answer.

"Anyway, I leave on Thursday. I'll use my return ticket and get back for the weekend with my family."

"Wow. So soon?"

"Yeah, it's best."

"So, what about Joanne?"

"She will stay and work. I'll be back in two weeks."

"Is it my fault you're leaving now?"

"Yeah, it is."

"I'm sorry. But I can't change my mind now."

"I know. Don't worry about it."

"I am worried about it. I really like you and want to be with you more."

"But the dojo is more important, right?"

Again-I had nothing more to say. We sat on the steps for another hour, talking with other foreigners and some Japanese as they entered and left. I didn't feel good about what I was doing and came close a couple of times to telling her I would stay at Taioso. But I didn't. We were sitting close to each other and we were both very quiet.

"Come on." She said. She led me upstairs to my room. I had a bottle of sake in the closet. She grabbed the bottle and left, saying she would be right back. She returned in less than five minutes after heating the sake in the microwave in the kitchen.

"We need to celebrate." She said.

She placed the warm sake on a tray that was provided for tea service. Then she poured some sake into each of two cups. She handed me one, raised hers for a toast, and we both drank. We repeated this a few times until the sake was gone. It was already late and time for bed.

"I'm coming back after this trip." I said.

"Really? When?"

"I have to ask my boss. But hopefully soon."

"How soon?"

"I'm hoping in another month." In fact, it would be many months later. But I was being honest and thought I could arrange it. She felt better. I felt better.

Chapter Twenty-One

"Never Heel Up"

I had packed my bags and had only to call a taxi to move everything to Ebisu and the Hoitsugan dojo. I had no idea how to call a taxi so just walked the few feet to Waseda dori, hailed one and gave him a map of the dojo in Ebisu. It was a quick trip, I guess because it was early morning. By six-am I was getting out of the taxi in front of the Hoitsugan. I would spend the rest of my one-month vacation here.

The training at the Hoits that day had been all basics. Nakayama Sensei was energetic and led us through some hard drills, counting loudly like he was a much younger man. It must have been my day. Sensei was next to me for almost all the drills, pushing my shoulders down, straightening my back, telling me to keep my eyes up and always admonishing me to keep my heel from coming up while moving in stance. "Never heel up." He said, in English, at least three times in the first half hour. I guess he got tired of saying the same thing to me. He stopped me mid-technique, grabbing my arm and shoulder with both his hands, and motioned for me to watch him. He did the same technique and picked up his heel, copying me. "Never heel up." He repeated. "*Moshi* (if), heel up, must heel go down." He demonstrated, first keeping his heel up after the initial step forward punch. Then he showed how I had to first put the heel down before making the next step forward, a waste of time.

The entire class was watching. Sensei explained that the push-off was from the back leg. When the heel was up, the ball of the foot would be the push-off point. Because the heel was up, there would be a slight delay while the muscles in the foot were able to create the necessary stability. It was kind of like the foot would become more of a shock absorber, wasting precious milliseconds until the rear foot had enough stability to allow for a strong forward movement.

Then Sensei showed the difference when the heel was down. There was no time required to move forward. Power was instantaneously transferred to the floor and movement was also instant, much different from the shock absorber example. Sensei told me to try again and keep my heel down. As he said, there was no time required to move forward and I felt the difference immediately. It was hard to do because I had already formed a bad habit of letting it rise, but eventually I was able to stop the bad habit. That one simple lesson made me faster, especially in kihon and kumite. Nakayama Sensei seemed happy that the lesson was understood. He smiled and patted me on the back.

"*Itsumo...ne?" Eeto*...every time, do". He was staring at me. "Never heel up. *Wakatta? Kore kara miru yo*. (Understand? From now on I will be watching you.)"

It was a great lesson, not just for the obvious improvement in my technique and speed, but also for the personal attention he gave me, the pat on the back, the fixed gaze. His eyes sparkled as he focused on improving my technique.

Lecture At Ebisu Honbu Dojo

Teaching Children's Class At Ebisu Honbu Dojo

Author With Nakayama Sensei

***

The Honbu lesson was led by a junior instructor and was half basics and half kata. It was a good class. We were encouraged to ask questions, very different from the other classes. He actually walked among us, pointed to each of us. There were many questions, all from us foreigners.

Class over, I headed for Ikebukuro. I wanted to have lunch, but also wanted to see Yumiko, so stopped by the ramen shop where she worked, walked through the door and started for a table.

"*Irashaimase*!" She was smiling and motioned for me to sit down at a table in the corner close to the kitchen in the back. In another couple of minutes, she was at the table, beer in hand. She sat a glass on the table and poured it full, then placed the bottle next to it.

"How are you?"

"Great. Training every day."

"Do you want to eat ramen?"

"Yes, absolutely. Yasai ramen."

"I'll be back in a few minutes."

I sat at the table and drank my beer. I had been thinking lately that it would be good to take a longer trip to this country. I liked everything about it. Of course, the karate was excellent, but also the food, the people and the culture.

There was much more to see and do. Life back in Flint, Michigan was boring. I had lived there all my life and deep down knew there was more. I had been here just a short time but had already met people from many different cultures with whom I could imagine becoming true friends, a change could possibly allow me to come out of my dull, lazy, isolated life. Most of them seemed tolerant and accepting of each other, unlike the majority of people I met back home, who were so negative and prejudiced. And of course, there were the bad memories. It was pleasant here. Even though I was on vacation, I thought this might be another option, to return for a longer period of time. I had no idea then, of course, how prescient those thoughts were.

Yumiko was back with my ramen.

"Can I sit for a moment?"

"Of course."

"You are leaving soon, right?"

"In two weeks, on Monday."

"You will go back to Michigan?"

"Yes. But I am thinking to make another trip to Japan soon."

"Why?"

"One month is not enough, I think. I would like to stay longer and learn more about your culture. You have an interesting country."

"Oh. Thank you. When will you come back?"

"Maybe in one month, if possible."

"Will you come back to Ikebukuro?"

"Probably I will stay at Takadanobaba"

"You moved to Takadanobaba?"

"Yes. But now I am staying at the dojo in Ebisu"

We chatted for a long time with many interruptions as she took orders and delivered food and drink.

"I want to take another trip this weekend." I had worked up the nerve to ask her.

"Where are you going?"

"Don't know yet. I was hoping you could help me decide. And that you would go with me."

"Oh?" She smiled.

"I can't leave until about noon on Saturday, but don't have to be back until late Sunday. Can you go with me?"

"I think so. Should I decide on a good place?"

"That would be great. Somewhere peaceful and not so crowded would be best."

"Have you been to Japanese *onsen*?"

"Japanese what?"

"Onsen. Hot bath. There are many not so far from Tokyo. You can relax in a hot bath while looking at the mountains."

"That sounds fantastic. Can you arrange it?"

"No problem. I know a good one. It is two hours by rapid train. It is not so cheap. Is that OK?"

"It's OK. It will be my last trip."

"We can meet at Saigo Takamori statue."

"Oh. That is the last Japanese samurai."

"Yes. He lost the battle of Shiroyama."

"What do I need to take?"

"Just some clothes and personal things, tooth brush and others. We will stay at Japanese ryokan. It is a small hotel, like an inn."

"Sounds great. I'm looking forward to it."

"Me too." She replied.

It was late and the shop was crowded. She had to get back to work.

"Ueno eki. Can you say *Saigo Takamori doko desuka*? (Where is Saigo Takamori?)"

"*Saigo Takamori doko desuka*?"

"Perfect Japanese. See you Saturday."

I finished my beer and headed for Takadanobaba, two stops away by Yamanote line, to see Victoria briefly one more time. Tomorrow Kawawada Sensei would teach the Hoitsugan class. It would be best to have a good night's sleep.

I had said goodbye to Victoria the previous morning, fully expecting to see her again that night. It was not to be. She left that morning to stay at a hotel in Narita, in order to catch a flight to Australia on Thursday. She left me a note, though:

Dear Michael:

"I enjoyed our short time together very much. I cannot say goodbye and will leave for home today. If you come back in one month, please ask for me. Junko will always know where I am. Or maybe I will be here again. Train hard in karate and have a safe trip back to America.

Love, Victoria."

There was nothing I could do as she was already in Narita. So, I returned to Ebisu. Thinking of her all the way back, and of our short time together.

Chapter Twenty-Two

I arrived at the Hoits. Antonio was already on the floor stretching.

"Sensei won't be here today." He said.

"Who will teach?"

"Juan teaches when Sensei is not here." It would be another experience I would not forget.

He started out with simple basics as a warm-up. After ten minutes, he had us get into the various stances and told us to sink as low as possible. He walked around, slapping us here and there, forcing us to go even lower. When we were all low enough, he had us move one step at a time into another stance. From a low front stance, we moved into a low horse stance, then into a low fudodachi. Seeming not to be satisfied, he told us to find a partner about the same size. Not knowing what was coming, and being too slow in finding someone, I paired with a British guy, who was quite a bit over six feet and a lot over two hundred pounds. Juan ordered one of each pair to climb up onto the shoulders of their partner.

My line was first to be on top. My partner bent down, and I climbed up and straddled his neck as he straightened himself.

"Down into front stance!" Juan shouted.

He had us do the same drills while carrying each other, moving through each stance as he yelled at us to get lower, always lower. I could feel my partner shaking, even though I weighed just a hundred seventy-five pounds. Then it was my turn.

I bent down and struggled to stay upright as my partner climbed aboard. Finally, able to balance, Juan again shouted for us to get low in front stance. We moved into kiba dachi, then into kokutsu dachi, then into neko dachi, where all the weight was on one leg, and back into zenkutsu dachi. I started shaking. Sweat was pouring down my face and into my eyes so I couldn't see. I tried to move without jerking, as Juan ordered, but my legs were shaking and starting to cramp. "Smoother" Juan yelled. "Stop wiggling." The students who were carrying their partners started to kiai loudly. I joined them, trying to bring out every ounce of energy.

"Hai, yame."

My partner jumped off. Immediately I felt my thigh muscles cramp into a knot and grabbed to squeeze them alive again.

"Change partners!" Juan shouted.

We rotated. I was across from a guy I had not met yet. He was also much taller than me.

"Hai, jyuu kumite."

"Oh shit", I thought. I could barely move. My legs were shot. "I'm dead," I remember thinking.

My partner attempted to drive forward with a front kick. His legs gave out and he fell onto the floor. He tried to get up but his legs were not obliging. Juan was there at once and told him to get out of the way. Then Juan took his place.

I couldn't move well at all. My legs just wouldn't do what I wanted. Juan kept shouting at me to move faster. I tried but was unable to put up much of a fight. Juan angrily and arrogantly started foot sweeping me and knocking me from one end of the small dojo to the other. I remember feeling relieved to be knocked against the wall because I could use it for support for my still cramping legs.

He was hitting hard and making sure that I understood his disgust. It was non-stop fighting the likes of which I had never experienced. I lost all feeling and was to the point of passing out. With one more foot sweep and face punch he yelled "yame". I was still on the floor from the sweep. "Get up!" He yelled. I got up.

"What the fuck was that?" I asked Antonio at breakfast.

"That was Juan."

"What did I do wrong?"

"You did nothing wrong. It was your turn with him. That is all."

"I still can't move my legs. They feel like jelly."

"Si, is like that."

"Maybe I cannot go to the Honbu today."

"No no. Is bad decision. If Juan hears about it there will be trouble."

"What? He will find out?"

"Yes. Absolutely."

But I can't move."

"You must go to Honbu."

I felt like running away to hide in my room, take Ibuprofen and sleep. Reading my thoughts, Antonio pulled out some white tablets from his bag and handed then over to me.

"What's this?" I asked.

"Is-how you say, like in banana."

"Potassium?"

Si, potassium, is close to Spanish. Take these two. It will help." I took them.

As we walked down the street towards the Honbu dojo, I felt more and more like staying on the road to the station and back to my room.

Again-seeming to know what I was thinking, Antonio said calmly; "You make it through next class. Then you be proud."

"I'm afraid I will not be able to make it."

"You must go to class. Is not important to be perfect. Today you must finish class."

"OSU"

The Honbu class was all kata with Osaka Sensei. Though it was difficult, especially when moving slow and heeding Sensei's command to stay low, I did not pass out or fall into a heap on the floor as I expected. That was reserved for the locker room, where I slid down on the floor up against a locker, feet stretched out in front of me, unable to move. I closed my eyes just for a second because my vision had narrowed and there was no feeling in my legs. It was not what I wanted to do, just pure exhaustion. My eyes opened a few seconds later though when one of the other students tripped over me on his way to his locker and nearly fell, cursing as he caught himself. I apologized as he staggered up from hitting his foot on the wooden bench leg. He continued to curse in a language I could not understand though I thought it might be Russian. But he forced a smile. "Good training", he said, in English.

Eventually I showered and walked across the floor, almost too late, it was noon. When I saw the instructor's class students frowning at me, I started to run but my left leg caved and I fell, very clumsily, my bag and me hitting the floor and my toiletry pouch and all its contents spraying outward to display itself to the entire class of instructors.

"*Nani yatteiru*? (What are you doing?)" It was one of the instructors.

"*Sumimasen! (Sorry)*" I replied.

"*Hayaku dette yo*!". It was the second time they had yelled at me to hurry up and leave.

"OSU"

I gathered up my bag and pouch contents and shuffled the rest of the way to the front of the dojo, turned and bowed off the floor. As I turned to leave, I could see three of the instructor trainees laughing. "Yeah, it is pretty funny", I thought.

It would have been easy just to crash but I had different plans and bought a ticket to Shinjuku, finding my way to Studio Alto, exit 2B. I wanted to feel the energy of this amazing city once more. For thirty minutes I stood outside, pretending to be waiting for someone but really just people watching. They were of all ages, housewives greeting other housewives, in groups of four or five. They would excitedly find each other, run up and hold hands and giggle like teenagers. Then they would walk off to have coffee in one of the hundreds of cafes. Salary men would do the same, minus the handholding and the giggling, and head off to an Izakaya or hostess bar.

Then there were the teenagers and university students. There were hundreds of them in groups of eight to ten, both male and female. It was hard to say girls and boys or women and men, they appeared to be neither, too young to identify as women or men, certainly by their behavior, shouting loudly and boisterously with complete disregard for the thousands of other people around them and bumping into them with their exaggerated gestures and horseplay. The female part of these groups all had an additional gesture that was both interesting and slightly alluring. On occasion there would be an uproar of laughter, then one of the females would cover her mouth, as if to stifle a laugh, then go down on her knees, which gave me the impression that she was laughing so hard that her legs became too rubbery to stand.

Since most of them wore very short skirts it was a sight to behold and I had to force myself to not stare.

Shinjuku – Studio Alta

Shinjuku was pulsing. I couldn't believe the number of people in such a small area, all of them in a party mood and ready to let loose. The neon lights in Shinjuku and other Japanese cities are well known. But to be there and see it, almost feel the electricity, was a completely different experience for me. There is nothing like it in the world.

It was time to leave Studio Alto so I walked up and down the streets and even found the same bar that served the wonderful grilled shrimps in Kabukicho where the young Yakuza had given the girls and me trouble, stopping in to eat two more of the giant ebi and drinking a cold Yebisu beer, still my favorite. This time there were small tables set up outside where I sat and continued my people watching.

The Kabukicho area seemed different than the rest of Shinjuku. It was hard to know why. Certainly, there was less of the neon for those few blocks, making the shadows come out, adding to the sense of mystery and roughness. It was also the conversations with the girls and with my dojo mates and the stories in the English language newspapers. But it seemed that things happened here that were not sanctioned or even known to the general population or the police. Of course, the experience of just a week before augmented this feeling.

After finishing my beer and forcing myself not to order another shrimp, it was time to walk over to the Golden Gai, an area that time forgot. It was an area that was frequented by rabble rousers, intellectuals, directors and writers in the late fifties and sixties. It is a row of plain store fronts next to Hanazono Shrine with few signs, no neon lights and very few people during the day, but comes alive (still without many lights) at night. A year later I found myself visiting Golden Gai many weekends and loved every minute of it, making many friends, both Japanese and foreigners, whom I still keep in touch with to this day, crying and laughing with them as we grow older, sharing our experiences together.

Walking down the street, I could feel the ghosts of the 1960's where novels and poems were written, screenplays imagined, plots against every imaginable political group were contrived but seldom acted upon, and deep conversations that strained the boundaries of intellect. The same feeling would return a couple of decades later walking up the hill in Montparnasse. I walked up and down the few mostly empty streets, taking peace in the silence so close to the craziness of downtown Shinjuku. But it was cold and though I wore a jacket and kept it zipped tight, it was time to get back to the neon lights that seemed to raise the temperature to a more comfortable level.

A coffee shop displayed a steaming cup of what the menu called "ウィンナーコーヒー". The pronunciation was *weenna koohee* but I later found out it was Vienna coffee. It looked delicious, with a dab of whipped cream on top. Walking in, I found a scat on an overstuffed couch with a glass table just big enough for my guide book. The waiter appeared and took my order. He started to leave when I noticed a cake menu on the table.

"*Sumimasen. Kore mo onegaishimasu.* (Excuse me, this as well please)"

"*Kashikomarimashita* (Of course)", he said, then left.

There were magazines on the table and more on a shelf a couple of feet away. Sticking my guidebook back in my backpack, I grabbed a couple and flipped through them, looking at the pictures and marveling at the advertisements. I didn't know it at the time but Japan was in the middle of what would become the "bubble", a period of high employment, huge profits from real estate speculation and manufacturing exports, and a high life never before seen. The magazines showed expensive items, mostly imported from the USA and Europe, watches from Switzerland, perfumes from France, jewelry from Tiffany's, all being worn by beautiful young Japanese women and men.

The waiter brought me my coffee and cake and handed me a hot towel on the end of a pair of tongs, still steaming, just out of the microwave. I sat there for an hour, just relaxing and enjoying life. The cake was OK. The coffee was excellent. Vienna coffee would become my favorite in the years to come. I would sit in many coffee shops, mostly in Tokyo and Yokohama, and usually order the same. One of the best was in Ginza, Tokyo, where the price for the delicious experience was one-thousand yen, no refills.

It was getting late so I left the coffee shop, swerved and jostled my way back to the train station and eventually back to the Hoits.

Chapter Twenty-Three

It is strange, looking back, I never thought of my first month in Japan as a vacation, though I certainly called it that. It was serious. Almost everything I did that month was done with karate training in mind, even when going out with the girls, having breakfast with my dojo friends and eventually when Victoria and Yumiko and I got closer.

I was, of course, serious during the actual class time training, never did I just relax or look back on the day's training as easy. Even now, with that in mind, I don't remember ever being relaxed while doing karate in the dojo. My mood is serious and almost austere, although laughing occasionally at Sensei's jokes. I know many students don't have the same serious, almost religious fervor as me. And I see it regularly these days. They are the students (and the Senseis) who have never traveled to other dojos and have never been exposed to budo and could not care less. Karate for them is not much more than a Japanese sport, reaching very high technical proficiency-but not budo. For me, it has always been a physical, mental and spiritual undertaking, not something I could call fun. Time always passes quickly at the dojo though and afterwards any stress I had coming into the dojo usually disappears.

I made it back to the Hoits after visiting a little shop outside Ebisu station and having *tsuki mi ramen* (ramen with an egg on top) and asked for two raw eggs instead of one. Both legs were cramping with every step I took. I had written down the name of the potassium tablets Antonio had given me so stopped into a pharmacy to buy some, finally, limping to my room, swallowing three of the potassium tablets, two Ibuprofen and a one-cup sake before crawling onto the bunk.

At eight o'clock in the evening, leg cramps woke me and forced me to roll out of the bed to stretch them away, in the beginning having trouble even grabbing my ankles. I was feeling better but took a couple more potassium tablets and two more Ibuprofen anyway, then went back to sleep.

***

Kawawada Sensei walked into the dojo at seven-fifteen. We all lined up, Juan at the head. The best thing about it was that Juan would not be teaching. Sensei led us through a series of kumite drills, Antonio was my partner. The hour flew by, the training was hard and fast but contrary to what I expected, my legs worked OK, probably helped by the other couple of potassium tablets I took during my commute to Ebisu, and with Sensei even cracking a few jokes and hitting a few of us on the top of the head when we didn't do the techniques correctly.

Juan joined us for breakfast. He was different than when he was teaching, a little reserved but intelligent and thoughtful. I talked to him about his many travels, he had been to the USA, Europe, China and now Japan. Juan would always be Juan inside the dojo as I found out in subsequent classes and years later, but outside the dojo he was a good person to be around, easy to talk to and well read.

We all walked to the Honbu dojo. It had been drizzling rain since leaving the Hoits, but now the clouds were starting to break up, giving me hope for a good onsen trip with Yumiko. The guys razzed me about taking her to an onsen after just meeting her, even Juan joked and said "good job!", as sexist as that sounds at this writing!

Chapter Twenty-Four

Ueno turned out to be a long train ride, taking an hour including my mistake of exiting down the opposite end of the platform. I asked, in my practiced voice, "*Saigo Takamori doko desuka*?" Mostly it was understood but often it was followed by a long string of directions that I could not understand which forced me to ask the same question all over again. But each person pointed me closer to my goal, as I finally paid more attention to their hand gestures than their language. The last person I asked, a young businessman, actually walked me to the meeting place.

Yumiko was there waiting. She smiled and said good morning. Then she bowed and thanked the young man for helping me. He bowed back, more to her than me, and walked backwards while still bowing for a short time, finally making a final bow and heading back to where he was going before I interrupted him.

"Shall we go?"

"Let's go", I replied. I had asked her to make the arrangements, including our destination.

"We will go to Onsen and we will go to Gora. There is a museum you will like. We can have gyoza nearby after that and then look for the onsen." She had prepared well. We traveled about one and a half hours on the Odakyu line and then switched to the Hakone Yumoto line. Then we again changed to the Hakone Tozan line for the switch-back ride up to Gora.

Exiting the station, Yumiko told me stories about the area, including the history of the museum we were about to see. It opened in 1969 and the foundation actively solicited art from all over the world, including Picasso and Henry Moore. There was little space between the sidewalk and the road and I felt uneasy being so close to the traffic. I saw many children walking with their parents but no one seemed to be taking any extra precautions.

We arrived at *Chokoku no mori*, walked up the wide steps and paid the entrance fee of eight hundred yen. When we emerged from the entrance hall I saw before me a panorama of art, all in a natural setting with gently rolling walkways winding around and through the art work. There were several buildings, the first being a restaurant and souvenir center. We decided to have lunch before starting our tour of the grounds, so waited in the cafeteria line, picking up our trays and choosing our lunches. Yumiko got a salad. I found a great little piece of smoked salmon and a bed of lettuce and tomato with a side of cheese and a few crackers. It was perfect. When we arrived at the cashier's, I also ordered two carafes of white wine and we found a table next to a window, from where we could see the grounds and a few of the art works. We relaxed and had a great lunch, talking about art, interrupted only by me making a second trip for two more carafes.

Lunch finished, we walked out to begin our tour. It was wonderful. We simply followed the wide sidewalks and stopped wherever we wanted. One of the first places we stopped was at the Henry Moore sculpture; I think it was "Reclining Figure". I had never been to an open air-museum so it was strange to see this kind of art outside, instead of inside a stuffy, hot, quiet room. I knew that it belonged outside. From further readings of Henry Moore, I found that he intended his work to be displayed and enjoyed in a natural setting.

We continued to walk slowly among the excellent pieces of art. After a while we came to the Picasso pavilion. I remember many pieces were from his "Blue" period. There was a display in the middle of the first floor that showed Picasso's transition from earlier to later stages of his life. It also showed the process of his famous "fish skeleton" patterns. It showed every stage in the process from Picasso grilling and then eating the fish, and finally cleaning it to be ready to be used as an impression. There were very good photographs of the master at work in his studio. We continued through the museum, seeing another Henry Moore, a couple of Rodins, some Miros and many less famous but fantastic art, all in a natural outdoor setting. We stopped every time we came close to the restaurant to have another glass of wine and talk about art. The wine, art and Yumiko combined to create a warm and sensual afternoon that I wanted to go on forever. But Yumiko wanted to take me to the Gyoza Center which was a short, ten-minute walk from the museum. They advertised twenty different kinds. I loved gyoza and had eaten a lot of it since coming to Japan. But I was not prepared for the delicious experience that was spread out on the table after Yumiko ordered. They had the typical minced meat and cabbage kind but they also had garlic gyoza, kimchi, pan fried, soup style, shrimp, beef, chicken, even natto gyoza. We ate it all and left stuffed.

Yumiko had made reservations at an Onsen. We walked back to the station, and hopped on the train. It was another hour before we arrived at a small town. From the station, we took a taxi to the Onsen, and entered the plain, one-story building which looked to be right out of the Meiji period. She told me the rules.

"You take off your clothes in the men's changing room. All of your clothes." Then she reached into her bag and pulled out a small towel. "You will need this."

"What for?"

"You can use it to wash yourself and to, um, steam your face. Also-you can use it for some kind of privacy, like this." She held the towel over her groin area and smiled. I wondered how women would be able to do that with only one towel.

She continued, "please put your things in the locker, here is your locker key, number twelve. Take the key bracelet and put it around your wrist, like this." I did as she demonstrated. "Keep it on your wrist all the time. After you undress, go through first door and you will see a small room with many stools and water, um, spigots. You must wash yourself with soap and rinse completely with hot water. Do not leave any soap on your body. Then you walk through the next door and enter the bath area. I think you will have two choices, onc very hot and another only a little hot. Please enter the not so hot bath first so your body will adjust. Then go ahead and try the hot bath.

"So, we will be in separate baths?" I was very disappointed.

"Oh yes. Most onsens in Japan now are separated. But there will be another door also. If you want, you can open that door, get into the bath and walk through a curtain area. This will take you outside where you will have a beautiful view of Mt. Fuji if the sky is clear. But you must be polite. The outside onsen area is for both women and men. Do not exit the bath, please stay in the water."

"OK. Are you going outside?"

"I will if you want me to."

"I don't want to go by myself."

"OK. I will go. We will meet outside at 4 pm. Please do not…how do you say…look strongly at the women."

"I will try." With that, we parted ways. I found my locker, opened it and starting removing my clothes. I was naked when I noticed an old woman who was sitting in a booth. I froze. Was I committing some kind of gaijin faux pas? But another man was there and was just walking through the door, holding his towel loosely over his privates. I guessed that I was OK and followed the man into the shower room, basically doing what he did, sitting down on the stool, shampooing, washing and rinsing. Then I walked into the bath area, holding my towel like the rest of the men, partly obscuring what everyone knew was there, quite different than the shower room at the gym in high school or even the locker rooms at the racquet ball club or karate dojo, where we all just walked around with nothing.

I followed my personal guide into the bath, being careful to enter at the opposite end so he wouldn't think I was weird. It was hot, but bearable. I soaked for five minutes, per Yumiko's instructions. Then I climbed out and walked over to the other bath. Sticking my foot into the water, I was shocked by the blast of pain that instantly turned it purplish red. The other guy simply walked down the steps into the bath casually, if slowly.

I tried it again. This time I went slowly also, first putting one foot, then the other foot down and then gradually gliding down the steps. I stood there for a couple of minutes, burning.

"*Atsui*? (Hot?)" My mentor was laughing.

"*Hai, atsui desu*. (Yes-hot)" I replied with a big smile.

I stepped down one more level about to my knees and stood another couple of minutes. Then, and I was not looking forward to it, stepped down one more time. The steaming water came up to my waist, scorching my testicles even though I had cupped them with one hand in preparation, as any red-blooded man would do. Even a good, swift kick in the groin beat the pain I felt. But I kept a stoic face, slowly releasing my privates and surrendering to the hot, sulphur depths.

And then it was OK. It was still hot as hell but I could handle it for a few minutes.

There was a large clock hanging on the wall, presumably to help us not stay in the bath until our skin peeled off. I had five more minutes until I was to meet Yumiko outside. But I had not seen any of the ten or so men go through that door. I stayed as long as I could and then moved over to the cooler bath.

It was four o'clock. I climbed out of the bath and walked over to the door, opened it and walked down the steps into yet another bath. This one was about halfway between the first two in temperature. About ten feet in front of me were the curtains that Yumiko had mentioned. I stood there, afraid to screw up. Maybe I had misunderstood her. I waited a few minutes, not knowing what to do.

"Michael?"

"Yumiko?"

"You can come out."

I moved one curtain aside and waded through to the outside. It was wonderful. The sky was indeed clear and I could see a snow-capped Mt. Fuji that hovered over everything. All around us were mountains, and naked people! Yumiko took my hand and guided me to a spot near a rock that shielded us a little from the rest of the bathers. At its base was a kind of carved out bench. We sat down, facing Fuji san.

"Beautiful?" she asked.

"Beautiful." I replied.

We sat there for a while, talking and dipping ourselves into the water to keep our shoulders warm from the cool mountain air. I tried not to stare and was pretty successful. Until a pair of young women climbed up out of the water, covering themselves with their tiny hand towels, and sat down on a cedar plank made for that purpose, I'd guess. They bent down, rearranged their six by six-inch towels, finally giving up, and laid down onto their backs, looking up into the now darkening sky.

"Some people do that. It is heated wood and feels great." She smiled. "Was that nice for you?"

I was caught so I just smiled back. "Yes. Nice looking girls."

I noticed that when I first entered the outside bath, most of the women squatted down so the water was up to their necks, hiding everything. Now, just a few minutes later, they were relaxed and talking with their friends, as if I was not there. And the water was certainly not up to their necks any longer. There were men as well, mostly with what appeared to be their wives or girlfriends. I saw no groups of single men but many single women.

The two women stretched upwards from the cedar plank and carefully stepped back into the bath. They did not use their towels at all this time.

"Do you want to try?" Yumiko asked.

"Is it OK?"

"Yes. You are a foreigner so some will stare. Just cover yourself."

We waded over to the same spot, climbed out and up onto the heated, pungent cedar wood platform. I could feel my back muscles relax. Yumiko twisted sideways. "This is kind of old Japan. Do you like?"

"Very much."

"Of course, you like the naked women."

"No no, I like this custom, where people are natural and not afraid to be seen naked. We are all the same, just different colors, shapes and sizes." It was a line of shit, and she knew it.

"It is OK. I wanted you to experience this too. We have to go back to the bath now. Others will want to come to this spot." We rose from the warmth and climbed down into the bath. A few minutes later, other women did take our place. It was a bit like a fashion model runway only no one was wearing clothes and there was a great view of Mt. Fuji.

Connected to the onsen was a small inn where Yumiko had also made reservations. We finally dressed, left the onsen and walked outside, down a short wooden path to the front door of the inn. Yumiko checked us in and we were soon emptying our backpacks and putting our clothes into the small closet, exchanging them for a yukata which was light and comfortable, if a little on the small and short side. "From now on we will wear these." She was just tying the cloth belt around her waist and then reached under and removed her underwear and dropped it into her bag.

"Sounds good to me." I guessed it would be fun to wear it for a while. I left my underwear on though, thinking that the yukata material was pretty rough.

We heard a knock on the door, "*gomen kudasai* (excuse me)". Yumiko let the two women in. They carried large trays with a dozen or so small dishes of food on each, which they placed on the kotatsu in the middle of the tatami mat room, moving quickly but delicately and noiselessly. The display was beautiful. Then they sat two large bottles of Yebisu beer on the kotatsu along with two glasses, pouring from one of the bottles into both glasses. Yumiko thanked them energetically and they left, amongst much bowing on both sides.

"Shall we eat?"

"Can't wait." I was very hungry.

We ate and drank, with a different older woman always seeming to know when more beer was needed. It was a feast and I felt mellow and ready to move on to other things.

"We will take another bath before we go to bed." she announced. With that, she rose from the tatami and gathered her small towel and motioned for me to follow.

"We will do the same way. You can skip the first bath and just go straight to the outside. But don't forget to shower first."

We met outside. The moon was not quite full but was still bright, especially in the dark countryside. Clouds drifted by, briefly blocking the light and creating a kind of sensual flicker on the steaming hot water. We sat together on the same wooden plank and talked. I was full of food and beer. Everything was a blur. Whereas during the day there was some semblance of modesty, now there was none, with both men and women walking around on the platform surrounding the bath, holding hands, and not even carrying their little towels. I remember thinking that I was, in fact, dreaming. There was no boisterousness however, and I was amazed at how they all managed to keep a suitable distance from one another. We talked and talked and walked around much like the other couples. A few times we even bowed and said a timid hello when our eyes accidently met those of a passing couple. It was all so civil and natural and utopian. I was certainly feeling the effect of the beer and the quietness and the moon shining on the bathers, but nevertheless I fell in love with Japan that night.

We got back to the room at about eleven o'clock and went to bed, skin still stinging from the bath, very warm and happy.

We woke at eight o'clock for breakfast which was down a hall and just inside the main building, between the rooms and the bath area. Everyone still wore their yukata and looked relaxed and seemed to be a little too quiet, as if they were sorry to see their vacation end. I know I was. I thought about asking Yumiko if we could stay another day but decided against it. I had to go back to the dojo and she had to work. Besides, I reasoned with my new-found zen logic, it is best not to anger the Gods in asking for too much pleasure.

The train ride back to Tokyo was quiet. I was still relaxed and felt like all the energy had been boiled out of me. Yumiko was also quiet, partly for the same reason and partly because, as she explained to me; "You are going back to America, I will miss you."

"I will miss you too. But I will come back real soon."

"When do you leave?"

"Next Monday."

"Can we meet again before that?"

"Of course, we can. Do you have time this week?"

We set a few options to get together before I left for the States. She then became happier and more talkative. We arrived at Ikebukuro station at three o'clock in the evening. I walked her to her apartment.

Chapter Twenty-Five

"We had some news today from Kawawada Sensei." Antonio was on the floor with me after chugging some can coffee Monday morning.

"News?"

"He told us there would be a tournament next Sunday near Shibuya. When do you leave?"

"I leave on Monday."

Is good. Sensei said you will compete with the Hoitsugan team."

"Huh, me?"

"Si. He said you need experience while in Japan."

"I'm not sure that's a good idea."

"Is not your choice. You stay at Hoitsugan, yes?"

"Yes."

"So, this week we train kumite all week. We have afternoon training here also. Honbu dojo is same. They have many tournament karateka".

"Hmm, sounds intense to me."

"Si, you will like, no?"

We talked a little longer and then went to bed. At the time we were the only ones there. As I drifted off to sleep, I heard others arrive. There was a rule to be quiet in the evening unless it was Friday or Saturday. I heard them, but still fell sound asleep.

Antonio was shaking my bunk. It was time to train. I had forgotten to set my alarm, for the first time since arriving in Japan. It was already a few minutes past seven am. Four others had arrived during the night, Richard and Juan included. Everyone was hustling to wash their face, some of them would brush their teeth but, as I was to find out, not all of them. Then they would climb into their gis. This would be repeated every day for the week.

By the time Nakayama Sensei walked into the dojo, we all had just barely made it. None of us had warmed up. Sensei did his customary greeting while stretching… "*samui desu ne.*" Then he hung his jacket on the hook in the corner. He stretched a little more, moved his arms around and did some slow knee bends. I remember watching him move. "Naw, he isn't seventy-one." But I knew he was.

We did a short warm-up and then Sensei led us through all the Heian katas. Then he concentrated on Jion. We went through it step by step, by his count, as he walked among us and made his adjustments. In all we did the kata ten times. Then Sensei had us pair up for one-step sparring.

"You will have a tournament on Sunday. Please remember that every technique is a one-step technique. Maybe you must combine many one-steps, but each must be a clear attack and must be full force with speed and power." Antonio was translating. We rotated through the one-step drills, changing partners every minute or so. Then class was over. I couldn't believe it, but it was over.

It was different now. I was hungry and badly needed coffee. Before, I always had time to prepare for the Hoitsugan class. Rolling out of bed with barely ten minutes to spare was totally different. I couldn't wait to go for breakfast.

But it was not to be. Richard kept the class on the dojo floor after Nakayama Sensei left. We worked on sparring drills, led by Juan, for another hour.

On the way to the Honbu class, I grabbed an eighty-yen can of coffee from the machine just outside the dojo and drank it on the way up the stairs. We didn't even change out of our gis. The Honbu class was all kumite and was led by Tanaka Sensei. He had us do one-step sparring as a warm-up. Then we went straight into free sparring. It was a very basic lesson. We got a partner then sparred for two minutes until Sensei's command to stop. Then we rotated to a new partner and started again. Sensei walked around and gave us all pointers. His instruction to me was explosive power. He watched my partner and me for a few minutes. Then he stopped us.

"You, not move fast, like bullet." He motioned me aside and stood across from my partner.

"Like this." He pushed off with his back leg and was inside my partner's defense in a micro second, ready to grapple him to the floor. "*Timingu wa taisetsu*… important. *Jumpu wa* no good." He demonstrated by exaggerating my footwork. Probably it was not much of an exaggeration. Sensei showed me how to properly work the legs by not moving up and down at all, just forward and back. Then he showed me how to attack.

"Not back. Never back, always front. Move with power, speed." He slapped me hard on the shoulder for emphasis. I understood. He demanded that I do better. He was deep into my space and expecting me to perform. I felt it and went into another world. Sensei had no mercy. He made me spar for a few minutes and then ripped me apart. Too slow, no power, no kiai. Over and over he made me work with my partner. The entire time he stared at me deeply and it was apparent that he expected better. He kept ordering me to move faster and use hikite and body rotation and fast movement to get to my target. He called over his junior instructors. They took kumite stance and were ready to attack me. I couldn't believe this was just for me. My entire life was full of good instruction. From parents, to high school teachers to university instructors and to the great journeymen teachers I had at General Motors during my apprenticeship and the instructors I had at the University of Michigan. Sensei pushed me hard again and this time I felt his power. I'm not sure if it was Sensei's regular teaching style or not. He was very threatening. His eyes again revealed the seriousness of this lesson. I understood and tried my best. Maybe the best I have ever attempted in my life. The junior instructors took turns working with me. I did not perform well and was swept over and over to the floor. I was sweating and to the point of passing out. Sensei shouted yame.

Sensei demonstrated again. He first shuffled back and forth and attacked from the back part of the shuffle. Then he did it again but from the forward shuffle which meant that after the shuffle forward, he pushed strongly with his back leg and then his front leg took over for the lunge punch. He also showed the same technique but used a reverse punch instead of a lunge punch, pushing off with his back leg after the forward shuffle. "Sometimes from back, is good, *da kedo* (but), from front is best." He had me try it. I understood what he was explaining but doing it was something else. I tried hard though and Sensei stood right there with me and made suggestions and comments. It was excellent training. I gained more efficiency in my attacks. This one training would come back years later when I needed it most, on the street.

When I think about it, while writing this, Sensei Tanaka's lesson was more than just a karate lesson. He was instructing me using his own personal experiences. He not only pushed me by verbal instruction but also by real threat, calling upon his juniors to help stress his point.

Chapter Twenty-Six

Richard, Juan, Antonio and I walked back to the Hoitsugan. On the way we stopped for breakfast. Tournaments were not uncommon for the Hoitsugan members. Since the main instructors were Nakayama Sensei and Kawawada Sensei they were often invited. I had participated in quite a few in the States, mostly in the Mid-America region which at the time was directly affiliated with the JKA. But this was to be something entirely different. Antonio told me that many of the Honbu students, including the instructor trainees, would also enter. This worried me even more. Some of them were responsible for bruises on my backside when I moved too slowly. And a smaller number of them left their mark during kumite practice. After breakfast we walked back to the Hoits. I assumed we were done for the day and joined them as they jumped into their bunks for a nice long nap, falling fast asleep as soon as my head hit the pillow.

"We train now, come on". It was Juan shacking me awake, just an hour later. I put on my wet gi and walked out with him onto the dojo floor. He was going to teach a few kumite drills. He lined us up, taught us one drill, and then had us practice with a partner over and over until I stopped thinking about it and just did it. I was all for that kind of training and had always learned best that way. For me, it was never as effective to learn a new drill, practice it a couple of times, and then move on to another drill. I enjoyed the luxury of repetition. Repeat we did. Juan had us practice his kumite drills hundreds of times. We finally quit at five P.M.

Then we went out to have dinner. Juan took us to an Izakaya on the other side of Main street, not far from Ebisu station. We all ordered our first beers, which disappeared almost as soon as the waiter left them on the table. We ordered more beers and plates of grilled fish, potato fries, tomato salads, saiko beef and other delicious dishes, some of which I had no idea what they were. But I ate all of it. I thought we were going to stay late and settled in to relax and enjoy.

But Juan suddenly called it to a halt and we made our way back to the Hoitsugan and, for me, a very deep sleep.

Antonio, assigning himself the role as my personal alarm clock, shook me awake for the Tuesday morning Hoitsugan training. I was tired and could hardly force my eyes open. My mind was foggy and I tried desperately to shake it awake. Nakayama Sensei had us again do all the katas, starting with Heian Shodan. Then we continued into the black belt katas. We did all of them, first by his count, slow speed, and then with no count, natural speed and power. Then Sensei lined us up against the back wall.

"You will perform your tokui kata, the kata you will do on Sunday at the shiai", Antonio was translating. He pointed to Juan first, who did an excellent Kankudai. Sensei made many suggestions though, and Juan accepted them with a loud "OSU". One by one we all performed our kata. Antonio did Jion. Richard struggled a bit through Unsu. We all did our katas twice, once while Sensei watched and gave comments, and again to see if we were listening. I did Jitte and tried to make all the improvements Sensei had taught the previous week, along with those he made that day. He still made some suggestions, but minor compared to last week. I had practiced the kata every day, many times. When class was over, we again did kumite until time for the Honbu class.

The Honbu class was all kumite again. Yahara Sensei taught. We did many spinning attacks and sweeps that left me dizzy and confused. A year later I would have the opportunity to train at length with Yahara Sensei and finally start to learn some of his incredible moves. We walked back to the Hoitsugan dojo after the Honbu training, stopping for a quick breakfast on the way. Juan did not let up. We did three more hours of kumite training, with a couple of breaks for water or Pocari Sweat. Juan took the time to explain that on Sunday, we should attempt to do our best and not be intimidated by whomever we had to spar. "Important thing is to fight hard and not give up. If you get beat, is OK. But make them work hard for their victory. Do not make it easy."

We had a quick bowl of ramen around the corner from the Hoitsugan. Then we all walked back to the dojo. Juan wanted to talk to the group so we sat down on the dojo floor.

"Kawawada Sensei wants us to perform well Sunday. We all have to do our best to keep a good reputation for our dojo. Therefore, we will keep this same schedule for the rest of the week. Tonight, you must go to bed early. No drinking. We will do kumite mini-tournament tomorrow after Honbu training. Kawawada Sensei will be here and will watch us closely. Do you understand?"

"OSU!" We all replied in unison. There was a little chatter but we were all tired and got ready for bed. I was reminded of my childhood, my brother in our shared bedroom and my sisters in the bedroom next door, hearing the noises of everyone settling in for the night, especially my sisters giggling, and then, unlike my childhood, the snoring of very worn-out adults. But I was so tired I still fell asleep and didn't wake until time for training at a little before seven o'clock the next morning.

Class began when a group of disheveled karateka made their way onto the dojo floor a little before the regular starting time, yawning and stretching and moaning. Juan was there and said that Nakayama Sensei had to go on a trip and would not be teaching. He led us through another set of kumite drills for the first thirty minutes and then called us to the middle of the floor, in pairs, for two-minute kumite rounds, which he refereed. After each two-minute-round, he ordered another pair to the center.

Fifteen minutes later, he had everyone line up in single file facing him. Then he had one person step forward and take free stance in preparation for sparring with him. The person next in line was to time the round at one minute. Then he was to yell "yame" and take the place of the one who just finished sparring with Juan. He would be sparring one-minute rounds with the whole dojo.

He sparred like a madman, attempting to sweep all of us and nearly accomplishing it. When I faced him, he wasted no time faking a jab to my face and following through with a whole-body twist, while projecting his right leg forward, in an arc, which cleanly took out both my legs. It felt somewhat like me standing on a chair and having it pulled out from under me. It didn't even hurt, until he fell on top of me with a reverse punch that found its mark on my sternum. Gasping for breath, I staggered up and out of the way of the next attack, running into the wall and falling to the floor again. He threw a few halfhearted kicks while I was down but nothing serious. Then he told me to get up. Thankfully my round was over.

Juan kept us way over the eight-thirty quitting time and led us through drill after drill. By the time we finished, we had just thirty minutes until the Honbu class started. All of us crowded into the bakery next door to the Honbu and bought pastries and ate them outside with canned coffee. Then we walked up the steps, ready to start the next class.

Osaka Sensei taught and had us perform all the advanced kata, including Gojushiho Dai and Sho, which I did not know. I was in the middle of the class so could copy easily but still felt embarrassed not to know it. For the second part of the class, Sensei had us line up in the back of the dojo. Then he pointed to each of us, in turn, to come up front and perform a kata that he chose. It was another excellent training. He gave everyone good suggestions, mostly on the finer details, hand positions on the turn in Nijushiho, foot sweep leg movement in Bassai Sho, and nukite hand placement in Unsu.

He pointed to me and said "Jitte". I couldn't believe it. I had practiced it at least a hundred times over the last few weeks and been critiqued by Nakayama Sensei twice. This was going to be a cinch. I stepped out, faced the class and confidently announced, in a loud, strong voice, "Jitte!" I slowly pulled my left leg back into zenkutsu dachi, while bringing my right hand down into a chudan osae uke, trying to time the hand and leg movement exactly. Then I started into the next movement at an angle to the left. "*Yame*", Sensei shouted. He walked over and had me start again. I stood at ready position with right fist cupped by the left hand and began the first move. "*Hai Yame*!", he shouted. "*Moo ikai hajime kara* (start again from the beginning)". I stood back into the yoi position. He stood next to me.

"*Koo yu fune*". He pulled his left leg back and went into the block. But at the end of the block he twisted his hips back towards the front and stayed in that position. This was different than I had been taught and I had seen no one ever do it that way. Sensei explained to me and the class the reasoning behind it. I did not understand it but did as he said and went through the rest of the kata with Sensei making suggestions on a few minor details, all good. It felt like another private lesson on Jitte, this time by Osaka Sensei.

The Honbu class ended and Juan, true to his plan, led us to breakfast and then back to the Hoitsugan. We took our one-hour nap and then climbed out of our bunks, back to the dojo floor. Today Juan had us do an hour of stretching while we all talked, sitting in a circle in the middle of the floor. After that, we did slow sparring for a few minutes and worked ourselves into fast mode. In walked Kawawada Sensei. We all stopped what we were doing, turned towards Sensei and bowed. "OSU!"

Sensei had us sit back on the floor. He talked for a good ten minutes about the need for strong spirit, both individually, and as a team. Antonio translated most of it which was great because I was in the dark.

"Sunday you will participate in individual and team kata and kumite. I expect you to do your best in all events. You will have opportunities to show your skills. Please make sure you do not embarrass or let down the Hoitsugan reputation. But more importantly, do not embarrass or bring shame on yourself. You will remember this for a long time. It must be a positive memory. It means you have to try your best, understood?"

"OSU!!" The walls shook.

With that, Sensei had us line up. He picked two at a time and ordered us to do three-minute sparring rounds while he watched. He picked out weaknesses in our techniques and gave us drills to improve. For me, predictably, he said I was not pushing off fast enough. Also, he showed me how to set up an attack by faking a shift-in reverse-punch twice, and then, when the opponent thought it was just another fake, pushing hard with the rear leg and throwing a real reverse punch, which, Sensei promised, would make contact because the opponent would not try to evade it.

"It has to look real", he explained. "Or the technique will not work. The first two times your opponent will naturally try to block or move away. The third time he will not." Kawawada Sensei was to use that technique with success a few months later against Kagawa Sensei and others, on the way to winning the first Shoto Cup. I was there to see it but it is still fun to google and watch over and over again.

1st Shoto Cup 1985 Against Koike | 1st Shoto Cup 1985 Against Kurasako

Against Yokomichi | Sochin Kata

Celebration First Shoto Cup Champion | First Shoto Cup Judges

We drilled for another couple of hours before Sensei called an end to it and told us to get some rest. I quickly showered and walked to the station to buy a ticket to Ikebukuro. I wanted to see Yumiko one more time before returning to the States.

She was working when I arrived at the ramen shop and, as usual, was all smiles when she walked up to my table.

"Good to see you. How is karate?"

I told her about the tournament on Sunday and that I had to train more than I thought. In between her taking orders and having to chat with regular customers, we were able to arrange a last date for the following evening. She would take a few hours off and we would go somewhere to have dinner. She would pick the restaurant. Downing my noodles and finishing my beer, I waved goodbye and headed to Ebisu to join my Hoitsugan buddies, who were already fast asleep.

Chapter Twenty-Seven

It was Thursday morning and Kawawada Sensei led us in simple sparring techniques. "Better to practice simple techniques and make them perfect." He said. We practiced the techniques for twenty minutes and then finished class with partner sparring, slow and controlled.

Kawawada Sensei took us to breakfast. He was fun and joked often about some of the Honbu dojo instructor trainees, mimicking the mistakes he had seen at the closed-door class. He told stories of some students coming into the class as hot shots, soon discovering that they were better at cleaning the floor with their gi. Another story was about a couple of Yakuza wannabes coming into the class after being waved on by the window clerk, wanting to fight anyone who would take their challenge. The Sensei that day told them very politely that this was a karate class and that since everyone here was a black belt, they would have to sign a waiver that gave up all rights in case of death. And that since they would most surely die, would they please write also to their next of kin? Much cursing by the two brave young men, but all on the way out the door. I asked Kawawada Sensei who the instructor was but he declined to say his name. I had heard the story before, like many of us who train seriously, and many times since. It is legendary, but it was told really well by Kawawada Sensei. Sensei also told us that often he and other teachers have to comfort new and old trainees as they experience tragedies, both in the dojo and with their personal lives, acting as father figures. He told this seriously and we took it that way as well. I could have listened to him all day. Antonio did a great job translating and Sensei even threw in a little English to help out. But it was time for the Honbu class. "See you soon!" Sensei said. "I will teach today."

Kawawada Sensei started the Honbu class with a fifteen-minute stretching session. He had us work in pairs, one person helping the other with various slow stretches, pulling or pushing the legs just past the limits while using good control so as not to tear our muscles. After that, Sensei taught us a few of the same drills he had shown us earlier at the Hoitsugan. We drilled slow and then fast, finishing up with one-minute sparring rounds.

We walked back to the Hoitsugan, knowing that another grueling training was in front of us. Kawawada Sensei stayed back at the Honbu so Juan told us to take a break for an hour and meet him on the floor at two P.M. It was, relatively speaking, an easy training. Juan had us go through most of the advance katas and ended the class with thirty-second sparring rounds, all of us rotating to get a new partner each time. At four P.M., I was showered and on my way to Shinjuku to have dinner with Yumiko. She chose an Italian restaurant where we had delicious pasta topped with strips of seared squid and *ikura* (salmon roe) and a couple of glasses each of Chianti. Afterwards we found a coffee shop near the Che Che restaurant I had visited during my first week in Japan. We talked for a couple of hours. I told her I would drop by the ramen shop as soon as I returned. She gave me her address and phone number on a nice washi-paper-wrapped note card. She made me promise to write to her. Then we walked back to Shinjuku station, stopping at storefronts in an attempt to slow the goodbye. At the station, she bought a ticket to Ikebukuro and I bought one to Ebisu. It was eleven P.M. when I crept into the Hoits, pulled off my clothes and slid into my bunk.

Waking at five, I tried to turn over and sleep more but finally gave up and snuck out to the dojo for some stretching. One by one the others came down to join me. They all had canned coffee and Antonio tossed one over to me when he stumbled through the door, still yawning and rubbing his eyes. Some of them had participated in tournaments before and we all talked about what to expect. I learned some things that would help me.

"There is contact but it is usually light, split lips, bloody noses and things like that are normal. There is a rule that if you draw blood from your opponent, you are disqualified, but the rule is never enforced." Antonio was finally waking up. It was early morning talk, just enough to keep us from falling back to sleep. We drank our coffee and started warming up with some slow punches and kicks. I felt stiff and needed to stretch out my leg muscles more but it was important to warm up the entire body before training.

A little after seven o'clock, Kawawada Sensei walked into the dojo. We all bowed and he had us line up immediately. "*Takui kata*." He pointed to Juan who was generally at the head of the line. Juan bowed and ran to the front, facing the rest of the line. He bowed again and announced his kata.

"Jitte." Juan went through the kata with good power, speed and dynamics.

"Hai." Sensei then pointed to the next person in line, saying nothing about Juan's kata. One by one I saw some very good katas performed. Some needed work but a few were certainly tournament ready. I wanted to do Jitte but felt strange about it since it was Juan's choice. So, when it was my turn, I decided, on the spot, to try Empi. It was not a good decision.

"*Sore, tokui kata*? (Is that your best kata?)" Sensei asked after I was finished. "*Shiai de yaru*? (You are performing that at the tournament?)"

"*Iie, Jitte yarimasu*. (No, I'm doing Jitte.)" I replied.

"*Dakara, dooshite Empi yatta? Shiai no kata to itta no ni*." I was getting lost with the Japanese but Sensei did not look happy.

Antonio helped. "Sensei is asking why you did Empi if you will do Jitte at the shiai. He told us to do our shiai kata."

I did not want to say why so just mumbled that I wanted to try Empi.

"Is not good", Antonio said. "Sensei said do tournament kata."

I turned toward Kawawada Sensei and bowed. "*Gomen nasai*. (I'm sorry.)"

"*Iya. Jitte yaru*? (Ok. You're doing Jitte?)"

"*Hai* (Yes.)"

"*Ja, yatte*."

I looked at Antonio. He simply said "do Jitte now."

I faced the class, bowed and did Jitte, trying hard to perform each move perfectly.

"*Hai*." It was Sensei's only response. He motioned for me to get back in line.

When all of us had performed a kata, Sensei told us to pair up for *jiyu ippon* (semi-free sparring) drills. I was happy to release some stress from the previous incident and pushed off hard and strong for each drill, thinking Sensei was probably watching me. I even noticed a little respect from Juan as he defended against my fast attacks and threw the same back at me.

We went to breakfast after class. It was a welcome surprise as we all thought there would be more kumite. Sensei did not go with us, saying he had to be at the Honbu. My ham & egg set came and I took a big gulp of the coffee before digging into the food.

"Guess I screwed up." I was talking to Antonio.

"No. Is OK. But you must do what Sensei says, si? Is important, no?"

"Yes. It is important. Kind of a stupid mistake."

"But is OK now." He repeated. "Remember next time."

"OSU."

"Sunday, where do we meet?"

"We will go together from Hoits. We will take the train to Shibuya and then a bus to the tournament location. Is about one hour, I think." Antonio said that after the tournament we would all go out for food and drink back in Ebisu. He had already made the reservations at an Izakaya. "So do not expect an early night."

We finished breakfast and went straight to the Honbu. Trudging up the metal stairs, again smelling the freshly baked bread and pastries, I stopped to look out over the street, thinking that this would be my last Honbu training since the dojo was closed for the tournament, immediately feeling depressed.

"I have to talk to you after class." I said to Antonio. "Is no problem." He replied.

Chapter Twenty-Eight

The Honbu training was again led by Asai Sensei. We had a long slow stretching session and a good warm-up first which Sensei himself led. Then he had us line up. I noticed during the warm-up that many of the instructor trainees were also in this class. It was not so rare that some of them came, but this time there were almost fifteen of them. Sensei had the trainees move into position across from the regular class students. We bowed to each other. Sensei explained that the trainees would rotate for one-minute rounds with all of us.

In my karate life, before and since, it was my hardest training. I had sparred with tough opponents in the States, at tournaments, in my dojo, at special clinics, and at Master Camp. But I was completely at the mercy of these guys. Over and over I was foot swept, hit hard in the face and body and even thrown to the floor in classic jujitsu moves. I tried to attack hard but every onc of them batted away my techniques as if they were annoying spider webs they had suddenly walked through. The harder I tried, the more frustrated I became and the more I was hit. None of the trainees said a word to me, no encouragement, but also no complaints. They just did their job being efficient kumite machines.

After each one-minute round, I bowed and moved to the left to face my new partner, who barely nodded his head in return, if at all. It was apparent they were doing what Asai Sensei told them to do. Their job was to give us a good lesson in humility. They were succeeding. I was awestruck at the entirely different level of skill I was facing. I was young at that time and fairly strong but they simply toyed with me. There was no way I would do well against these guys but I continued to attack, remembering Juan's and Kawawada's warning to do our best, no matter the consequences, but my movements were slow and cumbersome.

I remember at about the halfway point, trying to stand upright, deciding to learn as much as I could as to how they were so good. I saw, first off, that most of them were much more relaxed than me, never using a bit of tension until they absolutely needed it. I also saw that they moved back and forth and side to side, kind of sliding over the floor, not hopping or jumping at all. But what I noticed most is their extraordinary timing. Attacks were initiated when I was at my weakest position. Defense was easy because they seemed to know when I was coming and from where. Once I was swept off my feet and crashed into the next pair. The trainee yelled at me, picked me up by the arm and kicked me in the ass as he sent me back to where I belonged. I would fight him next.

I was dragging and ready to stop. But that would not do. Sweat was in my eyes and I had trouble seeing. It seemed as if every one of these trainees were floating, just above the floor, controlled by strings, like puppets, somehow manipulated by the puppet master who was also inside my head, knowing my every intention. Perhaps he was also a karate master.

I'm pretty sure I hit the floor ten times but it was easy to lose count since it was usually accompanied by a hard punch to the stomach or neck. I knew how to tense the stomach but couldn't figure out what to do against the neck punch since I had to be sure to pull the head inside to avoid banging it on the floor when I went down. I was intimidated and operating on autopilot. "Just get through this!" I kept saying to myself. I noticed that some did not get up and continue. They were taken to the side and were allowed to sit and watch the rest of the drill. It was very tempting, but I had to get back up each time because that is why I had come to Japan. I wanted to learn from the best and here I was. I kept thinking about the line at the movie theater and how scared I was and embarrassed, and how clueless as to how to handle the situation. Then I relaxed, slowed down my thinking and looked for my partner's weakness. There was little weakness to see but I was able to manage a good block and counter finally and even buried my fist into the next guy's belly twice, causing him to grimace. This was the same guy who yanked me from the floor. You couldn't see it clearly but I knew he felt it by the way his body shook and tensed, and the way he backed off a little. He also bowed after we finished, the only trainee that did.

Class was over and I struggled to walk across the floor to the locker room. Antonio was at the bottom of the stairs, waiting for me, a can of coffee in his hand.

"Let me buy a coffee too." I said.

We walked down the street to a vending machine. Coffee was available at the back of the dojo in the machines but I was always late walking across the floor and didn't have time to find my coins and leave before the instructor's class started. It was a warm, almost balmy day, but not much sunshine. Antonio and I stood at the entrance to a small park.

"I want to come back to Japan, soon."

"Si. Is not a problem. When can you come back?"

"Maybe in a couple of months."

"You will stay at the Hoitsugan?"

"I don't know. But how can I survive? Is it possible to work and make enough money?"

"Si, is possible. You can teach, like me, like Richard, like many foreigners."

"How can I arrange that?"

"Is not difficult. Look in Japan Times on Monday or ask other people. Maybe introduction is best."

"When should I find a teaching job? Should I wait until I come back?"

"Si. Is also not a problem. You can find work as soon as you arrive. Just ask others."

Is this really possible?"

"Many foreigners live here. Is a good life. People are nice to you, crime is low, is very exciting here. You can find nice girlfriend."

"Do I have to make a reservation to stay at the Hoitsugan?"

"No. Just come when you are back in Tokyo."

"It sounds like a dream. Do you think I can do it?"

"Of course. Anyone can do."

We talked for another hour. Antonio told me about visas and extensions and health insurance and various rules for gaijin, always carrying their passport, green card, or residence card and following the same rules as the Japanese. It all sounded like common sense to me.

We had the remainder of the day off to rest up for the tournament, although we still had Saturday morning's class to get through. I spent the day saying goodbye to some of the people I met. My first trip was to Takadanobaba. Junko was in the lobby when I arrived.

"Junko san, *nichiyoobi, America ni kaerimasu. Iro iro arigatoo-gozaimasu*. (Monday I will return to the States. Thanks for everything)"

"Ah, Michael san. *Doitashimashita. Mata nihon ni kimasu*? (You are welcome. Will you come back to Japan?)"

"*Hai. Mata kimasu. Tabun, raigetsu*. (Yes. Maybe next month)"

"Ah. Can I stay here?" I switched to English so as not to get it wrong. "Can I write to you and reserve a room?"

"*Hai, doozo*." She gave me her business card.

"You are welcome to stay. Please let me know in advance so I can save a room for you."

"Hai. *Domo arigato gozaimasu*."

I walked upstairs and knocked on Joanne's door.

"Hai, doozo."

I opened the door to find Joanne relaxing and reading on her futon.

"Hi there. Just wanted to say goodbye. I leave Monday."

"The month went fast, didn't it?"

"Too fast. I just talked to Junko san to arrange a room for next month."

"You're coming back?"

"Yeah. This place is fantastic. I'll try to find a teaching job to help out."

"It's easy. I have to turn down requests to teach. There's a lot of work here."

"Maybe when I get back you could introduce me to an English school."

"Sure, no problem. You'll have no problem finding a job here."

"Great. Have you heard from Victoria?"

"Yes. She's returning the first of the week."

"Too bad. I won't be able to see her."

"That's probably a good thing. She was pretty depressed when she left."

"Yeah. Guess I can't blame her."

"But we will both be here next month. We will stay for another year."

"Another year?"

"Oh yeah. Japan is good for both of us. It's very safe and it is easy to make money and travel."

We talked for a while longer and then hugged and kissed good-bye and promised to write. I left Taioso and walked to Takadanobaba station and bought a ticket to Shinjuku, walking around for an hour on the main streets of Shinjuku, taking in all the restaurants, bars and shops that Joanne, Victoria, Yumiko and I had visited. It was still day-light so the neon lights were not as dramatic. But it was still wonder-fully energetic, I did not want to leave. But there was another training tomorrow and we were supposed to get a good night's sleep.

I arrived at the Hoistugan about seven P.M. and walked into the dorm. No one was there so I assumed they were out to dinner. I went downstairs and walked around on the dojo floor, soaking in my recent experiences.

How many times had I hit the floor, swept by Juan, Richard, or one of the visiting university students? How much of my sweat was now soaked into the wooden floor, mingled with so many other karate students? How about the blood? Hundreds of broken noses and cut lips must have spilled blood on this floor, to mix with the sweat and become part of the wood that others unknowingly practiced upon. Sci-entifically we know that DNA cannot be changed by hitting the floor and being influenced by the blood, sweat and leftover skin particles of thousands of students. But what about the spirit? Cannot the spirit be affected by those who came before us and who have also worked hard and left their blood, sweat and yes, tears?

What would happen if one were to pull up the wood floor, place it in a controlled furnace, much like a crematorium, and burn it, at the same time collecting the smoke and fumes? Could it be bottled, condensed into a solid and sold, or better, be given away to future promising students to be inhaled as 'instant budo spirit'? And could it be given to past students, so they could, once a year, at New Year's for example, roll a small amount into a short joint-like cigarette and smoke it to infuse another year of combined knowledge and spirit? And how about the ashes? They could be added periodically to ceremonial dishes to make or keep students strong both spiritually and physically. The ashes could, of course, be added to the above joint to be given to the student who decides to travel to Japan, along with the letter of introduction. "Here is your letter of introduction, now smoke this!"

My dojo mates were back. Everyone was in a good mood. We sat in the middle of the floor and talked. I told them about my plans to come back and received assurances that an English teaching job would be easy to find. We went to bed at ten o'clock.

The Saturday Hoitsugan training was all slow-paced free sparring with Kawawada Sensei teaching. He again gave us a lecture about doing our best. We alternated between sparring and getting down on the floor and stretching. Sensei walked around among us and made comments about our techniques and how we could improve them. I was feeling depressed, knowing that this was my last training in Japan. At breakfast, Antonio said something about my mood.

"No worry. You will be back soon."

"I sure hope so. I feel worse than I thought I would."

I spent the rest of the day writing in my journal, eating all kinds of Japanese food, an occasional beer, and visiting a *sento* (bath house) to relax my muscles and my spirit.

Chapter Twenty-Nine

We made our way to Shibuya and then onto the bus headed for the tournament venue, which was held in the gymnasium of a community center. It was a quiet ride with most of my mates sleeping, but not me. I was too excited and nervous. The bus stopped and the driver shouted something that apparently meant we had arrived. Filing out of the bus, we walked the half block back and followed the make-shift signs into the gym.

About fifty people were already on the floor stretching and warming up. On the other side of the gym I could see the judges, referees and time keepers huddled together and saw others working to tape the floor for the three rings that would be used.

We threw our bags onto the floor in the corner just behind the double doors we had just entered. Antonio walked over to one of the officials, talked to him for a few minutes, motioned for us to pick up our bags, and led us to the locker rooms.

Gis on, we again found a spot to call home for the day and joined the others on the floor. We offered to help and ended up carrying chairs from another room down the hall and setting them up, four to a ring for the three rings. Then we carried more in to be used by the officials at the edge of the ring. Another hour later I heard a whistle and the muffled slap of a microphone as one of the officials called us to attention. He welcomed us and told us where to line up. We went through the bowing ceremony. The same official then read a long speech from a paper he unrolled and held at arm's reach, none of which I understood. Once the announcements were finished, we again spread out on the floor to stretch and warm up.

"Kata will be first, then kumite." Antonio said. "We must listen for our names to be called out." The registration forms had asked for katakana translations so hopefully we could recognize our name when the time came. There were around two hundred participants which I felt was an excellent turnout. Antonio told me that it was about normal. The corner judges were taking their seats and sorting through their scorecards. The three rings quickly became organized and the kata part of the tournament was about to begin.

Pairs of competitors were called out to one of the three rings and each bowed before entering the ring and bowed twice more when they reached the kata mark, once to each other and once to the head referee. Then they stood at attention while the referee flipped through the cards to determine which kata they were to perform. He chose a card, showed it to the competitors and announced it to the crowd. They bowed once more, shouted out the name of the kata and stood at yoi position until they heard "*hajime*".

Although there were three rings, it still took almost an hour and a half to get through the first round. Juan, Antonio and Richard from our group eventually made it into the second round. I was paired with a Japanese brown belt and we were told to do Bassai Dai kata. It was one of my favorites and I also went to the second round. The next time up Tekki Nidan was called out and I was able to win that one as well. The third pairing had me performing Hangetsu. I thought it went well but I lost and was now out of the kata competition. Juan had three wins, the last being against a very sharp looking Japanese yondan. Antonio also made it with a close match against one of the instructor trainees from the Honbu dojo.

After a fifteen-minute break, the fourth round began with a total of twenty competitors remaining, all of whom would be performing their katas in the center ring. All of us were instructed to gather around the ring to watch. One by one they did their *tokui kata* for the judges, one in each of the corners and one chief judge. The scores were averaged from what the judges announced and showed on cards. Antonio did well but the score was not good enough to put him into the next group of ten. Richard and Juan made it to the final ten, Juan performing an excellent Unsu kata.

The last round started immediately and Richard was called first, along with the name of our dojo. He announced his kata "Sochin" and performed it well, scoring a nine-point-five. Five more were called and then I heard Juan's name and our dojo again. Juan announced his kata "Jitte" which is the kata he had told Kawawada Sensei he would perform. It was strong and showed Juan's ability to separate the slow moves from the powerful moves, stressing the dynamic pauses and zen-like *kamae* (ready stances) that reside in Jitte. The audience applauded when he finished. The judges' score was nine-point-eight. It was the highest so far.

The next two performed their katas strongly but scored below Juan. That left one more to go. Up walked Ogura from the Honbu dojo instructor trainee class. There was applause even before he announced his kata, "Unsu!" The entire gym was silent during his kata except for when he made the signature jump. Then the audience exploded with whistles and shouts and applause. The score was called out, "nine-point-nine". Ogura won the *shiai* (tournament) with Juan in second place. But the Hoitsugan dojo had done well. We gathered together and congratulated Juan and Richard. They, in turn, congratulated us, true karate-do style.

In no time at all the kumite competition started. It was fun and exhilarating to watch such skilled fighters from all over Tokyo. There were, in the States, strong fighters but usually just a few in each dojo, sometimes only one. But almost everyone I saw that day was equal or more skilled than the top-level fighter I had met in the States. Karate was improving every year all across the States but the sheer history and head start the Japanese had was evident in this tournament.

The matches were announced and the fighters ran to their marks in one of the three rings, some of them bouncing in place, hardly able to contain their energy. The referees at times had to warn them to settle down if their excessive movement went against the neutral start rule. My first match came after about the fifth pair-up. Running to the mark, I bowed to the referee and to my opponent, a Japanese about my size. His belt was almost white, which worried me. The referee shouted "Hajime". We both took fighting stance. I expected him to charge at me at the start, Juan had warned us about the possibility, but he didn't. I remember us feeling each other out for a few seconds. Then he attacked with a left leg front kick, reverse punch combination. I blocked the reverse punch-the kick didn't come close, then I tried to sweep his left leg before he could gain his balance. It almost worked, he stumbled a little but I did not take advantage of it and there was no point.

We started again. I stepped across with a left-hand jab and reverse punch that pushed him backwards. Following him back, I again went for a foot sweep, this time against his back leg. It was clean and he went down, hitting the floor about a foot away. I dropped down on my knee with an elbow strike that stopped about an inch from his neck. "Ippon!" The referee was pointing at me. The four corner judges concurred. The first match was over.

Juan was in the other ring so I was not able to watch. But Antonio was up a few minutes later. He won his match with a good, solid barrage of round house kicks and reverse punches, the same thing he used in the dojo so well.

Richard didn't do so well. He was paired with a Japanese from one of the Universities, I think Waseda. His match lasted about ten seconds as his opponent thrusted forward with a fake jab and sweep, ending with a stomp kick to the groin. Another ippon.

The second round started and there was now just one ring. Juan had also won his match. Richard joined us, along with our other dojo mates. Out of the ten of us, six had made it to the second round, not a bad showing.

Juan was called first out of our group. He faced one of the junior instructors from the Honbu dojo. He did very well, finally winning with a front kick that was a bit too hard. His opponent was gasping for air but stood up to bow in acknowledgement.

Antonio was next. He had a long back and forth with a British guy who was practicing at the Honbu and had lived in Japan for almost five years. Antonio knew him, he said later, and they had shared a few beers. Antonio won, finally, all on half points.

After a couple more matches it was my turn. My opponent was Shinozaki sempai, one of the instructor trainees at the Honbu dojo. I was staring at a calm, relaxed and confident opponent. The referee shouted for us to start and I immediately took a sparring stance. Shinozaki did the same. He did not know me. He saw me once or twice at the Honbu dojo but whether he took notice I don't know. Therefore, he was cautious at first and waited for me to do something in order to judge my skill level. I waited until I thought there was an opening. Looking back, I'm sure it was a fake to lure me in. I attacked with the same step across jab and foot sweep technique I used previously, reaching out with my right leg and finding a tree trunk. He didn't move, instead he just blocked my jab and buried a reverse punch into my stomach. "Wazari (half point)".

We started again. I remember just barely taking a fighting stance and then a blur, and then stars. It was my first time to really, clearly, see stars. I was on the floor when I regained consciousness, with the referee and a couple of judges standing over me.

"*Daijobu*? (You Ok?)", the referee was asking.

"*Nan bon*? (How many?)" He was holding three fingers in front of me.

"*San bon. (Three.)*" I replied.

"Hai. You come."

I tried to stand but couldn't. The judges picked me up by both arms. I took a first step and fell straight to the floor which was made slippery by my own blood. They again picked me up and walked me over to the side of the ring and sat me in a chair. Someone was wiping blood from my face and stuffing toilet paper into my nose. I was in a far away place, with just enough consciousness to recognize that these people were taking care of me and that they were in charge. I looked around. Brown belts were busy with rags, cleaning the blood off the floor, which tracked from the center of the ring to the chair where I now sat. I laughed.

"*Daijobu*?" The referee was back.

"Hai." I said this automatically and knew there was not much conviction in my voice. I stood up and walked rubber legged, back into the ring. Shinozaki stood up. He had been sitting in seiza the entire time. He bowed to the referee, who had just given him a warning. Then he bowed to me, holding it a bit longer than necessary.

We took kamae again. I attacked as hard as I could after sensing an opening. I couldn't see anything and was not yet fully conscience. He blocked whatever technique I used and swept me to the floor with a solid reverse punch that landed hard on my chest, Ippon.

Shinozaki picked me up himself. "*Daijobu*?"

"*Hai, daijobu.*"

The referee walked me back to my mark. I bowed to Shinozaki, bowed to the referee, and looked around for my dojo mates. Antonio was there to help and we made it to the bathroom. He told me to wash my face. Then he surveyed the damage. Juan came in with a first aid kit. Between the two of them, my face was cleaned again with disinfectant, then a couple of bandages were placed just above my right eye. Juan then took some cotton swabs from the kit and told me to push them up into my nose. Antonio gave me three Advil which I swallowed with a handful of water from the sink. My head was throbbing. Shinozaki eventually won the tournament, beating everyone he faced.

I remember little about the trip back to the Hoitsugan. Juan and Antonio took me to a neighborhood clinic. I know the clinic was closed because it took an hour for the doctor to arrive. The doctor told me, through Antonio's kind interpretation, that my nose was indeed broken and that there was a slight concussion, possibly, he said, from a blow to the head, which was also responsible for the cuts over my eye. I'm not sure what a "slight concussion" is. Seems like there either is or isn't a concussion. He told me I should go to the hospital and get x-rays. But I had had enough. I thanked him and asked if he had anything to ease the pain. All he had, he said, was aspirin. He felt my nose again and, apologizing in advance, started manipulating it, pushing it left and right and sticking his fingers far up inside. It was excruciating and I told him to stop.

"You might need surgery." Antonio translated.

"Hai, OK."

Finished, I thanked the doctor. He gave me a prescription for pain. We left the clinic. It was already seven o'clock. We looked all over for a pharmacy but could not find one. Finally, I decided to not worry about it. "Let's go meet the others."

"Are you sure?" Antonio looked worried.

"Yeah. Let's get some food and some beer. That will make me feel better."

After a long discussion, Juan finally said, "let's go."

We found our way to the Izakaya where the others were sitting along the back wall. Our dojo mates were joined by some of the other students from the Honbu dojo. All together we numbered sixteen, eight on each side of the four tables.

They were finishing up their first round of beers and the tables were full of food. Juan sat at the end of the table, in the corner. My seat was in the middle, opposite the wall. Antonio was between Juan and me, on my side of the table. Richard held up his beer as the three of us settled in. "Kampai!" It was time to relax after a very tough week of training.

We talked about the tournament, filling in details for some of the students that hadn't participated. Stories were told. Antonio told my story to the entire table. I still didn't feel good but managed to laugh at some of his descriptions of the blood and how I basically just stood there and let Shinozaki knock me down at the end of the match. I started to protest but decided against it. Most likely I looked slow and defenseless after my broken nose and head shot. Guess it would have been funny to an onlooker. Indeed, I had been completely out of it.

We drank fast and ate a lot of delicious food. All of us needed to let loose. I started to feel a little better. The beer certainly helped. I couldn't breathe very well and remembered that my nose was full of cotton. Antonio described Shinozaki's moves. "He moved fast for a big guy. He shifted forward with a left hand backfist. That's the one that broke your nose. Then he came in with his roundhouse. That's the one that hit you in the head. You went down like a rag doll." Juan interrupted. "He didn't use any control. There is a no blood rule but nobody said anything about it."

I remember thinking it strange that Juan would say something like that. He was himself always lacking control and was not averse to drawing blood. Then an amazing thing happened. Juan rose from his seat, walked over with a full bottle of beer that the waiter had just delivered. I thought it was strange since we were all drinking drafts. He came around the table to where I was sitting, tapping me on the shoulder and holding the bottle over my now empty glass. "Pick up your glass", Antonio shouted from his seat. I raised the glass. Juan held onto my shoulder as he filled my empty glass. Everyone was still.

"Good job today." He patted my back.

"OSU." Antonio shouted.

"Thank you, Sensei, didn't do too well against Shinozaki though."

Shinozaki is a monster. You did OK." He motioned for me to drink. I took a large swig. He again filled my glass. Then he put the rest of the bottle in front of me on the table and walked back around to his seat.

I could still feel the pain and my vision was a little blurred, but my feelings for Juan changed completely, especially after multiple conversations with him that night. I was never to become a close friend, don't know if anyone did. I would train again with him and spar him often in the future. But I never again feared him. I was always careful and defended myself and respected his skills but I now knew his heart.

We talked into the night. I told everyone of my plan to return in a month. They were happy about that and I received many suggestions as to how to find work. As the night progressed the conversations became more boisterous. At one point, someone had the idea to play a drinking game he called *iki komi*. The object of the game was to quickly drink a *daijoki* (large draft beer) and then place the empty mug on top of your head. That was the starting signal for the next person on your side of the table to chug his beer and do the same. Fresh beers were ordered for this entertainment as it wouldn't do to have someone cheat by only downing a half a beer.

I'm not sure which side of the table won. We were all fairly well out of it. Eventually we left, my memory is weak on that part. I do remember Antonio having a serious discussion with the manager who said we were no longer welcome as this Izakaya was a family place.

We went to a second bar, the Japanese call this *nijikai*, and drank more beer and then switched to whisky. Somehow, I made it back to the Hoistugan. I'm sure I was aware at the time but I cannot remember anything about the walk back. I do remember Richard and Antonio waking me at eight o'clock on Monday as they had promised.

I had pretty much packed already and finished stuffing the rest of it into my two bags. They walked me to Ebisu station. There was not enough time to stop for breakfast or even a coffee. Antonio did stop on the way and bought me a can coffee from a vending machine. They helped me up the stairs to the platform.

"Sorry we couldn't find a pharmacy." Antonio said.

"No, I'm OK." I was lying but I didn't know for sure whether it was my injuries or the beer and whisky that hurt the most. I swallowed some of the aspirin the Doctor had given me with the coffee. The train arrived. Richard and Antonio shook my hand and then hugged me.

“I’ll see you in a month or so. I promised.

“We’ll be waiting.” Antonio replied.

Arriving at Ueno station from Ebisu, I caught the Skyliner to Narita where I stayed in a hotel for the night and relaxed, again writing in my journal. The next day, I boarded the plane back to Detroit. After lift-off, I ordered my first glass of wine. My ribs still hurt, especially sitting in the small seats with no way to stretch out. My nose was red and swelled and still started to bleed for no reason so I stuck a piece of the wine glass napkin into it. I just wanted to get rid of some of the pain so I quickly asked for another mini bottle and then told myself to slow down. I tried to relax and just think about all my experiences over the month. From day one, finding the Honbu dojo in the rain with the help of the postman, walking up the stairs and inhaling the bakery aromas on the way, talking to Tanaka Sensei and giving him the bottle of Jack Daniels, of meeting Yumiko, Antonio, Joanne and Victoria, Junko, Richard, Juan, and of course-Nakayama Sensei and Kawawada Sensei and the rest of the JKA instructors and trainees. I thought about the everyday commuting back and forth from Kimi and Taioso to Ebisu, the masses of people all headed to work that resembled the ants marching up the hill that we observed as children in my neighborhood. I thought about the training at both the Honbu and the Hoitsugan, the temples, shrines, the kind, orderly and polite manner in which the Japanese conducted themselves, the cleanliness of even the smallest ramen shop, the food… oh, the food! “I will definitely come back.” Then-a startling realization…I had gone almost an entire month without thinking of my two children and my cheerless, dreary existence, bordering on desolation, in Flint, Michigan. It is not that I wanted to forget it all, especially my children, I just wanted the memories to be pleasant, instead of tortuous. Today I have more or less accomplished this goal although I still have to remind myself occasionally to wrap those memories in a soft cotton cloud. And twice a year I still sometimes imagine what kind of adults my children would have become, and what kind of father I would have been. But this month I had smiled often, made friends, and looked forward to every new day. This was uncharted waters for me, at least for a number of years. And it was pleasant. Yes-I would go back.

Chapter Thirty

I arrived back in the States on a Tuesday, via Toronto, and crashed for two days, going back to work on Thursday. Nothing had changed. A few people asked about my trip but they were not interested in many details, just being polite, I think. Thursday night, I was looking forward to seeing my dojo mates again and telling stories. It was lots of fun and I felt good. But soon the days and weeks seemed to be returning to pre-Japan in terms of dealing with the same boring idiots at work who seemed to always want to cause trouble. And the supervisors who mostly put up with them, basically encouraging their behavior. There was one tough millwright who was always bullying people and had been arrested a couple of times already for fighting both at work and in bars. One time a couple of years previously, he had asked me "whaddya gonna do if I tell you I'm gonna kick you in the balls? Karate is bullshit." Me not saying a word, tacitly agreeing, he and his friends laughing and enjoying his bullying, which went on and on for a couple of years. The same guy approached me now and wanted to know what kind of "karate bullshit stuff" I learned in Japan. Rising from my chair slowly, I told him I learned how to get back up when someone knocked me down. Maybe it was the way I just looked him straight in the eyes, calmly, no smile and no anger in my expression, but pure confidence. He grinned awkwardly and walked away with no comment, never to bother me again.

A few weeks went by and I was stuck and starting to panic. I needed to go back. I needed to taste more of that culture and of that foreignness, to see my friends. And I needed it now. I asked my superintendent if I could take a six month leave of absence. He said he would "run it up the flagpole". He did-and the kind people in upper management decided that "your services are needed now, not later." I tried to adapt as best I could, and managed to make another short trip which helped. But by that time, it was just a matter of when, not if. Finally, I signed up for a Japanese language course in Ikebukuro by mail, sold my cars, my house, all my furniture, packed up the rest and took it all to Jim Nelson's house, destined for his attic, where it stayed for almost twelve years.

Epiloque

Recent Photo (2019) Same Bldg & Location - These Guys Loved Beating Me Up!

Visiting Japan was my Karma. I met people who became my friends and with whom I am still in contact with today, even though we live in different states and countries, including occasional face to face visits, long embraces and talks that last until we are exhausted. It was the karate mecca before the multiple splits, with every Sensei you can name all on the same floor at the same time and I was lucky to be a part of it. I trained with the best every day, and though they typically beat the shit out of me, I watched and learned. In Ginza, Tokyo, I even made friends with the police in the *koban* (police box) across the street from Sony Show Room and they invited me to train with them at their department headquarters gym.

It is impossible to overstate the importance of that one-month visit to Japan in early 1985, and my subsequent relocation to that wonderful country, for what it has done to propel me through these many years. Who knows what direction my life would have taken otherwise? Any arbitrary distraction along the way could well have dramatically altered my short time in this world. I was not going on the right path, this I know, and desperately needed a way forward. I became more psychologically and culturally alive and physically stronger and, of course, more skilled at karate and budo. I say karate *and* budo because I look at them separately. When we look at karate these days it is easy to distinguish those who know true budo from those that are certainly highly skilled karateka but do not know budo. This is a topic for another book, but there are many out there that know exactly what I am talking about.

Relocating to Japan during what was called the *bubble era* was good fortune for me, easy to find teaching jobs that paid so well I only had to work a couple hours a day to sustain my lifestyle. Teaching jobs that included going out after class with executives and being treated to wonderful dinners in expensive restaurants-and more that I will refrain from describing here.

Not only did I make many friends during my years in Japan, but Karma also decided that I should meet and marry a beautiful and intelligent woman. The broken bones, cracked ribs, and bloody noses were a very small price to pay for finding the woman I am so lucky to have shared my life with for close to thirty years. A woman who also performs beautiful kata as a nidan. Now living just South of Chicago, we visit Japan twice yearly and usually get a chance to train at one of the dojos.

Kawawada Sensei and Author – Hoitsugan Dojo - November 2019

Just last year, Kawawada Sensei flew to the Mid-West for his first time and taught a series of classes that left us all smiling and wanting more. With Tomoko and I being the resident hosts after classes and dinner were finished and everyone else went home, the three of us, sitting in the hotel lobby bar, reveled in old memories, crazy stories about the JKA and the other instructors, and some of the old students. Lots of laughter and promises to get together again in the near future. I thanked him profusely for teaching me those many years ago. He simply said "*Sore ga, watashi no michi desu* (That is my path)".

Visit To Central Illinois (Sensei Rick Brewer, Author, Kawawada Sensei, Sensei Tomoko Busha, Sensei James Hartman)

After Everyone Went Home (Private Time With Sensei)

About the Author

Michael Busha (boo shay) has been training in Shotokan karate since 1978 when he first walked into the University Karate Club just off the University of Michigan-Flint campus on 1st street, advancing to Shodan in 1982 at Ann Arbor, Michigan and Nidan in 1984 at the Master Camp in Philadelphia under Okazaki Shihan. He also trained in Aikido for a short time in Flint. In March of 1985 he took a one-month vacation to train in Japan at the Honbu dojo (Ebisu) and, as it turned out, the Hoitsugan dojo. Michael took one more trip to Japan later that same year, attending the 1st Shoto World Cup Karate Championship Tournament which Kawawada Sensei won in both kumite and kata. Eventually quitting his job as an electrician at A.C. Spark Plugs in Flint and moving to Japan, he taught English at a number of private schools and corporate offices, finally settling in at Sony Corporation where he met his soon-to-be wife, Tomoko. Michael continued studying Shotokan and also trained for a little more than a year in Aikido at the Wakamatsucho dojo and for a short time at Honda Sensei's Goju Ryu dojo near Kamitsuruma station.

Michael has been published three times before. Once in 'The Japan Times' for an article entitled 'Everything In Japan Is Not Small', which told the tale of a hiking trip up Yarigatake from Kamikochi with Paul and Allen that led to a Zen experience under the root of an old tree that had fallen over and in which he had taken refuge from a snow storm. An article on his recent vacation to Japan was also just published by Master's Magazine.

He was also published in SKM (Shotokan Karate Magazine), the best karate magazine out there. You can read his article 'UKE as IKKEN HISSATSU'.

https://www.shotokanmag.com/skm-back-issues/issues-140-to-149/809-shotokan-karate-magazine-issue-140.html

Michael (Central States Shotokan 5th Dan, and ISKF 4th Dan) and his wife, Tomoko (Central States Shotokan 2nd Dan) both train at the Central Illinois Shotokan Karate Association dojos led by Sensei Rick Brewer and Sensei James Hartman.

Very Early Times
(Swartz Creek Dojo)

Instructing (Early Times At Corunna Rd Dojo)

Instructing Class At Pekin Dojo

Instructing At Clinic At Bloomington/
Normal Dojo

Recent Training On
Business Trip

Saturday Breakfast Club At
Mapleton Dojo

Makiwara At Sensei
Brewer's House

Acknowledgements

Writing this book was one of the hardest things I have done. My wife Tomoko was there every day encouraging me. She was the one who suggested I focus on events leading up to and including my first trip to Japan. Thanks for always supporting me in my work, my karate and my life.

Without Nakayama Sensei and Kawawada Sensei and all the instructor trainees in Japan (now well-known senior instructors and in high demand world-wide), I may not have pushed myself as much as I did. Thanks for forcing me to 'get back up', so often! And many thanks to Nakayama Sensei for welcoming foreign students into the Hoitsugan and providing such a wonderful experience for so many karateka around the world.

Of course, without Sensei Golden and Sensei Jim Oberschlake, I may not have even discovered that Japan was where I would find my peace.

To Takashina Sensei-thanks for the wonderful lessons in Budo, the great advice regarding living in Japan, and for the thousands of repetitions!

To Joe Ferguson, Don Elford and Jim Nelson-thanks for sharing the early stages with me.

Lastly-thanks to Sensei Rick Brewer and Sensei Jim Hartman for tirelessly working to promote Shotokan karate in Central Illinois for these many years and for accepting me into their karate world.

www.ingramcontent.com/pod-product-compliance
Lightning Source LLC
Chambersburg PA
CBHW070025100426
42740CB00013B/2596

* 9 7 8 0 5 7 8 4 9 3 6 4 0 *